SPARKS FROM THE FIRE

· · · · · · · · ·

SPARKS FROM THE FIRE

A JOURNEY BEYOND SURVIVAL

. . . .

Eva Cutler

with Kelly Howe

Sparks from the Fire: A Journey Beyond Survival

Published by Wheatmark®
610 East Delano Street, Suite 104
Tucson, Arizona 85705 U.S.A.
www.wheatmark.com

International Standard Book Number: 978-1-60494-263-7
Library of Congress Control Number: 2009923978

Front cover illustration by Maggi DeBaecke.
Back cover photo by Stone House Studios.

You can email the author with comments or questions at
peacefulvoice@bellsouth.net.

I dedicate this book in loving memory of my brother Gyuri and brother-in-law Herb Kottler.

Contents

Contents

Prologue

I view my life as a series of episodes—situations and people that shaped me into the person I have become. In the pages that follow, my colorful collage of memories takes me as far back as my childhood, and the stories my mother told me fill in some of the moments I cannot remember. The past can feel like a dream, but a real dream and sometimes a bad one. I write to sort through that past—so that I can live in the present with heightened awareness.

When I first contemplated writing this book, I had trouble finding the format that would best convey my message. From the beginning, I did not want the book to focus on my Holocaust experiences only. Many books already offer perspectives on those events. Neither was I in favor of writing a memoir simply to air my woes. I fought hard against using myself as the protagonist, but whichever way I turned for advice on how to approach the book, the ball kept landing in my corner. I do not think of myself as a public figure notable to anyone outside my family and friends. Therefore, in many ways, though this book evokes a series of experiences from my life, it is not merely about me. It is also about people whose paths crossed mine, and what my often-short encounters with those people taught me. In *Sparks*, I bring to life experiences that helped me understand that regardless of color, culture, ethnic heritage, and religious affiliation, we all have the capacity for love and hate, for tolerance and intolerance, for noble generosity and the cruelest of selfishness.

Many of the stories that follow might never have made it to print had fate not brought me together with two other women who cared deeply about the project. During the early stages of my writing, despite having joined a writers' group and attending writing workshops and conferences, I still felt discouraged about how to find the best angle for the book and how to balance my personal stories with the larger reflections on human nature I wanted to offer. Just when I was about to trash the project once and for all, I happened to come together with my old friend Julie Sturman. Julie and I had been out of touch for a while, and not knowing about the project, she asked if I had ever considered writing a memoir. I confessed to her that I had seriously attempted doing it, but that I felt lost as to how to frame the project.

"I would like to help you, and I think I can," Julie offered. "I feel I know where you are coming from, and I feel connected to what you intend to put into words." At her invitation, I spent an entire week at her home where she helped me assemble all the bits and pieces I wanted to cover. Without Julie's editorial expertise, continued encouragement, and devoted guidance, this book would never have taken wing.

Later, while contributing to a Holocaust themed theatre-in-education project called *The Library: The Story of a Jewish Girl in Nazi Germany,* I met and bonded with Kelly Howe. Kelly was a member of the group of Muhlenberg College students who comprised *The Library*'s original cast, all of whom dedicated time and talent to develop the play. Simply because Kelly believed my story deserved to appear in print, she was willing to give the manuscript essential literary refinement. She helped me stitch together the individual passages of this book and smoothed my writing in ways that empowered it. That is how *Sparks* as it now appears came to be.

Many questions arose throughout this writing process of which only some were answerable. Would I have been complacent about the world around me without the Holocaust experience? Would I have cared to learn why so many people are mean-spirited while the spirit of love guides others? The only thing I can know for sure is that the lessons I was given, whether they brought joy or pain, were to make me wiser. I have made them into stepping stones, for myself and hopefully now for others.

To share what I have learned and lived in a way that is purposeful, to try to instill *love for peace*; these are the goals that mean everything to me.

Eva

By Julie Sturman

First you have to know that Hungarians all stick together. My father left home and came to America at 17. My mother came as an infant with her family. Their social life was centered around cousins who welcomed every Hungarian newcomer into their home. As the American daughter of two Hungarian "immigrants," I was infused with gypsy music and fed stuffed cabbage from a very early age. It became a part of my soul although I never learned the language and had a very typical middle class American upbringing.

It was pretty well submerged but there were subtle hints of the Holocaust all around me. My father's parents were killed by the Nazis, as were his two sisters and their 4 & 10 year-old sons. My father never discussed it, but on his deathbed he reminded me to have his body cremated, not buried. "If it was good enough for my parents," he said, "it's good enough for me." To this day, I get tears in my eyes whenever I think of the grandparents I never knew, the aunt who I am said to look like, the cousins I never had, and my beloved father, whose pain and survivor's guilt must have been unbearable.

My father was a "Holocaust atheist." From his perspective, there could be no God. My maternal grandfather with whom we lived was a quasi-Orthodox Jew so I had the whole spectrum of Jewishness around me. Looking back, it is easy to see why I identified first with being Hungarian (in every glamorous sense) and at the same time with being a Jew, if in fact, a very secular one.

I was nine years old when Eva came to this country at twenty-one. She was smart and pretty and extremely friendly and accepting which made me feel quite grown up. To me, she seemed like Cinderella, living with the wicked stepmother but destined to meet the prince and triumph over all. Because "Aunt and Uncle" were a part of the Hungarian Jewish community, my parents visited with Eva's family from time to time. During these visits Eva and I became truly good friends. How could I not admire someone who had been through the fires of hell and survived? How could I not be in awe of someone with Eva's dauntless spirit, her kindness, her talent, her inner and outer beauty?

By the time Eva married, I was a teenager. The mother of my best friend owned the apartment where Eva and Harry made their first home. Eva had everything a teenage girl of my generation wanted: a loving husband, a home of her own, a baby, and a cat. Eva was my role model.

She was also inherently wise, accepting, understanding and she became my confidant (she still is). Instinctively I knew her advice was always sincere and her friendship always genuine; she was a remarkable lady.

Throughout her adult life until she moved to Jim Thorpe and then to Florida, we always lived close to one another and though there were spaces in our relationship, it never faltered. The longer I knew her and the more I came to know what she endured "before and after," the more admiration and love I had for a lady who harbors no bitterness and no anger and who is still learning and giving and giving and giving.

Eva has an important story to tell. It is that of openness, of survival against all odds, of optimism and hope, and of love. When she asked me if I thought there was a book to be written, I finally had the opportunity to give her something meaningful besides my affection. I helped her organize her thoughts and get started. I did hours of editing with her at my side and alone. I believe in her, and everyone who reads her book will fully understand as I do that Eva's life has been a life worth living—meaningful, important, and a gift to all who have been privileged to call her their friend.

A Note on the Process of Writing *Sparks*

By Kelly Howe

The process of helping Eva with this project has been, like her friendship, a tremendous honor. We've been collaborating on it for the last five years. I helped her build on the foundation of excerpts she and Julie Sturman had already assembled. Sometimes we edited while bent over her computer desk for long weeks and weekends in her apartment in Florida. Sometimes our work happened from afar, over endless emails—Eva in Florida, me in Texas. Sometimes she wrote and then showed me excerpts. Sometimes she mused aloud while I typed her recollections. Sometimes the stories come in chronological order, sometimes they don't. In that way, their placement in this book reflects the mystery of how memories work, one sparked by another. The important thing to know is that, while the actual words in these pages are a mix of Eva's and mine, the stories, ideas, and opinions are hers. All I really brought to the table was an eye for order, sentence structure, and a word bank of action verbs. What Eva brought to the table, on the other hand, was her Everything. What a gift to have been welcomed into her life in such an intimate way. She is a friend, a mentor, a joy, a love.

I Was Born

The prevailing mood in war-defeated Hungary was not an ideal setting for romance, but that did not stop Margit Braun and Henrik Friedrich from getting married in 1919. I was born six years later, three and a half years after my brother, Gyuri.

CHAPTER ONE

Childhood and Adolescence

I see myself as a small child in the dingy three-room apartment. I'm on the first story of a gray, weather-scarred building built around a courtyard. I smell cooking odors from many apartments mixed with the stench of rancid alcohol from the taproom below. My mind's roving eyes spot the coal-fed wrought iron stove in the kitchen, grandmother Johannah's old mahogany dining-room set, and our full-grown Biri—the coward German shepherd father once brought home as a puppy tucked inside his pocket. I keep searching for little old plump Mrs. Volar's babushka-clad head next door. I find her squatting as usual, picking fleas off her cat. And I can't skip looking in on the filthy communal toilet, a few doors away, where we hold our breath to avoid gagging from the revolting odor. In this building, roaches and bedbugs grossly outnumber the tenants.

That scene is still vivid to me today. Blue-collar workers dominated our entire section of the city of Budapest. Poverty-stricken people lived in my building from the ground floor on up two flights. Some had no more than one room for an entire family. We were not exactly poor; we just didn't have the means to live elsewhere. Anyway, that was how mother put it. "Poor is the devil, because he is without a soul," she would say.

When I was a small child, I never thought of my parents as people, just as I never thought of myself as a person separate from them.

Growing older changed all that, particularly during adolescence, when my developing personality began to clash with theirs. Whether for disregarding curfew or disagreeing over my mother's choice of clothing for me, I was always in hot water. It was a good time for me to learn the values and the principles my parents lived by, but their innermost feelings remained hidden from me and perhaps even from themselves. Until the last stretch of their lives, that is, when due to illness, they lost control of their minds.

My mother Margit talked about her family and shared some of her painful memories about growing up in a household dominated by a demanding, violent gambler, her father. To escape his dominance and gain independence, she dropped out of school at age thirteen and apprenticed dressmaking. She married my father Henrik soon after he was discharged from military service. They moved in with his widowed mother Johanna on Szabolcs Street because, after the war, apartments were hard to come by. Shortly after they moved in, Johanna contracted influenza and died of pneumonia. Her sudden death awarded Margit and Henrik full ownership of the apartment, where they began building the foundation of their family.

My parents were cousins by adoption and had known each other through childhood. They were opposites in many ways. She was gracious and friendly, but reserved. Her personality attracted people's

-U. apartment on the corridor's upper left corner. Door to the infamous communal toilet is second to the right of the window. Photo is taken in 2005

affection and respect, but she kept much to herself, with little trust in anyone. Henrik befriended everyone. She was witty with a sharp tongue; he was humorous. Henrik was an agile, enthusiastic, multi-faceted man with a well-rounded educational background. Almost always working, he stole time for a game of chess or soccer for re-laxation. Margit was a bookworm. Books compensated for her lack of schooling, and through them she visited all corners of the world. While I never saw my father idle, neither did I ever see him with a book in his hand, unless it was work-related. His primary goal in life was to provide the best for his family, while hers revolved around be-ing at home with the family. They both loved music. Mother had a beautiful voice and loved to sing while father screeched on the violin and so our home was always filled with music.

Dad started out as a draftsman in an architectural office. During that period, he learned to build his own radio and cultivated his inter-est in photography. His education made him proficient in every phase of the building trade. When he established his own small building construction firm, the current building codes permitted him to build one and two-level homes and renovate existing ones. I remember my

Father working over the table (cca.1939)

father zipping around town on his motor bike inspecting the progress of ongoing projects, leaning over the drawing board for endless hours rendering home designs and floor plans, or laboring over a maze of administrative work under electric light. Neither of my parents was tall, but Father's 5'8 towered over Mom's 4'11. Even Gyuri and I looked tall next to my mother by the time we reached maturity, and I was merely one inch over my brother, reaching to a height of no more than 5'3. Mother compensated for height with authority. She had the knack of sending messages with just a look in her eyes. I can still see that look.

Margit was a wizard with limited finances. Money management was one of her most outstanding skills. The task was difficult but necessary because money came in spurts. Sometimes Father would have a large sum collected, which had to be stretched until another collection came due. Even in those in-between periods, we always had ample, simple, nourishing meals, deliciously prepared. Budgeting meant endless lists reflecting the priorities of our relatively democratic household. Each situation got equal consideration, but not all our needs could be satisfied at once. For instance, if Gyuri had to have a new pair of shoes and father needed new tires for his motor bike, the motor bike got the tires, and the shoes had to wait. Without the bike, Father could not work. It was his only means of job-to-job transportation.

When Gyuri was old enough, my parents bought him a three quarter size violin. It was his first. Father's childhood friend Tibor was a violinist and ran a music school. Our parents enrolled us both to take lessons from him. We shared the one violin. It was a long walk to the music school, and the two of us agreed to switch carrying the violin case halfway there. No matter how I tried to con my brother into taking it further, he was unbending. "A deal is a deal," he would say, and the matter was closed without further negotiation. We went on with the lessons for about a year, when I lost interest in trying to master that instrument. Gyuri, however, was obviously smitten from the start.

Early on, Father made us a small table much like a picnic table, with a bench on either side. Gyuri and I had our meals there until we were old enough and tall enough to join our parents at the dining table. My brother ate everything and never gave anyone a hard time. I was a picky eater and not particularly good at following the number one rule on Mother's endless list—not putting more food on our plate than we could eat. If we took more, we had to eat it all. Long after everyone had finished their fare, I could often be found sitting by myself, wearied, picking morsels off the poor semblance of what had once looked appetizing. It must have been a pitiful sight because Mother didn't have the heart to carry the punishment any further and released me. Her expectations for us to know the difference between enough and too much did not seem fair at the time, but her way of teaching not to be greedy and wasteful turned out to be quite successful in the long run. She conveyed that commodities should not be taken for granted.

Mother's form of democracy also allowed for free speech, which I practiced frequently. The fact that I was not the one to have the last word didn't discourage me in the least. Case in point was the failed attempt to achieve equal rights in the mashed potato case. My brother always got more mashed potatoes than me. As I watched the heavenly mush piled high on his plate, each spoonful added to my growing resentment.

"This is grossly unfair," I claimed. "Why do I get so much less than Gyuri?"

"Growing boys need more." Case closed.

I loved my brother, but I liked mashed potatoes at least as much as he did. Therefore, it seemed to me that Mother loved Gyuri more than she loved me.

No MATTER WHERE THEY LIVE, children need a place where they can congregate freely. For us, that place was on Szabolcs Street, a field behind our building, where Gyuri and I found the company of neighboring kids ranging in age from five to ten. Our playground might have been a city dump for all we knew, but it was the only open area accessible to us. We could live out our fantasies there, amidst heaps of junk and refuse, where even the burrowed creatures darting out, squealing, and scaring us half to death were part of the adventure.

Our courage was tested at a big gaping hole in the ground, where the big kids were showing off, boldly jumping into what looked like a waterless well. With circus-like showmanship the boys lined up. Inching their steps to the edge of the pit, they leaped one at a time, with eyes closed and arms spread like wings ready to fly. Their bravado left me awe-struck, but the thought of them expecting us "little guys" to follow in their footsteps made me ill. When it came to my turn, I looked down to what appeared to my five-year-old eyes to be a bottomless trap, I wished I were somewhere else. For an awful moment, I stood frozen at the edge, thinking I may never get out of there.

Backing out would have meant losing face, and I was not about to let those jeering name-callers intimidate me. As a last resort, I looked at Gyuri for encouragement. His "Don't worry Evie, I pull you out if you can't make it" contrasted with the mocking expression on his face. Still, those words were all I needed to spike my courage, ignore my wildly beating heart, and leap into the abyss. To my greatest surprise, I was able to climb out all on my own. The hole was not nearly as deep as it looked, after all. I was immensely relieved, but somewhat disappointed to find the extent of "heroism" displayed earlier tarnished. Self-decreed superiority motivated those older kids to incite competition, and we all fell for it.

THE OLD LADY WHO LIVED in one of the ground floor apartments walked laboriously. Hunched over, leaning on her cane, with wire-framed spectacles hanging low on her long, wart-studded nose, she sure looked like the witch off the pages of a Hansel and Gretel picture book. And for no other reason than that, we feared her. The temptation to challenge that fear drove us to torment the poor old soul. Taking our position safely behind the stairwell, we conspired to take turns ringing her doorbell and then withdrew to our hiding place to watch her open the door time and again. At first, she looked around, shook her head and disappeared behind the door, but, after several false alarms, she caught on to our game. Agitated, she furiously waved her cane, yelling and cursing in our direction. "Nasty kids!" she muttered at last, closing the door behind her.

Photo taken in 2005 the pass-through to what used to be our Playing field, is entry to back-yard gardens.

Cowardly hidden out of sight, snickering in delight, we felt powerful.

MOTHER KEPT WORKING TO HAVE enough money put aside for the future. She was an excellent dressmaker with an appreciative clientele. I often wonder how she managed to do such a demanding job at home in a small, poorly lit space—all while caring for two small children and carrying on her household chores. But she did it all, until Father's business began showing the promise of growth.

When dad began to renovate apartment buildings and traded part of his payment for an apartment, the sun began to rise on our horizon. I was seven when we left Szabolcs Street and its poverty-stricken lot, behind. Poverty never corrupted our senses, meaning that we gained an incentive to pull ourselves out of it rather than allowing it to defeat us. If anything, the experience heightened our understanding of social imbalance.

OUR FIRST MOVE TOOK US to Frangepan Street on the outskirts of the city in District XIII. The apartment was small, but we now had an inside toilet and one large room connected to a kitchen by a narrow hallway. All was new, clean, and bright. A year went by before we got a slightly larger place in the same district. It was on the third floor of a modern three-story building at #70 St. Laszlo Street, one of the community's busiest thoroughfares with a bus route to center-city. Without an elevator in the building, we had to walk the three flights, but it was well worth the effort because this time we had a full bathroom with a tub and a balcony to the street. The hallway connecting the kitchen and the all-purpose room was not nearly wide enough to dribble a soccer ball in, but Gyuri and I enjoyed the challenge—until the ball slipped away from us one day and bounced into the hallway mirror. Mother was furious over the shattered mirror and made sure we knew it. Of course, that was the end of the dribbling fun, at least for me. Gyuri, however, began to play soccer with the neighborhood team on Tarnay field, a nearby sprawling green.

THE DISTRICT'S ELEMENTARY SCHOOL WAS directly across the street from us, yet I often heard the morning bell reminding me I was late again. It was kind of embarrassing to arrive last, when kids from longer distances were already in their seats. Even the teacher's repeated scolding didn't break me from that habit because I slept so soundly that Mother didn't have the heart to wake me. Funny how she flexed her rules at times. Letting me sleep in like that went against everything she stood for most of the time, but she did it anyway.

PUBLIC TRANSPORTATION IN OUR NECK of the woods was sparse, and we were accustomed to commute on foot whenever possible or on a bicycle, when we were lucky enough to have one. The convenience of a job nearby was a blessing for many who found employment in walking distance. The two knitting mills on Frangepan Street and the lumber yard on Petnehazy Street (where Father purchased his building materials) employed people who lived in the neighborhood. Having all the convenience stores near by was also a plus, particularly when it came to food. Daily marketing was unavoidable in the absence of an icebox. "Running down" to the Eibenschutz grocery store at the corner was a cinch when we needed something at the last minute. The meat market, bakery, and dairy store were also only a short walk away, which made Mother's shopping easy, except when she opted to take the trolley over to the farmers' market. She made that trip on an average of once a week to bring home fresh poultry, fish, fruit, and vegetables. Mother would arrive absolutely exhausted but totally satisfied with the results of her task: a brimming basket on each arm.

The local drugstore provided the charm of its proprietor, whose scandalous affairs were on the tongue of all gossip worshippers. It gave some folks something to talk about, and they talked plenty. The owner of the tobacco shop, who also sold school supplies, was a jovial prankster at heart. One day, when I went looking for a small dish for a school watercolor session, Mr. Krausz produced a little ceramic bowl made for that purpose. I didn't like his suggestion because I thought the bowl was breakable, but before I could say a word, he tossed it onto the floor to prove me wrong. I was amazed to see it hit the ground. As if defying gravity, it bounced back into the air, then landed softly without as much as a chip or a crack on it.

"You see, it is unbreakable," said the man with a little laugh, and I believed him. I believed him so completely that I could hardly wait to get home and dazzle my parents with my newly discovered phenomenon. "Guess what! This dish is unbreakable!" I announced, bursting into the kitchen, where I found Mother and Dad. I breathlessly proceeded to perform the tobacconist's demonstration—only to see the little bowl break into smithereens on the ceramic floor. I stood there dumbfounded, with eyes nearly popped out of their sockets. I lost my tongue. The shock of such a deception was devastating. How was I, a gullible little twelve-year-old kid, to know that the magic behind Mr. Krausz's trick was a pliable wooden floor?

WE EVEN HAD A MOVIE theater on our street. The Beke (which means peace) Cinema was our place to unwind. Stepping into a world filled with adventure, beauty, and fantasy was the perfect escape from the routine of everyday life. Without an occasional visit to the Beke, life would have been an unthinkable bore. The Hungarian film industry—

still in its infancy then—lagged far behind that of Great Britain, France, and Hollywood. The thirties and forties were Hollywood's years of golden harvest. We supped up their elaborate musical revues, which included the likes of Sonja Henie on ice, *Broadway Melody* with Eleanor Powell, Fred Astaire with Ginger Rogers, Jeanette McDonald and Nelson Eddy, Judy Garland and Mickey Rooney. We watched the unforgettable performances of actors like Charles Laughton as *The Hunchback of Notre Dame*, Paul Muni in *Good Earth*, Spencer Tracey in *Captain Courageous* and *Boy's Town*, Irene Dunn, Claudette Colbert and others. They whetted our appetite for a world we wished to join. The silver screen colored our fantasies, broadened our horizons, and lightened our spirits. It made our daily life just a bit sweeter, particularly as we rarely overlooked stopping by White Mattie's Pastry Shop right next to the theater to savor his delicacies.

THE THREE-STORY BUILDING WE LIVED in towered over a spacious tenement project directly to the left of it. A ground-level row of apartments lined the yard in a half circle. Each dwelling consisted of one or two rooms with communal comfort zones for entire families. The impoverished people who lived there were essentially uneducated, lower working class. At the entrance to the fenced-in area was a small single dwelling. The little single structure was much like a farmer's hut, but definitely several steps up from the others with its low ceiling, cement floors, a kitchen, and two small rooms with windows. Six members of the Zsakai family lived there, my friend Anna (nicknamed Nusi) among them. Nusi and I were inseparable. We had been in the same class throughout elementary school and remained friends even after I entered middle school. Her parents were simple, decent peasant folks. Nusi's mother was our washerwoman, and her father, a short hunchback of a man, a retired street cleaner. No matter when I went into their house, I always found his head buried in the Bible.

One of Nusi's brothers, Sandor (or Sanyi, as we called him), was a talented artist. His uniquely executed miniatures won him recognition and an invitation to exhibit in Paris, France, where he received an award for one of his most impressive creations. Sanyi worked with an ivory-like plastic medium. I never tired of watching him cut intricate filigree designs into the material with a firmly held jigsaw in his agile hand. He maneuvered amazing patterns into pre-cut miniature parlor furniture sections with rapid, deliberate movements. Then he assembled those sections with painstaking accuracy. Sanyi's repertoire grew, and his creations became sought-after collectors' items, while he remained modest and unaffected. My parents bought several of his pieces I now treasure, along with fond memories of their maker.

Nusi and I developed a secret communication system to get around the temporary restrictions of my house arrests, which my mother enforced when I stepped out of line. Mother, the staunch disciplinarian, might have been short, but her stature was empowered by steadfast principals and an unusual strength of character. Due to my frequently revoked after-school privileges, Nusi and I borrowed our family canary's melody for the whistle tune to summon one another for a two-way conversation through the bathroom window. Standing on the edge of the tub, I whistled to let Nusi know I was grounded again. We would then chitchat long distance, as I naively thought I had outsmarted Mother. I should have known that precious little eluded my mother's attention. As she told me years later, she was on to my trick but kept it to herself because she admired my unyielding spirit. My family added that whistle tune to our ever-growing list of inside jokes. To hear it whistled by any one of the other three members of my family meant I was about to be teased.

When I went on to middle school, Anna remained at the elementary learning institution to finish the compulsory eight grades. Ironically, we would both become dressmakers in the end, but for different reasons. Anna would not be able to go on to higher education because her family could not afford it. As a Jew, I, on the other hand, would not be able to continue my schooling because the Nazis would come to power.

I WAS TWELVE YEARS-OLD WHEN we moved again, this time only a few blocks down the same street. The apartment at #56 St. Laszlo Street was in a very old, massive apartment building Father was renovating. The owner was a kind, elderly gentleman with whom Father struck his usual bargain for the nicest place we had so far. We were on the first flight off the stairway, with a large balcony facing the street. We now had a bedroom for me to share with my brother, a bathroom with a tub, and a separate little room for a toilet. Each of these amenities along with a pantry, branched off from the center hall. Straight ahead as we entered the hall from outside was the larger of our two adjoining rooms, separated by a glazed French door. It operated as our multifunctional, living-dining room during the day and transformed into my parents' bedroom at night with the use of a sofa bed. The apartment also contained a tiny room meant to house a servant, but as we had no servant, mother had intended to fix it up for me. Her plan, however, was outweighed by the need for a storage space. Thus, firewood, among other things, got stored there instead.

The kitchen was a comfortable, u-shaped workspace. One wall housed a small sink and a gas cooking range, the second, a credenza (built by my father), and the third, our table and chairs. During the winter, that homey nook became our little Siberia, where mother had to wear head-to-toe winter gear in order to do her daily chores. Cracks around the outside door allowed free entry to the cold air, which even the little fired-up potbelly stove failed to balance.

Each tub of bath water had to be heated. To take the chill out of the air, Mother lit a tall burgundy ceramic-tile wood stove in a corner of the living room. Leaning against those warm tiles was a delicious way to warm the body, as was the customary midday meal, which coincided with school dismissal. On my way up the stairs each day, cooking aromas were the first to greet my fine-tuned nose. I loved my mother's cooking, with the exception of one thing: cholent, a kidney bean stew, the smell of which always made me want to run the other way. That being a foolish mistake, I chose instead to give my mother a hard time, which was equally foolish because she gave it right back to me. Looking down at my plate of cholent with a disgusted grimace, I negotiated in an effort to avoid the inevitable outcome.

"Mom, do I have to finish this?"

"Why? What is wrong with it? "she asked, as if this was the first time she and I had confronted the cholent issue. Without waiting for an answer, she went on: "Don't make faces! Good food should be appreciated."

"Please, please, just looking at it makes me sick…and…God! I can't stand the way it smells!"

Wagging a finger, she scolded me sternly. "Watch your tongue, child!" I knew just what she was about to say next; this was a perfect opening for Mother to reiterate the story of earlier hardships in her life. We had heard her recite the same words so many times that Gyuri and I knew it well enough to impudently pick up the thread and mimic her: "*Yes, I wish I had this good food after the first World War … and think of the poor hungry people in the world who would gladly take your place …*" Mother had difficulty concealing her mirth in those moments, but she kept her composure intact. She must have known that to reason with us was totally useless, but after all, it was her duty to teach us proper values, particularly when it came to food. Sorry to say, her sermons didn't make any of our least favorite foods more appealing. As a matter of fact, the more she repeated the slogan, the less we really listened. So what if she had to go through hard times, we scoffed. What has that got to do with us? Why can't she stop bringing it up? And if she is so worried about the hungry of the world, she can pack up the yucky food and send it to them.

Of course, there was little sense arguing with Mother, because she always won. "Kids," she would say, "What do they know?" And she was right. We did not know enough to understand what she was trying to teach us. All the while, Father just stood by and let Mother be the bad guy. He focused instead on providing food for our table. My parents lived in ideal partnership. Each had their designated turf with a united front based on mutual respect and shared principles. House rules were simple and easy to follow, and the general mood of our family was far from rigid. As a matter of fact, it was rather congenial and flexible. For example, when it came to the question of cholent, I had the right to refuse eating it as long as I accepted the consequences of waiting for the evening meal with perhaps only some fruit in between. I didn't mind that much, as long as I could make up for it by taking a double portion of baked potato, winter squash, or bread and butter to go with the coffee in the evening. Nothing really bothered me much because I felt loved and cared for. I cannot remember ever being hungry or otherwise deprived, and I never suspected how my parents struggled to make ends meet on very little.

I knew we didn't have much money because Mother's great pleasure consisted of window-shopping. Walking through the shopping districts, we stopped to inspect the window displays. If either of us saw something we liked, Mother offered the same refrain: "*When we have the money, we'll buy it.*" This response got me used to the idea that we could not spare money for "frivolous" things. That did not mean we had to stop dreaming. However, I was also a realist. For instance, not considering myself a candidate for a class excursion that cost money, I never thought of asking my parents for the funds. The idea of not having enough money worked itself into my psyche. To this day, I still operate from a mentality of poverty.

Though Father's small construction business eventually would grow to the point that we could afford a little more luxury, we never had the good fortune to enjoy its fruit.

By the way, cholent is made with kidney beans, meat, barley, onion, garlic, and seasoning. A nice piece of smoked meat can enhance the flavor. At least that is how mother made it. Authentically, cholent was prepared a day ahead of Sabbath in the homes of observant Jews—and then sent to the baker the next day to be heated in the oven. Our family was not in the habit of following traditions. Therefore cholent could appear on our menu any time my mother's budget demanded it. Lucky me.

One of our neighbors on the floor above had a daughter named Dolly. She was the same age as me. Her father was a professional military man. Somehow our families never got to know each other even as our paths frequently crossed in the hallway. The Maytans kept much to themselves, though Dolly and I walked to middle school together. On our way, we stopped at the Catholic Church on Beke Square for her morning devotion. We could easily spare the few minutes it took for her to recite a short prayer, followed by some rituals alien to me. Nevertheless, since I was in the church alongside of her, I found it only natural to follow suit in dipping fingers into a water bowl, turning towards the altar, and curtsying while making the sign of the cross. As she did it, so did I. There was no thunder or lightning to protest my un-Jewish act. And I didn't feel any different after I left the church than I had felt before I walked in. I must admit, though, that the church's interior, bedecked with statues, had a strange effect on me. If anything, I felt an aversion to the idea of relating to the Spirit through clay-formed images. However, if it made Dolly happy, it was no skin off my back. After school, we always met in the yard at home to play with other kids. All was well until two years later, when her parents decided to transfer her into a parochial institution. The year was 1937.

> *"For me, the different religions are beautiful flowers from the same Garden or they are branches of the same majestic tree. Therefore, they are Equally true, though being received and interpreted through human instruments equally imperfect."*
>
> —Mahatma Gandhi

The very first day after Dolly returned from her parochial school, we again gathered in the yard again. This time, however, Dolly turned her back to me, pretending I was not there. I didn't know what to make of her strange behavior and decided to ask.

"Have I done anything to hurt your feelings?"

"I don't want you as my friend anymore!" she snapped back in a most irritated tone. I could not imagine what had come over her and decided to probe further:

"Why are you angry at me?"

Hearing that, she swung around, looked me square between the eyes, and shouted her accusation. "You are a Jew, and you killed my Christ!"

What she said made no sense to me, but it felt as if a dagger pierced my heart.

Defenseless in the face of such an absurd allegation, my lame retort came on the verge of tears. "What is the matter with you? I killed no one and I don't even know who this Christ was that you are talking about!"

But Dolly shrugged her shoulder, raised her head high, and walked away without a word. It had taken only one day for her to be taught to hate by the religious authorities of her school, whose words she was to accept without questioning. This sudden loss of a friend under unexplainable circumstances was the first of other similar losses.

In contrast, Nusi's and my friendship would end years later, thanks to the political edict that forbade Christians to socialize with Jews.

HUNGARY WAS STEEPED IN CHRISTIANITY from the time of King Stephen I. The young country evolved to embrace Christian ideology on every level during Stephen's reign, after he converted the pagan tribes of the land and established the Hungarian State. Fifty-five years after his death, he was canonized and recognized as the Patron Saint of Hungary. His legacy of Christianity became synonymous with Hungary's identity and was a motivational force for its ruling classes for over a thousand years even after the monarchy diminished. Thereafter, ruling classes suppressed non-Christians by assimilating them into the fiber of Hungarian society. In other words, the constitution recognized minority religions without restriction—at least on the surface. We were considered Hungarian nationals and part of the national tapestry, identified as Jews by religion only.

School activities reflected Hungary's commitment to Christianity. Such was the case with one of my favorite non-academic subjects, choir, directed by Aunt Izabella, an outstanding music teacher. She was a dwarfish lady with beautiful, abundant, rich brown hair. She twisted it into a prominent bun, which elevated her stature. She was well-suited to lead the choir of young girls, enthusiastically stomping her feet to keep rhythm and discipline. When we rehearsed Zoltan Kodaly's Easter cantata, Aunt Izabella invited the highly esteemed composer to observe our performance. The master was so pleased with what he heard that he arranged for us to audition with the Budapest radio station. Consequently, we performed Kodaly's Cantata on the

SPARKS FROM THE FIRE

air, broadcasted during the Easter season. It didn't make any difference to me that the lyrics for the Cantata were truly religious in nature. We lived in a Christian country, after all. We were accustomed to partaking in such endeavors without apprehension.

The public school system was well in tune with the national ideology. Schools reflected the country's Christian foundation by keeping girls and boys in separate buildings and mandating religious teaching within the standard curricular framework. Graded according to performance like other subjects, religion—which included Christianity (Protestant and Catholic) and Judaism—was taught by ministers, priests, and rabbis, respectively. The curriculum allotted each of the three belief systems two one-hour weekly sessions. The system did not seem out of the ordinary or unfair, as it was not in any way coercive. Students were not required to take a class that disagreed with their religious orientation. Those who were exempt could choose to observe or join another class's activity.

Curricular religious teaching had its pluses and minuses. On the one hand, I might never have approached the subject of religion on my own. On the other, the system helped raise walls of religious separation at a very early, impressionable age. My being Jewish became an issue *only* after I entered first grade. Grouped with other Jewish children to attend involuntary religious training, I was suddenly designated as a member of a sect, no longer one of the whole. I didn't fare well with my religious studies simply because I had no interest in them. Attending Friday night services at the Synagogue was compulsory. Biblical History interested me, but learning to read Hebrew to recite prayers in that ancient tongue made little sense to me. I resisted friends who asked me to join them in attending Talmudic instructions. I exerted little energy to comply with school requirements and earned a failing mark, which embarrassed my instructor more than it did me. I never had a problem with accepting Judaism as part of my historical heritage. On the other hand, however, the Jewish community expected me to adhere to dogma, a concept very much in conflict with my nature.

• • • •

A DEVELOPING ANTI-SEMITIC CLIMATE SWEEPING Europe under Hitler's influence only accentuated my inner conflict regarding Judaism. When people began turning against me because I was a Jew, it did not make any sense to me. I began to feel the effects of Nazi agendas in 1939. I was in my fourth and last year of middle school, where Gizi, a Protestant, and I were classmates and best friends. We always sat next to each other. Both of us participated in extra-curricular gymnastic activities and in the gym teacher's select performing group. We had a close relationship both in and out of school and often shared free time doing homework or skating in the school yard's skating rink during winter.

We totally disregarded our religious differences until our beloved homeroom teacher's vile bigotry inspired her to single me out. Margaret Czeiner (or Aunt Margaret, as we were to address our teachers) not only supervised homeroom but also taught math and geometry, which meant that we were in her class several times a week.

One day, she entered the room with her nose up, sniffing the air, and asking to have a window opened.

"There is a foul odor in this room," she commented, but nobody paid attention at first. However, her comment became a pattern over time, and she eventually rested her roving eyes upon me across the room, revealing the target of her disdain.

She then pulled me aside. She pretended benevolence, but with a wicked smile on her face, she said, *"You must learn to cleanse yourself properly to get rid of your offensive odor."*

The assault turned me red-hot with humiliation. Intimidated, I could only stare back at her, thinking: '*Why is she doing this to me?*'

I went home that day asking mother to smell me.

"What is this all about?" she demanded to know. "What brought this silly thing on?"

When I told her what happened, she looked away with a great big sigh and reassured me that the teacher was wrong. She advised me to "Ignore it." She never made an attempt to confront Aunt Margaret—something I did not understand at the time.

The day after that incident, I found Gizi moved to a seat far from me. She no longer wished to sit next to me because she said I smelled.

I had a rough time coping with the blatant betrayal of someone I had believed was a true friend.

Not long after that episode, Aunt Margaret opened our homeroom session by speaking with contagious enthusiasm of a great emerging German statesman. She praised the ideology of a humble man who had risen out of the ranks of average folks to follow his mission. "*Adolf Hitler is the man,*" she said—her face lit with admiration—"*who shall make our world a better place to live in.*"

Carried away with excitement upon hearing the good news, I rushed home to tell it to Mother. Her reaction to the 'good news' was not what I expected. Her demeanor stiffened. Her face turned a ghastly white. As she looked at me sadly, I barely heard her utter: "*My God, what will become of us?*" I had no idea what she was talking about, but I had the feeling that the news I brought affected her differently from how it affected Aunt Margaret.

Two of the girls who joined me in Aunt Margaret's homeroom, Jolie Mueller (whose parents owned one of the knitting mills on Frangepan Street) and Ellie Hoffman (from a family of bankers), had been my classmates in elementary school. Both girls, though from the affluent sector of our community, blended well with the rest of us. The only thing that set them apart was the way they dressed and the fact that, despite our classroom camaraderie, none of us ever got invited to their home, not even after we all transferred to the same middle school and remained classmates until graduation.

It was a surprise, then, that Ellie's mother made an exception when she hosted a graduation party in the honor of our homeroom teacher, Aunt Margaret. The Hoffmans opened their home to receive the entire class for the festive reception. It was the first time in my life I had a chance to get a glimpse at how people lived on the other side of the tracks. At first I felt self-conscious, as though I had entered a distant world. The pompous formality of the event left me with only one distinctly clear image in my head: open-faced party sandwiches beautifully arranged on trays, surrounded by an abundance of rich desserts, sweets and fruits on a large dining table. I cannot, for the life of me, remember anything else, or how the party ended.

One thing is certain: Ellie's and my paths never crossed again.

After that party, it became obvious that Ellie's family shared Aunt Margaret's affection for the new regime rising in Germany.

IN MY YOUTH, CHILDREN WERE largely able to remain undisturbed by the concerns of adults. I tended to be oblivious to anything outside of my own little world. The adults made sure not to discuss anything in our presence that would be over and above our comprehension or could make us fearful. Both my parents spoke fluent German, and I knew that they were listening to several of Adolf Hitler's public addresses with growing concern, but I paid no attention until a rapidly changing political climate intensified Hitler's presence in our everyday life. He mesmerized throngs with his fiery, hypnotic orations to such an extent, that, according to my parents, it was not difficult to fall under his spell.

IN 1941, I REACHED THE first plateau of my most precarious, formative years: my teens. I emerged out of the childhood cocoon and into a world of unknown challenges, the sort of trials and errors that honed my awareness and character. Impressions and experiences from one's teen years shape their views and actions later in life. Turbulant times placed undue obstacles in the way of our natural progression from childhood into adulthood.

My graduation from middle school at age fourteen completed the eight-year compulsory educational requirements. At the same time, Gyuri finished his twelfth year in the Gymnasium, a facility of higher education. Unfortunately, even though Gyuri was already a performing member of Hubay Music Academy's youth orchestra, the Numerous Clauses (an ordinance that restricted opportunities for Jews to further their career pursuits) prevented Gyuri from realizing his dream of actually studying at the academy in order to become a professional musician. Instead, my brother became a masonry apprentice in Father's small construction company.

The spoilers had the power to take control over our life but had yet to succeed in dampening our spirit. Gyuri never gave up his violin; nor was he discouraged from improving his technique. He measured his own skill by practicing his favorite piece, Tchaikowsky violin concerto in D, in concert with Jasha Heifetz's recorded version. My brother played to nurture his soul with a repertoire that also included Viniavsky, Brahms, Mendelsohn, Sarasate, Mozart, Rimsky Korsakov, Fritz Kreisler and others. We never tired of the music that filled our home as it resonated off the strings of his beloved violin.

The funniest and most amazing thing was to see our little green Hartz mountain canary going wild in his cage as soon as he spotted Gyuri setting up his music stand. We had to let him out; otherwise he would have gone nuts trying to break out of his cage. He flew straight to settle on the edge of the stand and tuned his voice like a singer would, while my brother tuned his violin. No sooner had Gyuri started to play than that crazy bird burst into his own melody with such gusto that we thought his stretched-out, throbbing little throat would burst. God forbid the bow would strike a false note! Pityu the bird (or Stivie, as we called him) would start crying in a whining tone. What a little performer that tiny bird proved to be! Mother got a mate for our troubadour, and they produced a chirping brood, but none of his sons turned out like him. He was one of a kind.

WHILE I WAS ATTRACTED TO people with academic knowledge, my own interests leaned more toward artistic design in a variety of mediums. I particularly disliked math and algebra and had to retake those tests to get my diploma. That meant I had to study during vacation time in the summer. Both Father and Gyuri excelled in those subjects and took me in hand. Trying to teach me proved to be more than they bargained for, and while it took some doing, I finally managed to stretch my dad's patience to the limit. He was in the midst of explaining a solution to some mathematical problem when he suddenly stopped, looked at me, and asked me to repeat what he had said. I looked back at him with a blank expression, for I had not the faintest idea because my mind was millions of miles away. "That's it!" he said. Angrier than I have ever seen him, he gave me the smack of my life.

That was the one and only time my father hit me, but I managed to pass the test.

BEING THE OUTGOING TYPE, I always looked for social involvement and never lacked friends. This character trait worried Mother, who thought that my trust in people might bring me down someday. When some of my former schoolmates introduced me to the Arena Street Synagogue's Cultural Center, I liked the place so much that I talked my brother into coming with me. As we had been squeezed out of the regular stream of society, the place became our second home. Gyuri's good humor and wonderful disposition won him many friends and popularity with the girls. The synagogue was not around the corner from where we lived, but it didn't matter much. We either walked or biked to get there. It was a great gathering place with overflowing cultural and social activities. The choir's conductor performed miracles with our mixed-gender group of non-professional singers, and it was there we met Feri (Ferenc) and Viki (Viktor), two boys who became our very best friends. They both happened to live on St. Laszlo Street. Feri's father was a horse-drawn carriage deliveryman, and their family lived in very humble circumstances. His sister Kati was a registered nurse and the librarian at the Cultural Center. Viki and his mother came to Budapest after escaping Vienna and Hitler's wrath in the nick of time. A well-meaning neighbor had informed them that the Nazis were tracking down young Jewish boys that very night in a house-to-house search and taking them into custody. Swiftly, the two stole across the border into Hungary and on to Budapest, where Viki's uncle gave them shelter.

At the Cultural Center, I also met Zsuzsa, and we quickly became friends. Skipping and hopping our way home from the center one day, we suddenly looked at each other and broke out laughing, "Let's be friends!" After so many years and a war that separated us, that friendship has never ceased. My mother, who was critical of all my friends, took exception to Zsuzsa, who truly deserved to pass the test of her discriminating judgment.

Concerts and the opera frequently occupied our agendas until the

Nazis revoked our right to enter public domains. The boys used to take turns standing in line for Opera House bleacher tickets starting as early as eight o'clock in the morning. They also secured tickets to concerts at the Liszt Ferenc Music Academy. But with the privileges of attending such events revoked, the Cultural Center picked up the slack. Jewish Cultural Centers city-wide booked prestigious Jewish performers who had been expelled from the legitimate entertainment world. Comics, musicians, and opera singers appeared in our small auditorium. Everyone tried to make the best of what felt like an increasingly dim situation.

The Cultural Center offered language courses as well. My infatuation with the English language might well be traced to seeing too many English-speaking movies. I even listened to the BBC Broadcasting Station on the radio, though I understood not a word of it. At the center, I opted to take English with Mr. Brown, while Gyuri, who studied French in school, enrolled in the French conversational class. Mr. Brown had lived in London for a considerable length of time, and he taught us to speak in refined British conversational mode, which did not turn out to be of much help in America.

Weekend hikes through the Buda Hills with about fifteen of us became the most cherished of all the activities during that period. We met at the "Banana Tower" with our backpacks full of food and supplies. The tower was actually a kiosk on a small, round, concrete isle in the center of town, where several transportation arteries merged near the Western Railway Station a short distance from the Margit Bridge. Our high-spirited group crossed the bridge over to the Buda side and continued to climb on up to Mount Gellert's most popular picnic grounds near the Norma tree. No sooner had we spread the blankets on the grassy mound than the boys had gotten into a soccer game, which we girls watched as we cheered them on. Those one-day excursions made us eagerly look forward to the weekends from early spring to late fall. Whether walking through the woods singing, picking wild flowers, or sprawling on the blankets eating in rustic picnic style, those days were refreshing breaks away after a week's work.

My parents were worried sick over us when air strikes began to come with increased frequency, particularly because we crossed the bridge on foot. Bombs frequently aimed at bridges and railroads, so choosing to cross was dangerous. We ran into just such trouble in the spring of 1943, when, while in the middle of the bridge on our way home, we had to stay still until the siren sounded to signal the end of the raid. By that time, the freshly picked violets clutched in my hand had nearly drowned in sweat. That was the end of our hiking days. A dark destiny approached, as the Nazi occupational forces took over the city of Budapest.

MY MOTHER HAD TWO SISTERS living in the United States: Barbara and Elisabeth. Over the course of my childhood, I had learned to love my Aunt Elisabeth through my mother, who adored her "little sister" and had nothing but the best to say about her. There were five Braun children. Among them, according to my mother, she and Elisabeth were a particularly inseparable team, until Elisabeth left for America. Elisabeth, like Barbara before her, settled in the United States with their Aunt Sophie and Uncle Gabriel. Sophie and Gabriel originally invited my mother instead of Elisabeth, but Mother was already married and reluctant to go and leave her husband behind. The opportunity passed on to Elisabeth, who accepted it in order for her fiancé Alex to follow her and avoid military draft as World War I loomed. Elisabeth's gamble worked, and she and Alex married in America. They had two children, Theresa and Bobby, born six years apart. The other three Braun siblings remained in Hungary, where they weathered the storm through two major wars and two bloody revolutions. After moving to America, Elisabeth continued to correspond with my mother only. Regrettably, Aunt Sophie, Uncle Gabe, and my Aunt Barbara died long before I had a chance to meet them.

From the moment Elisabeth had settled in the United States, my parents never abandoned their dream that some day she and her husband would help our family join them there, but the births of my brother and me temporarily halted those expectations. One time, Elisabeth and Alex suggested that father should immigrate on his own and send for us when he had established some form of security. However, it was not to be. Father could not leave us behind, and our relatives never attempted to take us all together. Therefore, the prospect of America was indefinitely suspended.

WHEN THE THREAT OF ANOTHER war began to rear its ugly head, Nazi propaganda succeeded in igniting the flames of dormant anti-Semitism, leaving us as Jews with more than ordinary threats of war to concern us. Worst of all, our country once again found itself in contract with the devil. The administration's compliance with Nazi doctrine kept tightening the noose around our necks. While there was still a chance to leave, some people escaped with the help of relatives living in safe places. In one instance, American relatives adopted a twenty-one year-old son to secure his immigration. This knowledge prompted my mother to approach my aunt and uncle to do the same for Gyuri and me before it was too late. Yet my relatives refused, saying that such an attempt could jeopardize their citizenship, something they were not willing to risk.

Mother felt betrayed, and in a last desperate plea, she warned her sister and brother-in-law that if they didn't help, that was the last time they would ever hear from her. "Furthermore," Mother said, "if anything will happen to our children, their blood will stain your conscience forever." Her final words went unanswered, and their communication ended.

Then sixteen, I was an idealistic, sentimental ignoramus not fully aware of the gravity of the situation facing us. Instead of trying to understand the fear and emotional stress that drove my mother to write that last letter, I was quick to blame her for what I considered irrational hysterics. I picked up the correspondence with my aunt where she had left, and I still wonder why Mother did not stop me. My aunt, however, responded generously, praising me for having a good heart. She and I kept in touch until diplomatic relations between our countries ceased and all communication between Hungary and the USA halted.

My brother was drafted into service at age twenty-one, which actually meant that he was transferred into one of several functioning Jewish forced labor units operating in the Carpathian region, a Hungarian mountain range that reached from Northern Hungary to the country's border with Russia. Gyuri was there during one particular winter, when, as I remember, my parents had to go and bring him warm clothing and food because the army only allotted the Jewish workers the bare minimum of rations. Eventually, when his brigade was transferred to Vac, not far from Budapest at the Danube bend, Gyuri had the good fortune to be placed in the KP unit, which often came to Budapest to replenish their supplies. We were able to see him on most of those occasions; in fact, sometimes he would show up unexpectedly in the air raid shelter during air attacks. He was a handsome young man, my brother: short, but well built with broad shoulders and narrow hips; gentle and quiet with large, soulful dark eyes and lashes you could sweep the floor with. He carried his violin tucked under his arm, Gypsy-like, to entertain his superiors and comrades. They loved him for it. To my knowledge, their unit was removed from the city of Vac following my deportation.

MY EARLIER FAILED ATTEMPT WITH the violin did not discourage my parents from trying to make a musician of me, and they figured the piano would be a more suitable instrument. Nevertheless, for that, we needed a piano. While Father was capable of picking a good violin at a nearby Gypsy camp, a piano was way out of his league. With the help of a colleague, who was also a pianist, they set out to find the right instrument. I have no idea where their search took them or what sort of incentive inspired the friend, but a far-from-ordinary, lacquered black Bosendorfer grand piano landed a prominent spot in our small bedroom. How they managed to fit it through the doors and into the room remains a mystery to me, but there it was. With Gyuri away in service, I had just enough room for a single bed and a wardrobe next to that magnificent obstruction. With the piano in place, Father's friend sat down to demonstrate his skills. The man banged those keys as if he were on the podium of a concert hall. The boisterous sound of that instrument shook the walls, but luckily did not harm the good old solid construction of our building.

My Father promptly hired Bora, the girlfriend of Tibor, Gyuri's

violin teacher, to give me lessons at home, but after two years, it became evident that even the Bosendorfer could not help me become
a musician. I went as far as attempting to learn the accompaniment
to Mozart's Minuet to surprise Gyuri when he came home on a furlough, but the surprise ended in embarrassed frustration. I was not
born to be a musician. However, I at least learned to understand and
appreciate music and acquired enough background to continue taking
lessons at a much later date.

Had it not been for the enforced Numerous Clauses, I might have
gone on to higher education. My parents wanted me at least to go to
a commercial learning institute and do secretarial work. However, increasing restrictions on Jews left me with the only option of selecting
a trade apprenticeship.

I fiercely resisted the idea of becoming a dressmaker like my
mother. "I want to be a photographer," I announced. To my disappointment however, the owner of a photo studio turned me down:
"The profession requires working with chemicals in a darkroom, and
it is not meant for girls."

Okay. Why not be a hairdresser then? So it happened that we made
a contract with a hairdressing salon, where, for six months, I learned
to clean mirrors and counters until they sparkled, opened doors to
coming and going customers, and cleaned smoke-filled stacks outside
in the dead of winter until my hands froze, caked with soot. Reaching
the limit of my endurance, I quit. The question was where to go next.

"You can't sit home while you make your mind up," declared my
mom. "Go and get work at one of the factories." So I did, and instead
of them giving me a chance to learn about the factory's manufacturing
process, they used me for a gofer. Doing menial work in a downright
subservient position made the prospects of becoming a dressmaker
look better every day. Father suggested we arrange a two-year apprenticeship contract in a small dressmaking establishment owned by his
lawyer's wife. Dr. Gartner's law service was on retainer by Father's
well-established construction firm. His wife was a dressmaker-designer, whose workshop consisted of one small room in their other-

wise lavish apartment in an upscale neighborhood. The Gartners lived separate lives under one roof to keep up appearances. Dr Gartner was a handicapped veteran of World War I. Their only child, Eva, two years my junior, felt emotionally neglected by her parents and took solace in my company. I became her elder sister and confidante.

As I was preparing to start my new position, I found my mother to be less than supportive for the first time. It hurt me to hear her say, "It will not surprise me to hear that you will have trouble holding the scissors and handling the needle." Was this her way of telling me to try my best? Did she challenge me to prove her wrong? Well, if she did, my mother's reverse psychology sure worked. I aimed not to please, but rather to spite her because she seemed to have lost faith in me.

Mrs. Gartner was a little skinny woman who never walked: she ran in rapid staccato steps. Her little beady eyes followed the movements of her steps, and she could have easily been mistaken for a scarecrow had she been found in the middle of a grain field with her brightly dyed, frizzy red hair. One thing I must admit to her credit: she was an excellent teacher, and she wasted no time to teach me basic sewing skills. As soon as I became proficient enough, she laid off the one employee she had on payroll. "Not enough room for all of us" was what she said, but she did not fool me. Her motive was not difficult to figure out. She paid me 4.00 Pengos for a week's unlimited working hours. There were times when her maid did not show up, and she would substitute me to do the house-cleaning chores. Mrs. Gartner gave me her personal items to mend when all legitimate work for customers was finished. Often she sent me to deliver finished garments across town to unfamiliar districts where I had difficulty navigating after hours in the war-darkened city and sometimes missed my piano lessons as a result. While a legitimate workday legally consisted of eight hours with an hour break for lunch and Saturdays until noon, she just plain worked me to death, ignoring the labor union's protection law. She counted on me not having the guts to stand up to her. I almost did not. It took almost a year to gather my indignation, but when I finally did, I gave her the surprise of her life. The last day I worked there, was a Saturday. Little did she know that I was determined to leave at noon, no matter how much work she would pile in front of me. I eagerly waited for the clock to chime twelve as the pile of my assignments continued to grow. Close to the hour, I began gathering my supplies. Looking cool and calm on the outside, I was plenty nervous and sweaty when I picked myself up, ready to leave. Mrs. Gartner looked at me absolutely stunned out of her mind.

"And what do you think you are doing?" she asked, an authoritarian threat in her voice.

"Something I should've done a long time ago," I replied. With that, I walked out on Mrs. Gartner and terminated the contract.

Magda, one of my friends from school, worked as a journeyman in an elegant center-city fashion salon. She recommended that I negotiate with Grete, the owner, to convince her to assume the remainder of my contract, as I needed another year to complete my apprenticeship. My interview with Grete went better than expected, and she took me on. I found paradise. Grete was demanding, but fair. She accepted nothing less than high-standard performance. Her clientele included wives of high-level foreign officials, as well as those of local dignitaries. In the tradition of other Haute Couture establishments, Grete Salon also staged seasonal fashion shows. Once I was given the honor to make a belt for a white pique number with a vertical woven pinstripe. The lines of the pattern had to be straight as an arrow, and when Grete inspected it, her "just about right" meant that she was pleased with what I did. Boy! Was I proud to have my first piece, no matter if it was only an insignificant accessory, accepted to be part of the show! Grete loved and respected her staff, including the apprentices, and we were eager to please her. Under the direction of Grete and her assistant, Sari, I honed my skills to the highest level. Grete was a middle-aged Jewess from Vienna whose paramour was a Christian military officer.

In March of 1944 came the full takeover of the city by Nazi occupational forces. At the very same time, I was about to graduate. I was to go to the union hall and produce a garment from start to completion, but shopping restrictions on Jews made it impossible to get material for my project. Mother, who was no stranger to improvisation, took apart a wool gabardine trench coat, dyed it navy blue, and cut out a dress for me to take to the union hall. I passed the test, got my journeyman license, and went back to the salon the next day. Grete was not there. Her paramour had her deported to Auschwitz.

SPRING OF 1944 FADED SLOWLY into a distant yesterday.

The Nazis mandated our move into an inner-city apartment building marked with the Star of David, a relocation that signaled the first step towards our deportation. The Gestapo hastened to devise methods to increase their efficiency in locating Jews for their twisted purposes.

The Blau family's five-room apartment in a large, old, and dingy structure on Dembinsky Street became our new, shared home base. Irenke and Lipot Blau were friends of ours. In fact, Irene was the only girlfriend Mother ever had, to my knowledge. They were a family of three, with one son Bandi serving in the Jewish military forced labor unit, like my brother Gyuri. Mother and Dad were unaware that Irene and Lipot were scheming to disappear. They spilled the beans just before taking off to an undisclosed hiding place. We had no idea of their plans, but their disappearance could have backfired on us, with unimaginable interrogation from the janitor who had to account for all the Jewish residents on a regular basis. The monitoring system had one loophole; sudden disappearance of Jews was not unusual. People were randomly picked off the streets, never to be seen or heard of again. With the yellow Star of David worn on our outer garment, we were easy targets for harassment, abusive verbal insults, and sporadic deportation.

The air was filled with tension. We had to watch our every move, action, and word because we knew that hostile people were implanted in those buildings to spy on us. You had to be mindful not to arouse suspicion of betrayal. We did not know whom to trust. Everyday life became increasingly difficult, as our future seemed to fade rapidly into oblivion. We lived with anxiety day and night, both during and in between air and ground attacks. We were constantly ready to walk three flights down to the earthen-floored damp cellar with a basket full of emergency supplies.

"Hurry, Hurry," Mother would say nervously, grabbing the basket on the run, as if our lives depended on that frequent exodus to the place that one misdirected bomb could have turned into a mass grave.

The frequency of nightly sleep interruptions finally got to me. 'What's the point of running down into that stupid cellar? If we get hit, it really doesn't matter where I'll be'—I reasoned—'so I might as well keep sleeping.' I made up my mind to ignore the next air raid. The following dawn, when the sirens blasted away, I pretended not to hear it. I was determined to stay in bed and did not heed Mother's relentless effort to get me out. Her increasing anxiety irritated me because I wanted to be left alone.

"Leave me be, I want to sleep. If anything happens, I won't even notice." I did not even open my eyes.

"Just get me my coat from the closet, I can't reach it," she commanded.

I angrily leaped out of bed, grabbed her coat off the rack, and blurted out, "This was a trick just to get me out of bed." Mother was small, but her hand was quick. A slap on the face brought me to full consciousness, and I realized, that as far as she was concerned, I had no choice but one.

As if we did not have enough to be concerned with, we also had a couple of canaries to worry about. One time we elected to stay in a friend's ground floor apartment instead of the shelter because the birds were not allowed there. At our friend's house, we placed their cloth-covered cages on the floor, and we all took our positions lying face down on the floor under the window to be protected against detonating pressure.

From the beginning of the air strike, bombs fell with rapid frequency, approaching their targets with an unnerving, eerie whistling sound as they fell. Each detonation sounded closer than the other, sending mother shaking with fright. She began praying aloud while the birds sang their hearts out. Each, the birds and my mother, voiced the helpless cry we all felt inside.

The moment of relief at the end of each raid was brief. We survived another ordeal, but what were we really spared for? We were sitting ducks.

I remember the day when father and I stood in front of our apartment, watching the sky. He anxiously calculated the time that elapsed between the flashing light across the sky and the sound of each cannon fire. He could tell that the front was very near. If the front had come closer, the deportations run by Adolf Eichmann–whom Hitler had placed in charge of the Final Solution—might have been halted. Unfortunately, time worked in favor of Eichmann's fanatic obsession.

THE THIRD REICH'S DAYS WERE numbered. Their defeat was so close. We could almost taste the sweet smell of freedom, but the cornered beasts fought harder and meaner to silence the city's remaining Jews forever.

We lost the race with time when, on the twentieth day of October, we awakened at dawn to the urgent announcement of our building superintendent: "I am ordered to call all remaining able-bodied Jewish men between the ages of 16 and 60 to assemble in the courtyard with supplies, ready to leave within one hour. The troopers will be here shortly." Indeed, they, the Hungarian Gestapo, known as the arrow cross guards, arrived without time to waste. They reconciled the list of Jewish occupants with the assembly to be sure nobody was left out. Attempting to hide at that point was out of the question. No one dared to risk the brutal consequences of that foolish move.

Destination unknown, the men, my father among them, were shortly out of sight. It happened so fast that we had no time to say goodbye and didn't know if we were to see him ever again. With Gyuri and now Father gone, Mother and I remained in stunned silence.

The intensified atmospheric tension pressured our oppressors to carry out the last details of a Final Solution. Eichmann orchestrated the detailed procedures to deport two transports of women from his Budapest headquarters. I was in one of them. Two days after the first shock of my father's deportation, they issued an ordinance requiring all women between the ages of sixteen and forty to assemble in the same rapid fashion. Mother was forty-eight. In her last effort to protect me she scraped together at least two days of ration from the little food left in our cupboard, and along with the meager food supply she filled my backpack with part of my trousseau to barter with. We embraced with hardly a word between us. Consoling words froze unspoken in our throats. What was there to say? Frightened to be left alone, my mother, whom I had known to be the rock of Gibraltar, looked forlorn, silently sobbing as she helplessly watched the last fragment of her hopes shattered. I felt numb with apprehension, fearing unknown dangers ahead. But looking at her, all my self-directed thoughts washed away. I could not bear to see her standing there alone like an orphaned child, a picture that never left my mind.

Gyuri and me (cca.1941)

CAUGHT IN THE FIRE

· · · · · · · · ·

Chapter Two

The War Years

Experiences up to and including Liberation

It was a dreary day. Heavy rain accompanied us as armed guards herded us in rows of two across the city like a flock of sheep. It was a most humiliating and degrading experience, as some passersby actually seemed pleased at the sight. The city of my birth was desecrated. We were alone and totally defenseless in a hostile world.

After hours of marching, we arrived at the KISOK soccer stadium. Exhausted and soaked to the bone, we spent the night on the bleachers. Everything in my backpack was saturated and my food ruined. I was hungry for the first time in my life, with no food in sight.

Lilly Braun and I were from the same building and became allies. She and I stuck together like glue all through our torturous march on the Viennese highway towards the Austrian border. Our destination was shrouded in mystery. The guards depended on day-to-day instruction from headquarters, where the officials themselves kept altering their strategy in accordance with rapid changes in the war zone. Our lives hung in the balance of unpredictable circumstances.

Winter was on the way. The temperature dipped, quickly reaching the freezing point. Without a shelter, we slept each night in roadside ditches, huddled together for warmth. My winter coat, scarf, and gloves barely fit the need. Wearing high-laced shoes, together with my extensive hiking experience, helped to keep up with the demand of daily marching order for some time.

Eventually we crossed the bridge over the Danube River to the

Buda side and camped out on the Tungsram (an electric supply manufacturing industry) public pool grounds alongside the river. This was
the second day of our journey, and food was still not to be had. Rumor
had it that the next day we would be given a ration. We awoke the next
morning to the pungent smell of burning leaves mixed with the familiar aroma of simmering split pea soup. It took us only minutes to line
up orderly in a single row to receive our portion. We stood and expectantly held our containers with outstretched arms. We were, however,
allowed only a brief look at the huge cauldron brimming with soup
over a fire of burning autumn leaves before, by well-calculated cruelty,
we were ordered to leave the scene and the soup behind.

Some people nearly fell into the boiling soup as they tried to scoop
some of the life-sustaining grub into their dish. The raw truth of our
quickly evaporating future was taking shape. Hungry, tired, and cold,
we marched on. The war in the sky and the enemy on land outlined
our destiny, which we had no chance to escape.

Walking through open fields, we frequently found ourselves
caught in the raging fire of air raids, sending us running for cover
back into the nearest roadside ditches, still the only available shelter
in site. Unprotected from the elements, we grew weaker each day. Lilly
and I decided to slip away and waited for the moment when we could
attempt our escape. In the fields, we passed randomly piled haystacks,
which offered inviting hiding places. We waited for an opportunity to
dash out of the line and burrowed into the closest haystack as adrenaline coursed through our blood. Just as we started to settle into our
prickly refuge, we heard the reassuring voice of a young boy announce
"Ladies, be assured of your safety; we know you are hungry, and there
will be warm soup coming for you to eat. I will call you when it's
ready." Lilly and I could hardly believe our luck. However, when the
boy summoned and we emerged from our hiding place, we discovered
there were several others sharing our haystack. The boy had deceived
us. Instead of heading for soup, he had summoned the guards, who
ordered us back to the marching line. The young boy, not more than
fifteen years old, grinned from ear to ear. To him, his act was an hon-
orable display of loyalty to the regime that posed the possibility of a
reward. To us, the deception was yet another devastating experience.

Back where we started, looking for anything resembling food, we occasionally came upon row potatoes and discovered them to be a very tasty treat. Sometimes we also found a vegetable that was used by farmers for cattle feed and had the taste and texture of kohlrabi. When we were lucky to find one, we savored it with careful rationing. Taking tiny bites between long lapses made it last longer. My memory fails to recall any food distributed at any time, except once, when, as we approached the border of a town, we met up with some sympathetic folks awaiting our arrival with hot soup. Those few people had the courage to defy restriction, which forbade them to have any form of personal contact with us. Nevertheless, there were also towns with others who, like vultures full of venomous hatred, tore away our meager belongings, saying, "Where you are going, you won't need any of this anyhow."

Their ugly words, ruthlessly hurled in our direction, carried the threat of death.

ONLY MANY YEARS LATER DID I begin to account for the differences between the attitudes of people I met from one town to the next. I have come to the conclusion that a community itself develops a certain personality. I believe this development happens for one of two reasons. Either like-minded people congregate together, or the leadership of the community sets the pervasive tone. In cities, for instance, I find that common cultural backgrounds and belief systems bind communities. In addition, in here in the U.S., each time an administration changes, so, too, does the mood of the general population along with it. Having recognized these phenomena, I have begun to understand that—whether in Hungary or the United States or anywhere else— larger cultural and national currents color human behavior. As a result, within a particular culture, exceptions to the rule stand out, just as did the women who offered us their soup and sympathy as we marched along the Viennese highway.

WITHOUT ADEQUATE NOURISHMENT, THE LONG and often-interrupted march began to have devastating effects on most of us. Wherever we were stationed, our work digging ditches became more difficult and exhausting as the winter gradually arrived with its frosty reality. The guards quickly disposed of those stricken by illness or exhaustion with a simple gunshot, leaving the lifeless bodies behind on the road where they fell. Fatigue took me over, and I could no longer lace up my shoes over my frostbitten feet. Walking became nearly intolerable in that condition, and I was on the verge of giving up the seemingly endless torment. The miracle that lifted my waning spirit came from the most unexpected source: a German officer assigned to our company. He offered a helping hand, inviting me to rest my arm around his shoulder in order to take the pressure off my feet as I walked. I do not remember even looking at his face, but his kindness sent a ray of light into the bleakness of the situation. That light gave me the strength to keep going.

We continued marching along the Viennese highway until reaching the last station on Hungarian soil. At this point, they began housing us in stables. For the first time since leaving home, at least there was a roof over our head, even if we slept on straw-covered ground. Digging trenches continued to be our routine and our small ration of soup (of undeterminable ingredients) and bread gave us something to look forward to when we returned from our work each day. One day, a young woman tried to escape and ran into the woods out of desperation. She was caught and made to dig her own grave. We were forced to watch her execution. A similar situation occurred when, in the adjacent men's' quarters, one of the prisoners kicked a Nazi guard's machine gun, sending bullets into the guard's leg. It was not determined who committed the offense, and, because no one was willing to tell, six men were chosen at random to avenge the 'crime' with their life. We had to witness their execution, too.

At one point, I accidentally pierced the palm of my left hand with a rusty nail. Shortly after, the wounded area began to fester, and a red line spread upward on my arm. I recognized it as the beginning signs of blood poisoning. In the absence of medical aid and in substandard sanitary conditions, I had resigned myself to expect the inevitable. But suddenly, the red line began to recede and, like a miracle, the infection cleared all by itself. This was the first of many seemingly miraculous occurrences that kept me alive so that I could fulfill my destiny.

NOSTALGIC RECOLLECTIONS AND DREAMS OF reunion with our loved ones filled what little free time we had. Talking about food helped to quiet our ever-growling stomachs. We also developed the habit of turning to the spirit world for comfort. We conducted séances, inviting supernatural entities to enlighten us about our future. Gradually, we lost track of time, and our outward appearances degenerated to the point that we became shadows of our former selves. Opportunities for cleansing were rare, and on the isolated occasions when bathing was possible, we had only an outdoor spigot and cold water available. Cleanliness was a thing of the past, a distant luxury. We began to itch and scratch long before our interment in the concentration camp. The shock of discovering we had become helpless prey to yet another invasion of our persons was almost more than I could take.

Having already endured the infection in my hand and my frostbitten feet, I made up my mind. I refused to work anymore, regardless of the consequences. Several others shared my decision. The following morning, they ordered us all to line up in the courtyard to face a German officer armed with a Luger and ready for an execution. He raised his gun, but, after looking us over, suddenly lowered it. He turned around and walked away with his head bowed. Spared yet again, this had to be more than mere coincidence or luck. It has often been said that cats have nine lives. Had I been a cat, I would have already used up at least three.

ON THE DAY WE WERE to be transported into Germany, we assembled early in the morning with all our belongings. Our superiors ordered their personnel to take us to the railroad station situated at the edge of a border town called Hidegkut, where we would be officially turned over to German authorities. This was really a formality because we were already under Nazi occupation, and there was hardly any distinction between Hungary's own generic Nazi/Arrow Cross and the

original hyenas (German Nazi SS). Hitler did not need to invade
Hungary because he had found a willing ally in our country's fore-
most leader, Miklos (Nicholas) Horthy, our regent. The Nazi ideology
swept through Hungary like the Plague, killing the heart of its people.
When Horthy, however, realized the extent of Hitler's willingness to
commit inhuman acts in order to achieve sole domination, the regent
attempted to negotiate and slow things down. As a result, Horthy was
eventually thrown out of office and replaced by Szalasi Ferenc, the
leader of the infamous Arrow Cross.

This forced regime change opened the gates of hell. Suddenly, ignorant masses ran rampant in their attacks on defenseless citizens. The
taste of power was intoxicating to the young and misinformed, who
enjoyed taking the liberties of killing or mistreating anyone at whim.
It was not unusual for a sixteen year old to harass an elderly Jew with
his bayonet, to strike someone with the butt of his gun, or even to
shoot at random just to demonstrate his authority. These self-impor-
tant individuals, along with German officers, comprised the group of
guards during the three-month ordeal that took us to Hidegkut train
station, where we arrived on the 1st day of January 1945.

As the process of transfer to the German authorities began, a tall,
dark-haired young gentleman stood before us in a trench coat. He announced, "Anyone holding a Swedish passport should leave the line.
Even if the papers are not with you, come over to me and I will take
you back to Budapest." He identified himself as a Swede, but I knew
of neither him nor any passport. I was too numb to recognize the
hint: Even without papers, anyone who wished to do so could take
him up on his offer. Only long after the war was over did I learn the
identity of that most courageous man, Raoul Wallenberg. He was a
Swedish diplomat who single-handedly managed to rescue thousands
of Jews from the jaws of death by heroic efforts and at great personal
risk. He disappeared at the end of the war, and investigations into
his whereabouts led to the Soviet Union, where he had been lured,
taken by force, and incarcerated on false charges. Speculations about
his fate were never confirmed because the Soviets denied having any
knowledge of him. According to the most recent accounts released by
Russian authorities, he died in prison soon after his capture. No clues

were offered as to the nature of his death. He was only 33 years old. I have often wondered why this remarkable young man had to meet his demise after devoting his life to save so many others.

WE ARRIVED AT HIDEGKUT TRAIN station in the midday. It turned out to be nothing more than a concrete platform without any sort of shelter. Our tormentors kept us in the dark as to when our train would arrive or where it would take us. Forbidden to sit down, we could only stomp our feet and rub our hands together to keep from freezing in the sub-zero weather. Had it not been for the pleading of my dear friend Lilly, I would have sat and had it all over with. She kept me going. When the sun went down, we were no longer under supervision; we sat on our luggage to spend the night under the sky. By sunrise, the death toll was great. Nature took many out of their misery.

When the cattle cars arrived, we were enormously relieved to be finally out of the cold. Anything seemed better than being outdoors in such awful, frigid conditions. How naïve we were! Jammed into a boxcar with standing room only, lice-infested straw on the floor, and just a bucket for a toilet facility, we found ourselves locked in a temporary moving jail cell. One tiny window way up high offered our only connection to the outside world. Neither food nor water was supplied for long periods. Each of us tired from standing in one spot all day and fought to gain a squatting space for relief. It became too much for some to bear. Several women broke down; the guards ended each one's crazed hysterics with a bullet in the head. Once or twice, we were released and ran like wild animals to grab handfuls of snow to quench our thirst—if not our hunger. By this time, we were all too aware that we could not expect anything more than this refreshing white nectar for sustenance.

The journey on the rails seemed to take an eternity. Heavy air attacks destroyed many of the lines and forced our train to take frequent detours. One of our fellow prisoners, hoisted up to the window, could determine only that we were somewhere in the mountains. When the train finally stopped and we were let out, the only visible sign informed us we had arrived at Bergen Belsen. Of course none of us had any idea where or what that was, but it did not take us very long to find out.

What followed bewildered me and left lasting, painful memories. Any possessions that had managed to survive the journey were taken from us. It was then that they revoked the last shred of our dignity and our very identity. Of all the things I held, photos of my family, my dear ones, were the hardest to give up. Female camp attendants, shouting out intolerant and intolerable orders, handled the check-in process. "Clothes—everything—no, you can't keep your shoes or your pictures, faster—keep moving—do as you are told." The attendants sorted our clothing and possessions and dropped them into individual heaps. We had no idea who these women were and found out later that they, too, were inmates, Hungarian and Polish women in charge of "reception." It was hard to believe that those who shared our fate could inflict such hostile treatment, but hatred finds its way without justification and has no limits. They resented us for having been spared the additional three months while they had suffered a more lengthy internment. It was an outrageous reasoning on their part to hold that against us. Being Hungarians—and from Budapest to boot—was, in their eyes, an even more unforgivable offense. The realization that their attitude could be traced to such a flimsy justification was my most bitter awakening. It was too painful to grasp.

After we were stripped naked, we were sent to take an icy cold shower without soap in an unheated common shower facility. Each given one randomly selected, ill-fitting garment, which might have belonged to someone no longer among the living, we were led to our assigned barracks. The entire episode mocked us, as it added insult and degradation to the humiliation we endured to the amusement of Nazi camp overseers.

Lilly and I were still together when we settled into our new "home," realizing our hope for freedom might never become reality again. Wooden barracks, which looked like large stables, contained rows of three-tiered bunks (also wooden) with aisles in between. Each bunk had one blanket and accommodated four people, two at the head and two at the foot. There was neither mattress nor straw, only bare wood on which to lie. I was one of the lucky ones because I had gotten a huge coat to cover my body. God only knew who might have been its previous owner. I received some sort of shoes as well, but my wardrobe needed no closet.

At this point, we were no longer with only Hungarians. We were in the un-blissful company of hostile Polish inmates. Our blockova, who was in charge of food distribution and served as an intermediary between the higher-ups and the inmates, was a little plump youngish woman named Yudga. Yudga and the others spoke Yiddish, which was a foreign tongue to most of us, making communication all but impossible. She distributed the limited food supply and dished out the first portions to her family and countrymen, leaving the bottom of the barrel practically devoid of solid nutrients that might have quieted our shriveling stomachs. All day we cried for water, which came only in tiny amounts, and often, some of us had to do without because the favored ones came first.

The bread ration was a small, solid piece of black bread that looked and tasted like it was made from sawdust but to us, it was like manna from heaven, and we never dared to eat it all at once. We got into the habit of hiding it under our heads when we slept to prevent it from being stolen. Survival had only a fragile chance, and soon it became evident the decision was not all Yudga's. God has ultimate power over all mortals, and he could not have spoken more clearly. In spite of Yudga's efforts to shorten our rations in favor of her own people, some of her relatives died even before being transferred into the krankhouse (sick house). First hunger and thirst killed, and then typhus began to run rampant. There was a person who was dying on an upper bunk across from me. I watched her, having my eye fixed on her hidden piece of bread, waiting for her to give way to the inevitable. When she stopped breathing, I rushed to reach under her head before anyone else, and I made it. Still, as I looked at her, I experienced an unbelievable feeling of disgust at the thought of going through with my plan. My hunger was not strong enough to overtake my humanity, even though bread and water were the two words on our lips, repeated and repeated with anguish and no relief. I crawled back to my bunk, feeling ashamed.

Every morning at 5AM, we had to line up in front of the barracks to be counted. The winter cold was getting less and less bearable, and finally, my body buckled as a result of harsh neglect, starvation, and the invasion of multitudes of lice. I got diarrhea, a sign of the dreaded typhus carried by the ever-present vermin. Finally separated from Lilly, I was moved into the krankhouse. Conditions there were almost beyond words. There were six emaciated bodies to a bunk instead of four; days ran into nights, death tolls were rising, and the stench of death, mixed with the odor of urine and feces, permeated the entire environment. There was a Russian woman next to my bunk who, in a sitting-up position, sang the first few bars of a song in her native tongue repeatedly and without let-up. One day she stopped singing. Her body was removed.

Being surrounded by death and dying became a way of life. By that time, food and water had become an elusive commodity. At a certain point, our bodies started to decompose from malnutrition. I would see the person next to me, breathing one minute, still and at peace the next. Was I to be next? Somehow, the question did not seem to matter anymore. In total resignation, I lay there, becoming comatose. Void of all feeling, the outside world ceased to exist.

LIBERATION

Am I floating? I am in a dark place…My eyes are heavy and will not open…I have a strange sensation of being immobile and in limbo. Where am I? Am I at all? Drifting…

Drifting…propelled like falling leaves by a gentle wind…drifting slowly out of the darkness. I am drawn, as if by a magnetic force, towards a lighted place, a strange destination with far-away sounds of human voices. Far away…I listen but what I hear makes no sense. Where am I?

The wheels of consciousness are in motion, picking up speed with accelerating urgency. My slumbering mind darts out of its vaulted cage.

The sensation of being back in my skin dawns, and, as if by a magic command, my eyes fly wide open. With barely focused vision, I look through the haze into buoyant eyes. I am stunned because they stare at me as if I was a rare relic. Shocked into full consciousness, I lay paralyzed with fear, not knowing where I am or whom those figures dressed in white, the owners of those buoyant eyes, might be.

"It's OK, it's OK, all is well." I hear these softly uttered assurances from one of the white-clad women leaning over me. She went on, obviously trying to convince me, I had nothing to fear, nothing to worry about. Her kind smile and soothing words worked wonders because they were in simple English, enough for me to understand. Suddenly the light dawned. Wow! Could it be true that my perceptions during what must have been my last conscious moments were not a dream but reality? The brightness made my eyes grow heavy once again. I closed them to try to reconstruct my fleeting bits of incoherent memory.

I recall lying on the top bunk, nearly wasted away in the sick barracks, hearing the rumbling sounds of tanks rolling into the camps and soldiers atop shouting "You are free! YOU ARE FREE!" in different languages. I heard them, but, in my delirium, they could have been just another delusion created to nurture my hungry, lonely soul in the midst of unimaginably sub-human conditions. Someone dying of thirst could compare the vision to seeing an oasis and helplessly sinking into the sun-soaked desert sand.

Even with freshly regained consciousness, it was difficult to comprehend the transformation. I observed my new reality slowly and with calculated caution. When I opened my eyes again, I surveyed the area, carefully noting every aspect of my new environment. What struck me first were the clean, sanitary conditions, which contrasted sharply with my last station. I gingerly caressed the white bed linens and sunk my head deep into the soft pillows. My nostrils opened wide to inhale the long-awaited clean air. I wanted every molecule of my being to be convinced that, after what seemed like an eternity of friendless abandonment, this was real. And indeed, it was.

The doctors and nurses around my bed shook their heads in disbelief at what they saw in front of them. If they only knew the thoughts and feelings running through my mind in those moments! Even I had difficulty sorting out those thoughts.

No one could imagine how I survived. "I really thought this one was a goner," I heard one doctor whisper to another. "Yes, she is quite a miracle," said the other one, and they promptly began to poke and prod as if they needed further proof that I was indeed not a "goner."

The little English taught to me by Mr. Brown in our Synagogue youth division came in handy. It also helped that Mr. Brown's British pronunciation was the same as my redeemers. The wonderful people around me tried to bridge the language barrier by speaking with careful inflections and elevated tones, waving hands and intensifying their facial expressions. As a situation comedy, the scene was surely worth high ratings, and I wanted to hear more and more.

"You are in the hospital," explained a nurse standing nearby. I was surprised to hear her speak in my native Hungarian. "This was the German military hospital. Quite ironic, don't you think?" She snickered from behind her surgical mask, and her eyes shone mischievously. Annuska was a Red Cross volunteer from England, where she had lived with her husband since the early thirties. She was assigned to our ward at her request, and we were grateful to have her as our interpreter and confidante. She candidly spoke of unsettled conditions on the continent, which raised many questions, especially about our loved ones. The future was ahead of us, but far from our view.

I wanted very much to speak, to question, but I could not. I was frightened because the free-flowing voice I once had now caught in my throat. My tongue refused to cooperate, and repeated attempts at speech brought forth only inarticulate sounds and burning pain. Why? Could it be because I had not spoken in a long time?

Annuska interpreted the doctor's explanation. My mouth was virtually destroyed by malnutrition. It would heal. I listened with rising panic and indignation. I was frightened; I could not speak. I did not quite believe the doctors' assurances. My helpless anger cast a shadow over the sterile white comfortable bed. My head ached. The thought that I might never be whole again was like a thundercloud on the horizon of my newfound freedom.

The large French window over my bed was open to allow the fresh spring air to revive our spirits and fill our lungs. We were in the mountains surrounded by woods. I ached to look out the window but, lying flat on my back, I could not. Scheming to pull myself up to a sitting position, I grasped the side rails of my bed and was thrown back in spasms of pain. That was the moment I realized I was covered with open sores stretching over the protruding bones of my skeletal body. Caught helpless, my first impulse was to let loose a flood of emotion, but something inside me fought against defeat and, instead, called for help.

Annuska came to my rescue. Sitting on the top of her ash-blonde hair, her little white nurse's cap fascinated me. I could not figure out how it stayed on and wanted to know, but sitting up was more important at that moment than satisfying my idle curiosity.

With Annuska's help, I was able to rise into a sitting position. It was wonderful to have someone who could make me feel as if I was all that mattered to her. "Have a look and enjoy the sights," she said, and I proceeded to turn my head toward the open window. As my eyes swept past the windowpane, I saw the reflection of a stranger staring at me. Surprised, I looked around to identify that skeletal being with cropped hair, but there was nobody there. I did not recognize myself.

They quarantined our ward for medical observation. Each of us had suffered different degrees of injury caused by long-term malnutrition. We were unparalleled specimens for medical researchers to study early stages of decomposition. Across the room lay a woman missing half her lip. The doctors promised that she, like the rest of us, could have reconstructive surgery as soon as she was improved enough to withstand it. Rozika, the girl in the bed next to mine, had a gaping hole in the side of her cheek. I had a perforated palate. She and I were in the same boat: communication was difficult—next to impossible—but we warmed to each other on our common grounds, and we managed to communicate.

Our hospital days were relatively uneventful, filled with the staff's daily routines and our eagerly anticipated mealtimes. Every precious moment and every morsel of food was a unique new experience to be savored. As a borderline survivor still on the critical list, my diet was carefully prepared to accommodate my condition. Unaware of the fragile line between living and dying, I had an unreasonable craving for baked beans: cholent. I hungered for it with a feverish obsession and begged for it until; perhaps because they did not want to deny me my last wish, they reluctantly brought it to me. The thought, smell, and taste of the beans held the key to my inner yearnings – for home, for family, for the distant past. Consuming the beans was a rather short-lived pleasure. No sooner had I swallowed the food than I convulsed with excruciating pain and lost consciousness.

Just when everyone thought I was as good as dead, I managed to return. Many of the people who were not hospitalized, however, suffered a different fate. They found themselves the unlucky recipients of well-intentioned generosity. The soldiers showered them with gifts of food, like canned hams and other foods unable to be digested by starved, shriveled stomachs. Thrilled to have plenty and ignorant of the ramifications, former prisoners ate the food and promptly died.

Hospital life continued on an upswing. Rozika (whose Czech name was Rozina Hirshova) and I became very close. Both of us longed to make up for the stolen years of our youth. She needed plastic surgery. My case was under advisement.

We had virtually no knowledge of life outside the hospital, but it came to our attention soon enough that, in newly liberated Germany, allied soldiers and young, ambulatory women survivors were like children in a candy store. The soldiers were just as hungry for relationships with the opposite sex as were the recently freed women. Once we were declared non-contagious, the outside filtered inside as people wandered through our wards looking for loved ones. Our room became like Grand Central Station as rumors spread that I knew a little English. I was bombarded with questions like "How do you ask for cigarettes? For Nylon stockings? For Lipstick?" The atmosphere filled with the spirit of victory, freedom, celebration, and we longed to be a part of it. Sarah, one of our roommates, gazed at the goings-on around her, longing to be part of the excitement. Half her lip was awaiting reconstruction.

All sorts of rumors floated around our hospital room, and we took them all with a grain of salt as life went on and we continued to gain strength. Then, after about a month, one rumor became reality. They would transfer those of us who required further rehabilitation to Sweden. The Red Cross filled its ambulances with bedridden patients, and we were off. Destination: Lubeck, Germany's North Sea Harbor. This unexpected turn of events was as farfetched to me as it would have been had we been going to China or Timbuktu. To me, Sweden was a far off land completely removed from the European culture to which I was accustomed. Looking forward, we were filled with anxiety. This was certainly not what we had planned and hoped for. Our homes pulled us like a giant magnet, but even if we could have returned, was there a home to go back to? Were there loved ones out there looking for us? Could we look for them? In the safe custody of our caregivers, we dreamed it would be simple. Sadly, that did not turn out to be the case.

Unexpected fanfare accompanied our departure to Sweden from Lubeck. A group of kilt-clad Scottish Celts gave us an unusual feast for our eyes and ears: traditional dances to the rhythm of drums and bagpipes. Happy laughter filled the air; gratitude filled our hearts. As we boarded the Red Cross ship to Sweden, we felt alive, validated, cared for, and free.

AWAKENING

· · · · · · · · ·

CHAPTER THREE

After Liberation

SWEDEN
MAY, 1945-46

My family's financial circumstances had never allowed us the luxury of travel. Growing up, I had never trekked farther from Budapest than to some near-by rural town, and the only "big" body of water I had ever seen was the River Danube. Whatever I knew of other lands and their culture was from maps and from what I learned in school, but somehow, the only thing I desired to see in my lifetime was the ocean. Any ocean.

That wish was granted, as were so many of my other wishes later in life, but the time and circumstances were not what I would have chosen. I was a barely surviving Holocaust victim carried on a stretcher aboard a Red Cross vessel en route to Sweden. Alas, the sea, with its infinite range and expanse, was there in my full view. Still, while the ongoing rhythmic murmur from its dancing ripples and waves could barely escape my attention, I wished to be looking into the often-murky waters of the Danube instead. Longing for the familiar brought to mind the summer my family spent at Romai Part (as it was then called) when I was still very young. Romai Part, a resort on the Buda side of the Danube, was the poor man's Riviera; it overlooked the flowing waters from its down- to-earth, primitive rural environs. The amenities where we stayed consisted merely of simple wooden cabins, outhouses, and wheel-operated water well. Father joined us only on weekends. Mother, there the whole time, paid a daily visit to the farm-ers' market near the resort for a supply of fresh produce.

For Gyuri and me, the well quickly became our center attraction. We found turning a wheel to fetch water a novelty worthy of watch-ing over and over again. The suspense and thrill of the entire operation peaked each time the bucket emerged full and splattered cold water over us as it swung back and forth on its rope. Over time, we got used to seeing the same operation repeated—until one day, when a little green creature hopped out of the bucket as a fellow resort vacationer was about to empty its contents into another vessel. Startled, the two of us jumped out of the way and plowed into the man holding the bucket, causing him to stumble off balance, spilling its entire contents all over the ground. The chain of events happened so fast that we real-ized that this was our first encounter with a real live frog only as it hopped away.

Strange, how looking at the waters of the North Sea opened the pages of memories of that long-ago saga, offering a thread that tied me to my loved ones to chase the blues away. This is just one occur-rence that brings to mind how I feel about the existence of a Higher Power. Things that we wish for do not always happen when and how we want them to come into our lives. Something larger than us, in its ultimate wisdom, is in charge.

And so, as the ship set sail towards our destination, I could look at the sea at last and say to myself, by golly! This sure is a lot of wa-ter! Way, way larger than the Danube … and yes … more fascinating as well. And I even managed to smile.

I KNEW LITTLE MORE OF Sweden than its location on the map. When I was in school, I thought the peninsula that contained Sweden, Nor-way, Lapland, and Finland looked a lot like a leaping tiger. There was such a geographic distance between Hungary and the peninsula that I felt no connection to any of those countries, except for the knowledge that the Finns and the Hungarians sprang from the same Finno-Ugric roots. Had it not been for the magical sounds of music by Norwegian composer Edvard Grieg and the works of Swedish scientist Alfred

Nobel (founder and benefactor of the Nobel Prize), the leaping tiger would have remained a faceless spot on the map—and Sweden the last place on Earth to visit. (World War II changed all that, bringing Sweden closer to us). Yet there I was on the top tier of a hospital boat heading towards its shores by a strange twist of fate. I was in no condition to return and face further hardships in war-torn Hungary. I could not help feeling disappointed by the unanticipated detour that indefinitely delayed my homecoming, even though I did not know if I would find any surviving members of my family when I did return.

Thinking on positive terms, though, I was grateful to recover in Sweden, a country of blessed neutrality.

AFTER SEVERAL DAYS OF TRAVEL on high seas (and lots of creamed scallops), we reached the ports of Sweden at the harbor of Malmo.

It is hard for me to recall the thoughts that might have crossed my mind throughout that tumultuous period of transition—or how long it took us to disembark. Excitement around our reception brushed all other trivia aside. Carried into a large terminal, we were lined up in rows and greeted by a group of benevolent ladies buzzing in an indistinguishable language, eagerly distributing hot chocolate and sandwiches.

On what seemed to us like a stage where we were characters in a convoluted play, those well-meaning ladies appeared as though they had been miscast in their roles as social missionaries—particularly compared to the uniformed and organized personnel who had been directing our affairs since liberation. The words of our welcoming committee in Malmo ended in an upsweeping tone. Sighing often, their rapid, singsong chatter heightened the amusement of an already surreal sequence. We had little time to muse before we were transferred to a hospital, where the strain of our journey ended in the fold of a protective environment. I was happy to find myself sharing the same room with my friend Rozika and four other Hungarian women. While her bed was near the door at the head of the room—far from mine across the room, it was reassuring to have a friend among strangers. It appeared as though fate had brought us together like soldiers, remnants of a battle. We derived a sense of security in the nearness of others like us. Our soon-burgeoning camaraderie seemed to unite us, much like in the pages of recorded history, where whole groups have been lumped together under one defining banner.

FOOD, *GLORIOUS FOOD!* SWEDISH CUISINE held many surprises in store. The first meal served to us in the hospital was certainly newsworthy. Breakfast fruit, eggs, oatmeal, butter, and milk were familiar repast by now, but the bread? I was sure they had made a mistake and given us coffeecake instead. Wrong! Fluffy, white, and sweet, but it was bread. *Where, o where was yesteryear's crispy, crunchy Hungarian crusted rye bread?* Lunch brought yet another jolt to my unsuspecting hungry palate in what appeared to be little white potatoes in cream sauce on a plate of meat and vegetables. Yummy!! Potatoes, what a treat! I greedily bit into one, only to withdraw with a shudder at the unexpected sensation of the soft, mushy texture of a tiny creamed onion. I pushed them aside on the plate, but not without my guilty conscience poking at me: "*Hey! Was it that long ago when…*"

"True, but the time when any food would have been acceptable is over," I silently reasoned. Nevertheless, my value system would always remind me not to take food for granted.

> *"Hatred ever kills, love never dies. Such is the vast difference between the two. What is obtained by hatred proves a burden in reality, for it increases hatred."*
> —Mahatma Gandhi

Soon we began to receive outside visitors. Some were Hungarian Jewish emigrants living in Malmo, others interviewers from the Hungarian Embassy there to help us any way they could. The opportunity to speak our own language was tremendously helpful in restoring a feeling of well-being among us.

Much to our chagrin, however, the camaraderie in the room turned out to be an illusion when ambulatory visitors from other wards began streaming in, looking for relatives and friends. A girl named Suri

discovered that she and Rozika were from the same town in Czechoslovakia. Their joyful squeaks led into an animated discourse in Hungarian, which abruptly became a more somber, rapid word exchange in
their native Czech. Their mode of speech sounded more like a speed
contest than an ordinary conversation. Their meeting electrified us silent observers. Things like that did not happen every day, and having
shared the room, we felt like we had a part in it. No denying, a tinge of
envy did cloud our hearts, but not in any way that would have damp-
ened the spirit of our provisional relationships. Therefore, I did not
hesitate to call over to greet Suri. She did not seem to hear me. I then
called to Rozika, but when she didn't respond, I waited until Suri left
the room to address her. When I did, Rozika looked at me strangely,
as if she saw me for the very first time. She shrugged her shoulder and
silently turned away.

The rest of us looked at each other, baffled by this stunning change
in her attitude, for we knew of nothing that could have warranted her
rude behavior. Connecting the dots of the preceding events, I suspected that Suri must have said something to influence Rozika into
giving us the silent treatment. In any case, we were disturbed by the
thought of spending the rest of our hospital days bound together in
the same room with someone who had so flippantly dismantled our
unity. Suri's visit the next day confirmed my suspicion, when the two
women immediately withdrew in the manner of some secret society,
making their intention to segregate the rest of us crystal clear. Barely
holding back tears, I called over and asked what the problem was.
After exchanging a conspiratorial glance, the two turned to face us,
grimacing as if a foul smell suddenly hit their nose, and Rozi opened
the floodgate of venomous words still in my ear:

"You Hungarians stink! We have no need for friends of your
kind." Facing me, she coldly added, "And **you** from Budapest! You are
the worst of all!!"

I could hardly believe it was real. But a quiet stupor fell over our
ward like the calm after a storm, and the repulsed stares of both Rozika and Suri indicated that it was very real indeed.

Callous behavior is unacceptable at any time, but in our vulnerable, super-sensitive early stages of recovery, fresh out of the Devil's

den, for a fellow survivor to shun me for such a totally insane reason was an outrage. It was hard to fathom that they chose to focus on our identity as Hungarians (whom the Czechs held responsible for revoking their country's political autonomy) rather than as Jews sharing the unfortunate tragedy that had befallen all of us.[1] In any case, how could we be blamed for the fate of their state? How could this animosity not be left behind in the ashes? We were all pawns in the Nazis' political chess game, which they played with complete disregard for the humans whose lives they disrupted or destroyed in order to win.

Much to my horror, what happened in that hospital room in Malmo with Rozika was staggeringly similar to my childhood experience with Dolly, who charged me with the crucifixion of her Christ, an act for which the Jews have been held collectively responsible. Both Dolly's and Rozika's accusations were misplaced; furthermore, their stance fermented hatred. In fact, Rozika's actions hit me harder than anything Dolly or the Nazis had ever done to me. In time, the shadows of painful memories faded, but the wound inflicted on my sensibilities at that moment would remain unhealed.

Unfortunately, hate is an illogical, intrinsic human trait, which transcends all ethnic, religious, and national boundaries. Like a contagious disease, envy, ignorance, and fear of the unknown are the germs infecting all whose minds and hearts are not immune to them. I believe history must be taught with an emphasis on the humans who

---

1   In 1920, during the aftermath of WWI, the Treaty of Trianon carved up Hungary. Two-thirds of Hungary was lost to Czechoslovakia, Rumania, Yugoslavia & Austria. The Czechs thrived economically and socially until 1938, when Hitler, in order to appease his Hungarian allies, gave them back the lands that had been taken from them (even though it was not his to give). The Czechs had no desire to become Hungarian and were not given a warm welcome, so tremendous animosity developed between the people born as Czechoslovak citizens (in what had originally been the northern regions of Hungary) and the people who had remained Hungarian following the divisions made by the Treaty. When Hitler swept through Hungary, Jews in the outlying regions (including both Hungarians and former Czech citizens like Rozika and Suri) were the first Jews to be deported, unlike Jews like me, who had been relatively safe until the war was nearly over, at which point the Nazis began deporting Jews from the city of Budapest.

lived it in order to expose the ugly face of hate for what it is: **the felon, #1 enemy of all humankind.** What future generations must learn from history is that the enemy is within, not without, and that the responsibility rests on each person's shoulder to turn the tide so that past mistakes may not be repeated.

A COUPLE OF WEEKS IN the hospital worked wonders. Little by little, as my strength returned, I was able to get out of bed, try to stand on my wobbly feet, and take a few steps. My remarkable recovery allowed them to transfer me to Loka-Brunn, a camp for Hungarian women, one of many camps set up for the rehabilitation of ailing survivors. Rozika (Ruzina Hirshova) was most likely placed elsewhere with her Czechoslovak compatriot.

LOKA-BRUNN

Human life as we know it goes hand-in-hand with nature. Each change on the path of life offers a new beginning, each season a different chapter. Just as the rising sun of each new day heralds the passing of the old, it also offers new and unexplored pastures. My arrival on Swedish soil coincided with nature's awakening after a long, dismal winter sleep.

Time was drawing near to leave the hospital and the name of Loka Brunn surfaced as our destination. The name sounded awfully strange, but then again, so did the entire language, and I wondered if the place was some little hole-in-the-wall community stashed far away from civilization somewhere in the boondocks. I asked one of our frequent local Hungarian visitors, a very nice elderly man I had grown to like, if he knew about Loka-Brunn. His eyes lit up at the mere mention of the name.

"You are going to love it there! Loka is a well-known Royal Spa in a little hamlet tucked within the mountainous fold of South Central Sweden. I was there some years ago and enjoyed it so much, I promised myself to return there someday."

"As a matter of fact," he continued, "you might as well know that Loka-Brunn is not just any place."

Loka-Brunn was known for its mineral springs during the middle ages, when it functioned as a sacrificial well. It opened to the public as a spa in 1720 and became a Royal Spa in 1759: "One legend attributes the recovery of King Adolf Fredrik's migraine headaches to hot and cold baths and mud-packs he received while at Loka-Brunn. This little hamlet attracts visitors from the world over year round to enjoy the healing powers of its mineral waters."[2]

"So, I am actually going to live in a health spa?"

"Come to think of it," the man said," it makes good sense. After all, you were brought here to be healed."

Not only was I surprised that he knew about the place, but the enthusiasm of his reaction took me off guard. Needless to say, I was greatly relieved. I thanked him profusely for painting exciting, vibrant colors on the canvas of my future. God! I had something exciting to look forward to.

I was to be whole again!

OUTSIDE OF THE USUAL HOSPITAL gown, we did not own a stitch of clothing. The Hebrew International Aid Service (HIAS) changed that as we were about to leave the hospital. It was a first for me to be on the receiving end of pooled clothing and other necessities for the needy, but instead of feeling degraded by it, I was humbled by such good will. They gave us assorted basics, including personal hygiene accessories, with the intent to make us feel well cared for. This distribution was the first of many throughout our entire stay in Sweden.

When I found myself dressed in "civilian clothes," traveling by train like "normal people" for the first time in what seemed like an eternity; it felt strange, but strangely good. There is hardly a way I can reflect upon the emotions running through my entire being as I sat and watched nature's magnificence unfold in my view through the window. Spring was at its best, and I was taking it all in. The panoramic view alone was enough to lift my spirit. When the train arrived

---

2   Loka-Brunn publicity brochure, 2002.

at our last station, a motor vehicle was waiting to take us to Loka. Seeing the resort for the first time surpassed all my expectations. I fell instantly in love with the rustic little community, nestled between mountain slopes and two lakes. Out in the open, the scent of spring in the air brought back the time of days spent walking the Buda hills with my brother and friends on the other side of Pest across the river Duna (Hungarian for Danube).

An unpaved main road ran through Loka's natural terrain. Upon the hilly landscape, several rather primitive one and two story wood buildings were scattered. Private owners, after whom many of the structures were named, had originally built most of the buildings. These rustic living quarters, wired for electricity, contained dormitory-style rooms furnished to supply the basic elements of comfort with a little potbelly stove. Each floor had its own communal indoor lavatory.

In our newfound freedom, we were still not entirely free, as we were under the supervision of the Swedish camp administrators. Getting used to this was difficult at first, but in time, life in Loka-Brunn proved to be heaven on earth with only one cloud over the rainbow: our continued deep concern over how we could reconnect with our loved ones from such a distance.

I LIVED IN A ROOM with two other girls. My roommates, Ilona Ellenbogen and Lilly Guttman, were about the same age as me. Ilona was small, Lilly relatively hefty, and I skinny, flat as a board, crowned with short-shorn hair, barely the length of a boy's. Because of my physical appearance, my new friends began to call me Adam.

It was not long before we have gotten to know each other well. Living in one room, the three of us became a team. We often walked together downhill to the common dining room, where volunteer cooks from our group prepared our meals. We began to get used to seeing the breakfast table waiting for us, set with fresh milk and root beer in pitchers, butter, sugar, and cooked oatmeal. We often took leftover milk to our quarters to allow it to set into cottage cheese. Finding a drowned mouse in the setting milk one morning discouraged us from continuing that project. To decorate our barren room (which included three iron beds, a table, three wooden chairs, the stove, and hooks for clothing), we produced fancy paper cutouts for doilies. Later, we got hold of a wide-mouthed bottle and collected field flowers to grace the table. Those simple little personal touches created a homey atmosphere.

With hardly anything to keep us busy, we were pretty much left on our own to fill the day with activities and create our own entertainment. The women in the camp were of different ages and from different parts of Hungary. "Auntie" Stern was a good-humored elderly woman with a ready smile and ageless vitality. She volunteered to keep our sidewalks clean and was always ready to lean on her broom and tell us stories about her life in the United States, where her children were waiting for her return. The woman was a victim of unfortunate circumstances, as she was trapped in Hungary while visiting relatives in Budapest when the war broke out. Her American citizenship was ignored, and she ended up in Bergen-Belsen with the rest of us. We liked talking to her because she was unique among us, having close ties to America and a family waiting for her.

Next to the recreation hall and the common dining room was the post building, where we gathered each morning after breakfast to wait for the arriving mail. Disrupted mail service worldwide slowed our search for our loved ones. However, relatives living in the U.S., Israel and Australia were able to search for surviving family members through the Red Cross and HIAS. As a result, my cousins Clara and Ica, who lived in the area referred to as Palestine (later to become Israel), succeeded in tracking me down. I had last seen them when they left Hungary in the early thirties. Daughters of my mother's elder sister Frida, Ica and Klara were about fifteen and thirteen years older than me, respectively. Clara had followed her fiancée to Palestine, to which he had immigrated as a civil engineer, a pioneer in the irrigation of swamps. He wished to have a part in creating a Jewish state while in the Middle East. Soon after Clara and Ica found me, they sent me an affidavit, hoping I would come to live with them. I was deeply touched and thanked them for their concern but declined, hoping that soon I would get a similar offer from Elisabeth, our mutual aunt in the USA. In truth, though, I had another motive for declining: Even though I was in favor of establishing a Jewish homeland, after what I had been through, I was not prepared to find myself in the turbulence of such a disputed territory. Nonetheless, I continued corresponding with Clara and Ica long after I immigrated to the USA.

As for Aunt Elizabeth, since she did not appear to be looking for us like my cousins had, I wrote to her from Loka-Brunn. Her address had never left my mind. I informed her of my survival and asked her to bring me to the United States. A response was slow in coming. If she had been so taken by the generosity of my heart during those days when Mother had stopped corresponding with her, where was she now? Why did she have to be prodded?

ON THE SECOND FLOOR OF the post building was a room with a small balcony. The kitchen crew lived in the room, and the balcony became our lookout. There we could spot the approaching mail truck from a distance. The space on the balcony could hold only four people, and each day a different group of four would have the privilege to announce the coming truck with the ring of a bell. One day, when it was my turn to be on the lookout post, the conversation turned to clothes. One of the girls had a wish list. On top of it: a pair of white slacks. Just as she finished telling us about her wish, we spied a man coming towards the building wearing white trousers. We had but one man on the premises, Arne, a young Swedish cleric, and the stocky man we saw was not him, so we knew it had to be a stranger.

Struck by the happenstance of having the white pants she had wished for appear as if on cue, the girl mischievously called to him in Hungarian: "Hey buddy! How about giving me those trousers? I want a pair just like that." Hearing this, the man looked up with a grin from ear to ear. To our astonishment, he responded in the most perfectly pronounced language of our own: "Ladies, please don't take it off me, this is the only pants I got."

It took only a moment or two for us to catch our breath before we all burst into uproarious laughter. Afterward, he introduced himself as a doctor who, himself a survivor, had been summoned from a nearby recovery camp for Hungarian men. We were not aware that such a camp existed. We had heard, however, that a doctor was expected to join the staff; we just never figured they would select one from among our compatriots.

As for Arne the cleric, he was a tall, blonde, and good-looking young man who found himself attracted to the fact that our complexion—and our particular Hungarian zest—set us apart from Swedish women. On a discreetly camouflaged hunting expedition for female companionship, his handsome young roving blue eyes locked into those of Irene, an attractive 5'8" slender brunette from Budapest. Their blossoming fairy-tale romance soon took on headline proportions in our little community, catapulting Irene out of anonymity and into the limelight. It was hard for the rest of us not to be curious about the one chosen out of so many. We soon learned that Irene Fuchs (Fox in English) was a widow. She married in her late teens, but her husband died while serving in one of the military's infamous Jewish forced labor units. I suspect she knew about his death before her deportation, so to see her happy was all we really cared about under the circumstances.

OUR CAMP DIRECTRESS, INGEBORG WACHTMASTER, in charge of the entire management of our community, appeared to be a cool, impersonal administrator. For instance, when the tall, slim yet big-boned woman showed up in the mess hall during mealtime to make announcements, her demeanor could have easily been taken for that of someone who was there only to perform a job. However, the simply dressed woman—though always proper—had nothing pretentious about her.

I don't know when, but somewhere along the line, I developed the habit of making eye contact with people when they spoke, and that is how I realized there was more to Mrs. Wachtmaster than her outward manner revealed. Perhaps because the confidence I once had in people's sincerity was shaken, I intuitively searched for genuine feelings veiled behind spoken words. The warm look in Mrs. Wachtmaster's eyes belied her exterior. Those eyes spoke of a different, very humane self.

Mrs. Wachtmaster called to my mind a Swedish fable, according to which a couple received two invitations mailed simultaneously. Both invitations requested their presence at two successive occasions, both to be held by the same people. The first of the two was a black-tie affair, the second, a costume ball. Much to their chagrin, the couple arrived dressed in their costumes for what was actually the formal gathering, but because their host greeted them cordially, as if he had seen nothing out of the ordinary, they did not realize their mistake until they were ushered inside to join the rest of the guests, who, like their hosts, paid no attention to the folly. If anyone had the impulse to comment or even raise an eyebrow at the couple's appearance, it certainly was not apparent in their polite expression of indifference.

Remembering this fable, I began to realize that although Mrs. Wachtmaster (like the guests at the party) usually concealed her emotions that did not mean that she was not motivated by a deep, caring concern for us.

Mrs. Wachtmaster revealed that concern for us particularly when she proposed that we assemble a Hungarian folk-dance group. I suspect she did so because she understood our need to have a creative outlet through which we could recapture our sense of self-worth. For those of us to whom the suggestion appealed, we were eager to get started and break the monotonous routine of our daily lives. We sprang into action, attempting to recruit other members for the dance team. Francine, one of our own, a former ballet dancer at the Budapest Opera House, volunteered to take responsibility for directing and choreographing the entire production. For starters, she decided that the size of our group should be limited to six couples and therefore selected twelve girls, I among them. Because we had no boys in the camp, girls played their roles, too. With my already boyish figure, it was natural for me to become one of them.

Francine was an excellent teacher. With the graceful and firm body of a dancer and abundantly sprouting locks of red hair framing her slightly freckled peachy complexion and hazel eyes, she embodied a painter's dream. She had lost one of her fingers while in the concentration camp but did not let that hinder her enthusiasm. She succeeded in training a group of amateurs into a colorful assembly of Hungarian folk-dance performers. Mrs. Wachtmaster was preparing to take us to perform in Karlskaga, the town Alfred Nobel called home. All of us were so intoxicated by the prospects of this engagement that we became nearly oblivious of our lingering infirmities. We had great fun creating our Hungarian national costumes and rehearsing. Having something exciting to look forward to gave extra special meaning to our days.

WE TRAVELED TO KARLSKAGA IN a bus driven by Mrs Wachtmaster. When we arrived, a delegation of township officials escorted us to the Town Hall auditorium, where the performance would take place. Our dressing room was behind the stage. The room was not large, but everything we needed was there: dressing table, mirrors, stools, a rod to hang our clothes on, two armchairs with a little table between them, and even a cozy looking upholstered settee. Too keyed up to relax, we got our costumes out of the trunk and hung them on the clothes rod, even though we were hours away from dressing. When the time finally came to prepare, as everyone frantically rushed, we kept bumping into each other like people trying to get somewhere on a crowded train.

"Hey girls, cool it!" Francine calmed us. "There is no need to worry. We have plenty enough time to go through our routine on the stage to be geared for the real thing without any problem. Just remember, we are doing this for fun." FUN? Of course! How could we have forgotten that? The word put everything into the right perspective. We made some last-minute minor adjustments in our routine before bouncing onto the stage with cheeks blushed and stars in our eyes. Our souls' freedom sang as we danced our heart out to dazzle our hosts with a fiery, Hungarian-spirited folklore presentation. I felt much like I used to feel while dancing in the school assembly so long ago.

Years later, it occurred to me as strange that not for a moment did we ever consider the irony that it was so natural for us to be the salutary representatives of Hungary, a country that went along with the Nazi regime in order to disclaim our birthright and destroy us.

Regardless, at the time, our audience responded to our performance with thunderous applause, and although we did not understand the words of the elderly gentleman who spoke afterwards, the approving nods, smiling faces, and the rousing cheer at his concluding word of salute broke the language barrier.

Hungarian folk dance assemble { I am the third boy from left)

BACK IN OUR ORDINARY GARMENTS again, we followed Mrs. Wachtmaster into a large banquet hall, featuring a long table festively set with extravagant food. The atmosphere in the room was fit for important foreign dignitaries. For us to be elevated to such a lofty position was impressive, but, by that time, I could think only of the food on the table. Finding my place was easy with name cards at each setting, and when I finally was seated, I found myself staring into the eyes of a fish glazed and decorated as though it were a cake. Thinking it was some fancy dessert to be served after dinner, I admired the skill of the baker who could make it look so real. Imagine what a shock it was to have it served up for appetizer and to realize that the fish *was* real, eyes and all. Needless to say, I could not get myself to touch it, let alone eat it.

Eva Cutler

Once again, it crossed my mind how only a few short months ago I would have given my right arm for just a bite of anything that resembled food.

At a long table, the twelve of us girls sat in pairs, scattered between our prospective Swedish hosts, with whom we would spend the night and following day. Piri (one of the girls) and I sat next to each other, with Mrs. Wachtmaster at the far end to the left of us. I don't know how the others felt, but, for me, sitting around the table with our interactions limited to politely exchanged glances and awkward smiles with our hosts was like watching a foreign film without subtitles. Mrs. Wachtmaster, on the other hand, was deeply engrossed in an animated conversation with a couple across the table from her. From their occasional glances in Piri's and my direction, we assumed that, whatever they were discussing, it somehow involved us.

Finally, dinner was served. After several unusual courses of Swedish-style edibles, I welcomed the dessert trays laden with assorted delectable-looking creamy pastries. My weakness for sweets, pastries in particular, was in my genes, passed on through generations of pastry freaks. Little wonder, then, that just looking at the tray of assorted look-a-likes of French, Swiss, and Austro-Hungarian buttery baked delicacies absolutely sent me into a tizzy. It was as if the doors of heaven opened, but the challenge to select one from the array of delightful creations proved a difficult task. Finally, after some agonizing deliberation, I settled on what looked the most promising of all to satisfy my craving, but the first forkful of what turned out to be salty icing sobered me quickly. Indeed, the butter-cream icing of those generic pastries was made with salted butter, which, to my mind, no self-respecting European pastry chef should ever dream of using.

IT WAS QUITE LATE IN the evening when the festivity ended, but the best was yet to come. On the way out, Mrs. Wachtmaster summoned Piri and me and introduced us to the couple with whom she had been conversing at the table. We were correct to assume that their conversation revolved around us; Mr. and Mrs. Nordquist were to be our hosts for the night. During the short ride to the Nordquists' home, Piri and I exchanged only a few words. Both of us felt a bit strange in our position, but all that changed as we stepped over the threshold of the Nordquists' spacious home. Both Mr. and Mrs. Nordquist were formal and kind; they made us feel as if we belonged.

At the end of such a long and exciting day, we were ready to turn in. After a warm bath, Mrs. Nordquist clad us in flannel pajamas, tucked us in bed, and bid us good night as she placed a block of chocolate for each of us on the nightstand. Piri and I slept in the room of their daughters, Marta and Agneta, who were away in school. What a sweet night that was! For the first time since leaving Hungary, we awoke in the morning to the smells and sounds of a home, and what a home! I had never known people who owned a house where every member of the family had his or her own private room. The kitchen was bright and warm, with Mr. and Mrs. Nordquist waiting at a breakfast table richly endowed with assorted cold cuts, cheeses, bread and butter, jam and the cutest of all: soft-boiled eggs in eggcups with tiny knitted caps over them. Thank God for my little English and Piri's limited German, we could at least have a simple verbal interaction with the Nordquists, as they spoke both languages.

The Nordquists owned a skiwear producing plant. After breakfast, our hosts took us there and showed us around. The plant was closed for the weekend, but we got a chance to see how the garments were made from start to finish. The tour ended at the shipping warehouse, where our hosts outfitted us with ski pants and boots, saying we would need them for the winter. I had never dreamt of taking to the slopes. Coming from a modest middle class background, I considered skiing right up there with tennis: extravagant sports granted only to a privileged few in the upper, affluent classes of society. I accepted that and never aspired to such luxury. However, skiing in Sweden was not reserved for special classes; it was a way of life – particularly in the mountains during the winter. In light of that, the Nordquists' generosity served a practical purpose.

Each moment spent with the Nordquists was a very special experience. Our stay there offered us the chance to interact intimately with foreign customs, and we had Mrs. Wachtmaster to thank for making it all happen. In fact, throughout that whole weekend, her efforts gave us confidence and motivated us to revitalize our sense of potential, which had eroded over time. We needed an accepting environment to do that. I could never have seen it then, but now, I understand her intentions to help us overcome our sense of worthlessness. All I know is that each time I recall that weekend in Karlskaga, it still reignites the pride I felt so many years ago.

WE HAD A FULLY EQUIPPED sewing room available for those of us accustomed to making our own clothes, and that is where I developed a friendship with Magda and her mother, 'Aunt' Bella. Aunt Bella was a professional dressmaker-designer who had owned a dressmaking salon in her hometown, where she taught Magda her trade. I was drawn to them out of sheer loneliness, so despite the fact that sewing was our only common ground, I was willing to overlook most of the unpopular, abrasive traits that kept others in safe distance from them. The mother-daughter team was least-liked by most and with good reason. With a superior air about them, they looked down on everyone, particularly when a wealthy relative from America made contact with them. They flaunted their good fortune inappropriately, callously rubbing salt into others' wounds.

Magda's only brother Geza had died in a forced labor camp even before she and her mother were deported. After we all arrived at Loka-Brunn, the two were among the first to establish communication with people back home, and the news from there was not good. Magda's fiancé had married another woman, while her father mysteriously disappeared on his way home from a concentration camp—an event that coincided with rumors that Russians captured returning camp inmates and took them to Siberia with an insane justification that, if the inmates could work for the Nazis, they could work for them as well. (We often wondered if something like that might have happened to my brother.) Overall, the mother and daughter had not much reason to return home. They decided to go the USA, where relatives offered them a safe haven and a bright future.

· · · ·

SPRING AND SUMMER SEEMED TO roll by quickly. The turning of leaves and cooling temperatures ended our daily swimming in the lake, and before we knew it, winter was on its way. If ever I fell in love with old man winter, it was during my stay in Loka-Brunn.

I still needed a warm winter jacket to complete my ski outfit. We had a monthly allowance of 5 Kronor to give us modest shopping power at the general store in the little nearby village. At first, the transactions between the storekeeper and us played out in body language and elevated articulation; it was both humorous and frustrating. As time went on however, we became more familiar with Swedish expressions, and the shopkeeper could relate to us more easily. Five Kronor was more than we ever expected to have, but it did not go far enough to buy wool for the winter jacket I had in mind. The problem got resolved when, out of necessity, I looked for alternative resources and found it in a surplus army blanket. To give my project eye appeal, I decided to get an affordable contrasting yarn to knit the sleeves and collar. What surprised me most was that I even enjoyed knitting it; I had loathed my needlework assignments when I was in school, where I had to comply with strict rules without room for challenging creativity. Following uniform details bored me, and I always fell behind assignment deadlines. Once we had to knit a scarf with designated dimensions, and it just did not seem to grow. Finally, when it was almost time to turn in the project, I loosened the stitches and got the iron to stretch it as far as I could, which of course rounded the ends and narrowed the width. I failed miserably, but I never forgot my basic needlework skills. Invariably they served me well.

Sitting on the rail, sporting my new ski outfit in Loka Brunn

I am not much for rules, but in

the case of knitting the sleeves and the collar of my new jacket, the basic knowledge I had learned in school came in handy. I even figured out how to shape the pieces without the use of a pattern or instructions. In the end, I produced the missing link to my ski outfit, which turned out to be a smart-looking lumber jacket. With it, I was ready to face winter.

To KEEP THE FIRE BURNING in our room's potbelly stove, daily my roommates and I hauled wood from the barn, where the supply never seemed to deplete. When snow fell and generously layered the countryside, the slopes, populated by a colorful array of people, came to life in the early morning hours. Adults and children commuted to work and school, respectively, on skis. I will never forget how the little kids on skis, with long-tailed hats trailing in the wind and backpacks in tow, made a scene fit for a travelogue. Our icy roads posed a daily challenge, but it was par for the course. Walking to the dining hall turned out to be a great balancing exercise each step of the way. Since all the activities centered around the main building, we avoided going back to our room as much as possible and made hay spending the day outdoors skiing and sledding. Following breakfast and mail delivery, we rushed to the storage room to borrow skis and sleds (called parkas). The parkas were like dog sleds, with a seat up front and extended tracks in the back, where you stood to steer the handle bar while going down hill.

Ilona (sitting) and I riding the Parka

The small supply of skis and parkas had to be shared. Sledding was something my roommate Ilona and I loved to do together, so we usually shared a parka. For downhill skiing, however, I teamed up with Magda. The two of us would take turns climbing uphill on the main road and beyond for the thrill of an adrenaline high as we descended. We did so repeatedly, until our bodies' heat made us forget the biting cold. We stopped reluctantly only when it was time to return the skis.

1945 WAS COMING TO AN end, and with 1946 on the way, Lilly (my roommate) and I volunteered to be in charge of the program celebrating the New Year. Ready for some honest-to-goodness fun, the two of us were full of good ideas. Our personalities complemented each other; Lilly's biting humor and my love for parody combined to form our signature brand of comedy. When she, as Carmen, gyrated her ample body to the tune of Habanera in front of my self-conscious, skinny Escamillo the Torreador (nervously biting on the rose between my teeth), we nearly brought the house down. In another hilarious satire, Lilly sang the Popeye to my Olive Oyl. Spliced in between our numbers were two singers performing a mélange of favorite Hungarian tunes in a pub scene, which was accompanied by a pianist. Lilly and I ended the program by reciting a poem we based upon our life in Loka. The stanzas—full of hilarious to naughty commentaries—left nothing to the imagination. We left the best of our gags for last: a punchline about Irene 'the fox' (Fuchs) pursued by Arne 'the hunter.' It hit the jackpot.

For the first time in a long time, we had a reason to celebrate the New Year. We did so with gusto and renewed hope for a peaceful future.

ON VERY COLD DAYS WHEN the lakes' surfaces froze to a solid base, some people drove over the ice to shorten the distance to their destinations. The weather bureau closely monitored and reported surface conditions for the benefit of those who traveled the lake route. Keeping abreast of the reports was of monumental importance; warnings of the slightest change in ice conditions could not be ignored. In addition to potential thinning ice, drivers during those days also had to keep in mind the fact that their cars ran on an alternative form of fuel less powerful than gasoline, the supply of which was limited following the war. This sort of information did not filter down to us immediately because it had no bearing on our way of life—until an unfortunate accident befell two of our campmates.

One night, two girls went on a date with men from a neighboring town. As the foursome drove across the lake on the way back, they had nearly reached dry land when the car ran against a mound of ice. Because the car used inadequate fuel, it lacked the power to push forward over the icy obstruction and slid back instead. The ice broke under the rear wheels. The car sank, and all four passengers drowned.

This incident altered the originally welcoming mood of surrounding communities toward the residents of Loka-Brunn. Prior to the accident, many men found themselves intrigued and tempted by our all-women camp. They did not come into our territory but instead waited and approached us when we were out in public places. Many of the Loka girls found the opportunity to be out in the world with an escort hard to resist, and, with no reason not to, they often accepted dates. Single women from local villages, however, began to consider us competition, while the married women were upset that we had supposedly lured their men away. The accident brought local animosity towards us to a head, and we found it ironic that, because of the mistakes of a few, we were once again victims of a generalization.

The deaths of our campmates shocked us terribly. To meet an icy death after having survived the fires of the Holocaust was a nightmare that could have been avoided. It was a sobering reminder that playing roulette with life can be dangerous.

His name was Gyuri, like my brother. Seventeen years-old, the lanky, bespectacled boy was the sole survivor of his family from Nyiregyhaza, a town in far northeast Hungary. He lived in the same men's' camp from which our doctor (the one in the white pants) had come. The doctor came to Loka-Brunn regularly, which gave Gyuri easy access to come along and hang out with us. He struck me as a very lonely, vulnerable young boy starving for the warm embrace of female companionship. Because he came around so often, somebody began calling him Mancika (a female nickname), and it stuck. Gyuri either did not notice the mockery or found it amusing; either way, to him it seemed the hallmark of acceptance. Unfortunately, by going along with the joke, he opened himself as an easy target for ridicule. It pained me to see how his infatuation with fifteen year-old Gabrielle was not only rejected, but also made fun of. Mancika also opened the door for the likes of Aunt Bella and Magda to feel superior by never missing a chance to put him down. Aunt Bella liked referring to him as "a little hick-town ignoramus," even though she herself came from a rural town much like Mancika's. She assumed her town near the Yugoslav border a bigger, better, more advanced community—and fancied she and Magda more polished. Even if that was true, it did not give her the license to be cruel.

I found it disturbing that a woman of Aunt Bella's age, particularly after what she herself had been through, was capable of antagonizing another person in order to feed her own ego. I remembered the satisfaction and power we as little children had derived from torturing the poor old lady with our pranks on Szabolcs Street, and I consciously began to monitor my own behavior.

WHEN THE LONG-AWAITED LETTER FROM my Aunt Elisabeth finally arrived with a $1.00 bill tucked inside it, she said she was very happy to hear of my survival and announced that a package was on the way for me, but no word about inviting me to start a new life under their protective wing in the United States. I was too happy to hear from her to pay much attention to what I assumed was an oversight. I responded immediately. I told her I did not know what had happened to my family, as none of my letters to them were answered, and asked again if she would sponsor my immigration to the USA. Soon, another letter and another dollar bill arrived, along with a package of some hideous clothing but no word of encouragement about the prospects of sponsorship. Again, I figured it might have skipped her mind, so I asked once more. This time I mentioned how others in my camp had been receiving invitations and affidavits from relatives and even from strangers. I told my aunt I was sure that she and her husband, as family, would do the same for me. Instead, in her next letter, she skirted the issue, so soon I had to realize that without any given reason, she did not intend to encourage my endeavor, even as I was stranded after such a horrendous experience. I could have remained in Sweden as so many others did, but I lacked the confidence and courage to face the world alone, and when I made that perfectly clear to my aunt, she finally complied. When the affidavit for my immigration came, I noticed another party had co-sponsored it, which gave me the impression that my aunt and uncle were not financially solvent enough to make the offer on their own. She did not tell, and I did not ask, but at that point, I realized that perhaps money was the reason behind her hesitation to bring me to the U.S.

I proceeded to prepare for my journey. In the meantime, in a last desperate effort to search for my family, I sent a letter to Mr. Alzner, our designated contact (and my father's friend and chess partner). *If* he had survived *and* my letter reached him, I would find out if any member of my family was still alive.

By February of 1946, nearly a year had passed since our ship pulled into the harbor at Malmo. During my time in Sweden, health had been mine again to enjoy—except for the fact that my prolonged malnutrition had caused damage still waiting to be repaired. I had a perforated palate, and the opening capacity of my mouth was limited to merely two centimeters. At the hospital in Karlskaga, I underwent successful surgery and a month of daily therapeutic exercise to widen the opening of my mouth, but nothing could be done for my palate due to an enormous amount of bone loss and weakness of surrounding tissues. During my hospital stay, Mrs. Nordquist, with her daughter Agneta, came to visit, carrying a basket of goodies. I have no idea how they found out I was there, but it was a lovely surprise.

After the surgery, I took the train to see the Hungarian Consul in Stockholm about reinstating my citizenship status to obtain a visa for my travel to the USA. Gyuri (Mancika) and I traveled there together because he too was in the process of immigrating to America, having been invited to live with family members in Detroit. Mancika and I had bonded in a sister-brother relationship from the moment we first met. We had a great time browsing through shops in the big city like two little kids giddy with the zest for life.

The year at Loka-Brunn passed swiftly into another spring. Living in the mountains had introduced me to a new way of life, different from what I had known as a rudimental city dweller. No matter what fun I was having, however, my family was never far from my mind. For instance, one night I had a dream that resurrected an unpleasant exchange between Mother and me back in the days leading up to the war:

The escalating dangers of our situation had produced debilitating effects on my mother's mood to the point that she hardly paid any attention to her housekeeping regimen. In my youthful arrogance, I was annoyed with her and threw myself into compensating for her lack. Becoming the cleaning nut to make sure my friends would see a well kept home became my top priority. Windows had to be washed and floors waxed, things had to be orderly displayed, etc—until Mother got annoyed with my obsession.

We had a large French window I felt needed a good cleaning. To reach the top of the window required a stepping stool, which I set up for my project, prepared with the necessary cleaning objects. Mission accomplished, I stepped off the stool and thoughtlessly tripped on the telephone cord running beneath it. As I stumbled, the phone fell, and I grabbed onto anything I could get hold of on the way down, but I fell against the window, which, fortunately for me, only cracked in the process. Still, Mother reacted hysterically, slapping me on the face. Absolutely furious and hurt, I had no idea that her nerves had become strung so tight that even the slightest discord could send her into frenzy.

I was probably sixteen or seventeen at the time all that happened, but I soon forgot that day as danger approached. But during that dream one night in Sweden, it all came back. My roommates were awakened by my uncontrollable sobs. They shook me from what seemed to be a disturbing dream. The crying spell stopped as soon as my eyes opened, but I was totally spent. The dream revived that long ago day with a slight twist:

I was standing on a ladder, cleaning the glass on our entry door. Somehow, I lost my footing and fell, breaking some of the panes in the process. Mother angrily slapped my face, but this time—instead of getting mad at her for doing it—I grabbed her hand and kissed it.

WITH ALL MY PAPERS IN order, my relatives were able to purchase me a fare on a ship bound to sail on the 15th of May from Goeteborg, Sweden, to New York. Around the middle of April, I received a letter from my parents, an answer to the one I had sent Mr. Alzner in search of them. They were ecstatic, and so was I, knowing that the three of us survived. My brother, however, was still missing.

With the discovery that my parents were alive, I was ready to cancel my trip to the USA, but, after a frantic and agonizing correspondence via telegrams, they urged me to carry out my plans. With me in America, they believed, they would have a chance to follow me there.

THE JOURNEY FROM GOETEBORG HARBOR on the Drottningholm (my ship) to New York took a week. I traveled together with several others from Loka, including Magda and her mother (who—incidentally—traveled on first class, unlike the rest of us poor suckers). Mancika's trip was delayed until a later date, and though we kept corresponding until I got married, I never got to see him again. Upon leaving Loka-Brunn, I made a vow to return someday. I had come to understand why the elderly gentleman who visited me in the Malmo hospital had made a similar promise to himself. My love for the Swedish people remained in my heart forever.

Sailing on the Drottningholm towards the US.(I am on third row center left)

Not like the brazen giant of Greek fame,
With conquering limbs astride from land to land;
Here at our sea-washed sunset gates shall stand
A mighty woman with a torch, whose flame
Is the imprisoned lightening, and her name
Mother of Exiles. From her beacon-hand
Glows world-wide welcome; her mild eyes command
The air-bridged harbor that twin cities frame.
"Keep ancient lands, your storied pomp!" cries she
With silent lips. "Give me your tired, your poor,
Your huddled masses yearning to breathe free,
The wretched refuse of your teeming shore.
Send these, the homeless, tempest-tost to me,
I lift my lamp beside the golden door.

—Emma Lazarus (1809-1847)
Engraved on the pedestal of the Statue of Liberty in 1903

CHAPTER FOUR

Beginning Life in the U.S.

Nearing America's shoreline the ship gradually slowed, gliding into port. Leaning against the railing, I focused my eyes on the horizon, waiting to catch a glimpse of the Statue of Liberty. Watching the phantom-like figure emerging through the haze with New York's skyscraper-studded skyline behind it sent goose bumps up and down my spine; it was every bit as phenomenal as I imagined it. Emotions among the Holocaust Survivors were running high at the sight of the illustrious Statue greeting us *"huddled masses yearning to breathe free."*

It was a significant moment for us, and we fêted our successful entry with shouts of joy and laughter amidst tears, hugging and kissing whoever was near. In the spirit of the moment, we exchanged addresses and wowed to keep in touch. I made such a promise to Magda and her Mother, who sought me out as well. I held onto them the way a child holds onto their security blanket. As anticipation heightened, people began pacing the deck. We were close to the end of a long journey, but again at a crossroads. Looking forward to meeting new family members, strangers to most of us, even I began to feel uneasy. I was excited about entering a new world where I hoped to be accepted, but I could not ignore the possibilities that I might not be.

These thoughts disappeared, however, as the captain's voice blasted over the loudspeaker. The ship anchored, it was time for us to prepare to go ashore.

"Have your credentials and entry visas handy to be examined by the Immigration officials on your way out," the captain announced, "and I ask that you form a single line to make your exit flow swiftly. I fare you well."

The announcement produced furious activity on deck. Exhilarated by the prospects of crossing the threshold of our new homeland, everyone was eager to get in line. At that moment, looking toward a new beginning, it was easy to believe that far, far away from everything familiar, the past could be laid to rest.

HOLDING ON TO ALL MY earthly possessions in a small travel-case, I descended the gangplank with steady steps. At age twenty-one, I felt much like a young child whose gift was waiting to be unwrapped: eager, excited and curious. Except when I looked into the crowd of people waiting behind the terminal gates, my knees weakened. Doubt and fear returned, until, to my relief, I saw Aunt Elisabeth. She recognized me the minute she saw me. My Aunt, Uncle Alex, who accompanied her, and their close friends, Emma and Bela Molnar (the co-sponsors to my entry), genially received me. My Aunt was a beautiful woman. She had a full head of snow-white hair and warm brown eyes, but not a trace of resemblance to my mother, whose delicate features were accentuated by high cheekbones and almond shaped grey-blue eyes. Instinctively, I was looking for something in my mother's sister that would bring my Mother closer, but I found nothing.

I COULD HARDLY WAIT TO see New York! Unfortunately, my first impression of the city was not in the least favorable. In fact, the neighborhood around the harbor—with its dark gray weathered tenement houses, laundry hanging out windows, and litter strewn all over the street—was nothing like the glamorous United States depicted in the movies. Concealing my disappointment was not easy, but it was a good thing I did not say anything because, as I later came to realize, New York City, though much larger, was no different from major cities elsewhere. The glamour is reserved for the rich or for show. Broadway is not real life, even in America.

• • • •

THE RIDE FROM NEW YORK to Philadelphia's Logan district took about two to three hours with Uncle Alex behind the wheel. When we arrived at Aunt and Uncle's house on the 1100 block of Sommerville Avenue, the abstract idea of their home etched in my mind became a reality. The conventional two-story brick house, aligned and connected to several others, was not anything I had seen before. We walked up several steps from the pavement to enter a glass-enclosed porch that led into the rest of the house. Inside, I was enveloped in darkness until someone switched on the light. The railroad design of the interior did not allow much light to filter into the downstairs, and the second floor was no cheerier than the one below. I was surprised to find the house so bleak, as Logan was supposedly a sought-after, upper-middle class neighborhood. I mention this only because my first impression of how people really lived in America was very different from the images fancied abroad. The bedroom designated to me was adequate for sleeping. Though its small, shallow wall closet had only hooks to hang clothes, it was still enough for me at the start, as I had next to no wardrobe anyway.

I REALIZED RIGHT AWAY THAT my Aunt was determined to make me conform—both in appearance and conduct—to American standards. That of course meant that I had to abide by her values rather than my own. I had wanted learning how to live the American way to be up to my discretion, but if plucking my eyebrows and wearing lipstick could improve my appearance, I was willing to try it, even if it was out of character for me.

However, some of Aunt's other instructions for getting by in America left me even more perplexed. For example, she warned me never to turn my head to stare at black people, but it would never have occurred to me to do so in the first place. Aunt Elisabeth's comment aroused both shock and indignation. So many of the images transported to Europe featuring highly acclaimed black American citizens (Marion Anderson, Josephine Baker and Paul Robeson, for examples) conveyed the impression of racial equality in American society. If such equality really existed, why did Aunt Elisabeth feel she needed to warn me about such behavior? Something about it did not feel right to me, but I did not believe I was in a position to question her.

Within the first week of my life in America, I was introduced to downtown Philadelphia. My Aunt took me to Lit Brothers' popular department store bargain basement, where she filled in some basic needs in my wardrobe. Traveling by subway was a novelty; Philadelphia's underground rail system was much more extensive than Budapest's. Standing in the center of Philadelphia, I had to pinch myself to believe I was there.

Meeting my cousins was somewhat disappointing, for neither of them generated much warmth. Bobby was fifteen and still in school. He understood Hungarian, but was reluctant to speak the language. Theresa spoke a broken Hungarian, but already married, and she and her husband Mort had no interest in including me in their circle of friends. Bobby and I managed to overcome our language barrier in time and warmed to one another. He was very quiet and reserved with hardly a spark in his personality, but living under the same roof, we got used to each other's presence.

My uncle owned the Ace Electric Motor Company, furnishing motors to a variety of manufacturers. Two weeks following my arrival, he took me to a blouse manufacturing plant owned by one of his clients, where he arranged a job for me. After a brief introduction, the owner promptly assigned me to a machine and proceeded to demonstrate the assembly of a collar I was to produce. I noticed that—with the exception of the owner, his son (the supervisor), and the in-house mechanic—all the machine operators were women.

Once I learned that Uncle Alex had a lucrative business, I realized my relatives were not hurting for money. I began to wonder why, if not for financial difficulties, they were slow to respond to my request that they sponsor my immigration. I would not learn the astounding answer until much later.

Though my uncle picked me up after the first day of work, after that, my relatives expected me to navigate the city on my own. They wanted me to become self-sufficient. But it was too soon for me. My relatives disregarded the fact that I was uncomfortable finding my way around a strange land without basic English communication skills.

My Aunt's attitude was based on her own experience; she thought that if she survived it, so would I. Somehow, I overcame my fear of the unknown and the experience did not hurt me one bit. In fact, my first job turned out to be a valuable learning experience. The Italian women in my workplace were benevolent; the other Jewish women were suspicious of me because I did not speak Yiddish. To my good fortune, I could communicate with a very friendly Hungarian lady. She became a helpful ally, guiding me through many difficulties as I got started.

WITHOUT WASTING MUCH TIME, I enrolled in a night-school class in pursuit of my citizenship. There I met Ella, who was my own age, a Czech-Hungarian survivor. Discovering our mutual history helped to bond us quickly. Ella's parents were exterminated, but she discovered her three surviving brothers living in Israel. It was of paramount importance for us to gain citizenship without delay. Citizenship was not a privilege that would benefit us only; it would allow us to apply for our relatives' immigration to this country. Ella wanted to bring her brothers; I wanted to bring my parents.

Mother and Dad were under constant pressure for refusing to be-

photo I received from my Parents after the war in 1946

come members of the Communist party, which then occupied Hungary. Leaving the country legally at that point was next to impossible. In order to avoid serious consequences for disobeying regime rules, my parents liquidated all their assets, hired a guide, and set out to sneak across the Austrian border. Unfortunately, when the hired "guide" deserted them in the middle of nowhere, finding their way through unknown territory while trying to avoid searchlights was difficult. By some miracle, however, their treacherous journey ended after crossing the Austrian border. Fortunately, both my parents spoke fluent German. Shortly after their arrival in Austria, Father sought employment. When he found out that the occupying American authorities were looking for someone to supervise the construction of homes for stationed military personnel and their families, he applied. With his extensive professional background, Father was hired on the spot. Fearing continued hostility toward Jews, they masqueraded as non-Jews. After a year in Austria, they were eager to leave. Since I was not yet a citizen, I still was unable to send for them, so when the opportunity arose for them to move to Toronto, Canada, sponsored by Mother's cousins, they decided to take it.

Uncle and Aunt were furious with my parents' choice not to wait another year and come straight to the United States.

"How can you judge them when you don't know what it was like to live there under duress?" I retorted. "After what they went through, how could you expect them to keep living in constant fear and uncertainty in the midst of a simmering human volcano ready to erupt any time? Was it not better for them to leave, and be somewhere to feel secure?

"How dare you open your mouth to us?" they snapped back. We will not tolerate such impudence!"

So I was impudent. Speaking-up on behalf of my parents was disrespectful, and I had to be reprimanded for that. It was a blow. Were they not listening? How could Uncle and Aunt be unsympathetic towards Mother and Dad, when they knew all my parents had endured, especially the loss of my brother? Right then, it occurred to me that perhaps my relatives did not really want us to be here.

This hypothesis was supported when I found out that Aunt Elisabeth and Uncle Alex had sponsored a young German Jewish man's immigration to the U.S. at about the same time that Mother had asked them to help rescue Gyuri and me. The young man's name was Wenger, just like theirs. Needless to say, this fact provoked and disturbed me.

I STAMPED OUT COLLARS BY the dozen in a factory for a year before I found a job where I could use my sewing skills to better advantage. Following a newspaper advertisement for a center-city specialty shop looking for an experienced dressmaker, I began my career altering commercially produced clothing for Teddy Benjamin, a woman of few endearing qualities. Virtually sweating through three years in her poorly ventilated cubbyhole workroom, I learned to detest the woman for her contempt toward "refugees." Knowing that she considered me the 'exception' to whatever she held against "those others" was no comfort. I found her wickedly maligning attitude ironic, especially because she herself was Jewish, a second-generation American of Russian descent. Furthermore, she 'liked' me because I was vulnerable and easily intimidated. Each time she had to select one of her helpers to lay off during the slow season, she chose me, because she trusted I would come back when needed. Upon my return, invariably I had to correct all the botched-up work left behind by the person awarded the privilege to work instead of me.

Teddy also wanted to "improve" my appearance, particularly the way I dressed. Her coercion was difficult to fend off. When I finally succumbed, she insisted on selling me a dress at cost from her inventory and proceeded to guide me in complementing the dress with a selection from a stylish shoe store. This little extravagance created a fall-out with Aunt Elisabeth, who claimed that I could not afford such luxuries because I had to save the money for my parents.

"And if you do this again," she threatened, "you can pack your things and be out of here."

I was flabbergasted, hit hard by Aunt Elisabeth's continued insistence upon controlling my actions without considering my needs. Eventually, I resigned myself to try to make the best of a demoralizing living situation, recognizing I was on permanent probation.

AUNT ELISABETH WAS A VERY talented seamstress and a master of creative needlework. She was also an excellent cook and baker and a model homemaker. These traits—and her love for books—were the only similarities I found between her and my mother. Once my Aunt rendered a beautiful rose and butterfly design with sequin embroidery onto two black tunics, one for Theresa and one for me. It was one of those rare occasions when she treated me and her daughter equally. I loved the blouse, which had to wait patiently in the closet until there was an opportunity to wear it.

I tagged along with my Aunt and Uncle to many of their social activities, which usually involved their association with the Hungarian-American club. Their friends, like the Molnars (my co-sponsors), were all deeply rooted in Christian-Hungarian customs. This social scene did not interest me. My relatives and their friends were not in my age group, and, regardless, I was ready to forgo Hungarian customs for an American way of life.

DURING THE THREE YEARS I worked for Teddy Benjamin, I saw several poorly qualified applicants hired to assist me in the workroom come and go. They either left quickly because of the poor working conditions or were fired for their lack of knowledge. In the end, I was rewarded for putting up with all of the nonsense; my first important social contact happened through one of those transient employees. Ilse (a German "refugee," according to Teddy) mentioned that she was the member of a Jewish youth organization, Junior Hadassah. Ilse's cousin Inge chaired a chapter of Junior Hadassah in the Olney section of the city. Ilse offered to take me to one of their meetings and I accepted. The prospect of encountering other young people excited me.

However, a less than cordial reception by her cousin Inge made me wonder if I had made a mistake.

"Why did you come here, and not to the Logan chapter?" she asked.

"Well," I said defensively, "Ilse brought me here, and I didn't know of any other chapter. Is there a problem?"

"No" she replied coolly. "You can stay if you want." She shrugged her shoulders, as if to say 'It makes no difference to me.' Suddenly, the idea of returning for a second meeting lost its appeal.

To some people, an exchange like the one between Inge and me might not have been a big deal. However, because of my experiences, I interpreted it as a rejection. When I mentioned this to Ilse the next day, she was just as puzzled as I was.

That evening I received a telephone call.

It was Inge, calling to apologize. She had not realized she had offended me and invited me to join them again. I was struck by her sincerity, and I became an active member in her chapter. Hard as it might be to believe, this was how my life-long friendship with Inge began, and it grew deeper with each passing year,

Membership in the Junior Hadassah proved satisfying. I met some fine girls, as well as young men invited to attend our social events. I had never dated back in Hungary. I had had several very close male friends during my teens, but the closest I ever got to a romantic involvement was from afar, with a pen pal in the Jewish military service I met in person only once.[3] Therefore, I was hesitant when I entered the dating scene at Junior Hadassah. My language skills did not permit much conversation, but I did manage to develop a relationship with one young man. Martin. He was a speech therapist, and he loved my accent. Marty was refined, intelligent, and educated. On our first date, he took me to the Philadelphia main library on Logan Square. I gasped as I stepped in its doors, awed by its enormity. More like a temple or museum, there seemed something sacred about it, to have all those works in one place. Much later, he admitted he took me there

---

3   It was not uncommon to develop fantasy relationships during the war, especially in our precarious circumstances. In fact, some even rushed into marriage either wanting to grab hold of life while there was still a chance, or because rumor had it that married girls would be exempt from being taken for forced labor.

as a kind of test. As someone who loved learning, he thought watching how someone reacted upon stepping into a library could tell him a lot about whether he could have a meaningful relationship with them. He also enjoyed diverse cultural experiences, and he introduced me to the Hedgerow Theatre, which produced primarily Shakespeare and other classic playwrights. Accustomed to attending plays by Shakespeare, Moliere and Pirandello as a young girl in Hungary, I loved going to the theatre, and I appreciated that Martin wanted to share it with me.

He was serious about me, but I did not realize that at the time. We dated on and off for about two years. Though I liked Martin very much, I was still straddling the threshold of a new way of life, and I had to shed what I had been previously taught about how to relate to men. My mother had instilled in me that proper behavior for a woman meant restraint, waiting for men to call you and not the other way around. I was never the one to initiate dates, which Martin took as a sign that I was not interested. Eventually, he became discouraged, and we parted ways.

I VISITED MAGDA AND AUNT Bella in Brooklyn on a regular basis. Just about four years after our arrival to the states, Magda met a young man who fell in love with her. Although the feeling was anything but mutual, mother and daughter decided that she ought to marry him because "it was the practical thing to do."

According to Aunt Bella, Norman and his background were less than impressive, but he could be molded. And that is what she and Magda prepared to do. Mother and daughter spoke of marriage like a business deal. To me, it was disillusioning, but I accepted Magda's invitation to be her maid of honor at the wedding. Aunt Elizabeth and Uncle Alex were invited, and I was to bring an escort. Though I was still dating Martin at the time, I of course shied away from calling him, so I went alone. I wore a lovely gown my Aunt made me for the occasion. She really outdid herself, wanting me to shine. I believed it was a gesture from her heart.

The wedding was a pompous affair, with all the traditional trimmings. No extravagance they could possibly afford was spared. However, the affair ended on a strange note; the bride went home with her mother, and I with them. The groom would pick his bride up the following day. As soon as we got back to the apartment, Magda and Aunt Bella rushed to pile the monetary gifts on the table and began summing it up, pleased with their profitable venture.

My Aunt sent my parents a photo of me in my full regalia. The gesture may have been well meaning, but it struck me that Aunt Elisabeth might have had other motives. She seemed particularly eager to display how it was she—in other words, not my mother—who had brought about my transformation. I worried about how my mother would respond to that.

I FIND LIFE AN UNFATHOMABLE mystery. One may never know when and where life-altering situations will present themselves. In addition, while the choice to respond to any opportunity is ours, a Higher Force seems to govern the direction one takes. Accepting that as true has helped me come to terms with all that has happened in my life, a large part of which I spent in turbulent matrimony with Harry.

I met him on a beautiful sunny day in May 1951, when a mutual friend from Temple Sinai's youth group invited Inge and me to a picnic. Located in the Mt. Airy section of Philadelphia, the congregation was popular and had a quite large youth group. Members were urged to invite guests, which meant the group bought together people from many different parts of the city. Inge came with a date, but neither of us knew anyone other than the friend who invited us.

Once the activities began, we started to feel more comfortable. I stumbled on a volleyball game, but not having played since my school years, I decided to watch for a while before joining in. I soon found out that standing so close to the sidelines was not such a good idea, when a loose ball hurled straight toward me and struck me in the right eye. Startled by the unexpected blow, I staggered as I tried to steady my balance and waited to regain the focus of my vision. Realizing that no permanent damage was done, I was about to leave when the fellow responsible for the foul aim stopped me to see if I was injured. Profusely apologetic, the young man offered to escort me back to where I stayed, but I assured him that was not necessary. A little while later, as Inge, her friend, and I were about to settle down to eat, that same man approached me with a paper and pencil in hand to ask for my name and phone number.

"Are you taking census for the organization?" I asked.

"Have you never been asked for a date?"

I did not know whether to laugh or be annoyed. I found his arrogance unappealing.

Noting my hesitation, he tried another tactic. Harry—as he then introduced himself—offered to bring us a sample of his supposedly highly praised potato salad to appease me. I figured what could I lose? Moments later, he returned with his fare, which I silently judged acceptable, though certainly not above average. However, I took the offering as a token of his contrition. Somehow, his brazen persistence captured my interest.

It was then I noticed the mischief in his eyes. Dark and provocative, something about them seemed familiar. He lingered with us for a while before he mustered the nerve to ask for my phone number again. This time, however, he made a point to tell me that he was asking me out on a date.

I decided to give it a chance, for I had a feeling that he was someone I could trust. More than a week passed before I heard from him, and another passed before our first date. When he finally called me, I learned the reason for the delay. The piece of paper he had written my number on had been torn, leaving him missing some crucial digits. He called several combinations until he hit the jackpot. His determination fascinated me.

Before I met Harry, Aunt Elisabeth and Uncle Alex had moved to a one-story ranch house in Melrose Park, a classy neighborhood just outside the Northeast city limits. Especially after the darkness of the house in Logan, it did not take long to get used to a lovely, bright new home on a well-manicured half acre. My aunt set up one of the house's two bedrooms for me. Easy public transportation between our neighborhood and Philadelphia proved helpful to Harry, who lived on the opposite end of town, in West Philadelphia, and did not have a car. I was terribly impressed when I realized the distance he had to travel to spend time with me. That he was so willing to make the journey each time made me start to believe that ours was a destined relationship. Being around Harry felt so natural to me.

Harry confessed that from the moment he saw me he decided that I was the girl he was looking for. When we first met, he was a student at Temple University working towards a small construction engineering degree. At night, he ushered at a movie theater. When we began seeing each other more regularly, he was able to use his father's car, a huge old Packard that only a prayer kept rolling. Harry was not much of a talker, but with my broken English, there could hardly have been much of a worthwhile exchange of ideas.

Harry and I dated for six months before reaching an impasse. He seemed quite comfortable with the way things were, in no hurry to make a commitment. I, on the other hand, wanted to get married and have a family. At 25, I did not want to wait indefinitely for Harry to come around, so I told him I wanted to call it quits.

Just as I broke up with Harry, my parents arrived in Canada. Aunt and Uncle, who had been planning to spend a week at a resort in the Catskill Mountains, decided to take me with them and extend their vacation to travel to Toronto to welcome my parents.

Looking forward to meeting my parents for the first time in six years stirred up dormant emotions. It was difficult to imagine what it would be like being with them again, especially when we would be without Gyuri. We still had not heard from him. Mother and Dad were staying with Mother's cousins Erno and Eva. Before learning of my parents' plans to travel to Canada, I had not even heard of these relatives. I never thought to ask how the two couples made contact. Things like that were way down on the bottom of what seemed an endless list of questions.

During the long car trip through New York State, we stopped to see Niagara Falls, with its massive body of water roaring downward into its frothy abyss and a misty rainbow hovering above. Despite my nerves about the visit to come, I felt peaceful in the presence of nature's infinite unfolding.

WHEN WE ARRIVED AT ERNO's home in Toronto, we found him, his wife Eva, sister Rozsi, and husband Gabor sitting in the garden.

With them were Mother and Dad.

I was so excited that I could not quite remember whether I ran towards my parents or they jumped from their seat to run towards me, but before I knew it, the three of us clutched each other in an emotional embrace.

It was also quite moving to see my mother and her sister reunited, as the two has been apart since Elisabeth came to the US before World War I broke out. Father also seemed delighted to see Elizabeth; their relationship also stretched back to childhood days. Even Uncle and Father had known each other, though vaguely. So it was a reunion for all.

Mother and Dad reunite with Elisabeth and Alex in Toronto

The spotlight of the day, however, continued to fall on Mother, Dad, and me as we hugged, letting the tears fall freely. It was hard to believe that the three of us came through and could be together at last. Never the less, it was painfully obvious that our joy could never be complete without our Gyuri.

Seeing Mother and Dad for the first time face to face made me feel a powerful mix of past and present all at once. In my mind, my parents had remained the same. I was not prepared for the changes that time had bestowed on all of us. Even the ring of their voices sounded strange to my ears. And I had changed as well. I had grown into an adult in their absence. I no longer saw them as my authority figures. Instead, I saw them as the two people whose nurturing love had given me the strength that carried me over the gates of hell. I now loved them with an adult love that came from knowing my parents as exceptional human beings. What extraordinary people they were had become more obvious to me when I was tossed out into the world among so many others.

We had so much to catch up on, but there was hardly any time. The week slipped away quickly, filled with shared stories about the years that had elapsed since last we had been together. When we drove away, Father's lighthearted grin was more reassuring than Mother's heroic smile because I still could not help noticing her misty eyes. As for me, I left relieved that they were safe in Canada—no longer waiting on the other side of the ocean, fearful and uncertain.

On the way to the Catskills, I had time to ponder over my parents' account of what I had "missed" by not returning to Hungary.

Budapest, Hungary, 1945-46

When the International Red Cross took me to Sweden to recover after liberation from Bergen-Belsen, I could not possibly have fathomed the trauma my parents and others would face in the midst of chaotic post-war conditions. A politically volatile Europe made it all the more difficult for people to rebuild their shattered lives. And while my parents' personal accounts rendered those conditions vividly in my mind's eye, it was still hard for me to believe it all.

It was the fall of 1944. The Allies were closing in from the West, and the Soviets from the East, but Adolf Eichman was not about to abandon his mission. Determined, he gave the orders to rush the execution of all remaining Jews living in the Budapest's ghetto. When they herded the remaining captives toward the Danube for execution, my parents Margit and Henrik were among them, and made a frantic move to escape.

Father quietly instructed Mother that, when he signaled, she should tear off her yellow star and hold onto him.

"Don't think, just follow me,' he implored.

The opportunity for escape came when my parents passed a trolley stop. No one noticed as they slipped out of line and into a departing car. Reaching the home of a Christian friend, my parents were sheltered until liberation.

Those who had not managed to escape the transport, however, were taken to the Danube as planned, and a firing squad carried out Eichman's orders. The blue waters of Johann Strauss' Danube flowed red, colored by the blood of innocent martyrs.

THE WAR WAS OVER. BUDAPEST, the city of my birth, was in shambles. Furious air and land attacks had transformed the landscape so even memory could barely reconstruct it. Known to the West as the *Pearl of the Danube,* Hungary's capital was mostly rubble.

Though the Nazis were gone, danger and disorder remained. Soviet Communist occupational forces took over Hungary. It was chaotic. After all everyone had been through, liberation was not quite the experience people had expected. Acute shortages of foods and other necessities pushed many over the edge. All over, women were raped, and shops and homes were looted. No one felt safe on the streets. The battle for survival had just begun. The hatred and animosity the Nazis had worked so hard to fuel was not about to dissipate overnight. It was as if the flames of hostility would never be extinguished. Gloom hung over the city. With the future of the country in doubt, people longed for a return to relative normalcy.

As soon as possible, my parents wanted to return to their abandoned apartment. Tired and still frightened, they pulled a little wagon packed with their earthly belongings as they waded through heaps of ruins and dead bodies on the way to the outskirts of the city where the apartment was located. They were relieved to find the dwelling intact (though vacant). Sadly, though, stepping across the threshold of the apartment—once filled with joy and laughter—only drove home the fact that their family was not complete. Where were Gyuri and Eva? Were they alive? Were they well enough to find their way home?

But there was a surprise waiting when my parents returned. On the wall still hung the unharmed oil portrait of their children! Was it meant to be a sign, a symbol of their survival? With hope in their hearts, my parents began a prayerful vigil.

EAGER TO FIND THEIR FAMILIES, deportees began to return home from the camps on a daily basis. Most of them made the hard journey home driven by sheer force of will. They longed to resume their interrupted lives. Few had the good luck to be reunited with their loved ones; there were more broken hearts in those days than one dares to count.

A year passed before my parents learned I was alive in Sweden. Of the many letters I sent, only the one addressed to Mr. Alsner found its way through the still poorly functioning postal system.

Mr. Alsner—known as Louie to my father—was a simple man. He was the neighborhood barber, as well as my dad's chess partner, friend, and confidante. Louie was also a man of strong political convictions, even under the most precarious of circumstances. He was the only member of his entire family to defy the Nazis. Mr. Alsner *dared* not to relinquish the friendship with my father, and, most importantly, offered to take custody of my family's valuables until one of us returned to claim them. Though in those days many people made such promises to their trusting friends, not everyone kept their word. Louis, however, was an exception. He returned all of our valuables to my parents unharmed. While many other Christians had turned their backs on us, to me, Louie Alsner embodied the true spirit of Christianity.

Before the Nazis invaded Budapest, Louie had offered to be our go-between; if separated, we would contact each other through him. As a communist, he survived Nazi interrogations and harassment. Had he not lived through the war, my letter might never have reached my parents. When he received my correspondence, the courageous and loyal friend ran through the streets, ecstatically waving the letter.

"Look Friedrich!" he shouted. "Look what I got for you!"

MORE TIME PASSED, AND MORE survivors streamed through troubled borders. Still, there was no sign of Gyuri.

My parents waited anxiously, until one day a strange young man knocked on the door and introduced himself as Gyuri's friend.

"We met during deportation and remained together until liberation," he explained. "When we encountered a lot of confusion between the liberating forces and returning prisoners on our way home, we decided to meet at this address if we got separated. I expected to find him here. Please let me know as soon as he returns."

He never did.

Hopes of his return faded in time. For years, we waited for a miracle.

We looked for him in every face, at every turn of the corner on every street.

We kept hoping that he too was looking for us somewhere in this dismembered Universe. We called into the wind for all to hear:

Gyuri, where are you? **Gyuri, Where are You?**

ONE DAY MUCH LATER, LONG after my parents had joined me in the U.S., my mother reminisced with me about a curious, almost mythical incident that haunted her.

"You remember," She said, "we always opened the window to air out the place. It was not long after we settled in the apartment when I noticed a great big butterfly flying about the room. It circled several times before landing on the oil portrait [of Gyuri and me] for a while. Then it frantically raced toward the window, attempting to go outside. A very strange feeling came over me. Somehow, I felt Gyuri's presence in that butterfly. With a heavy heart, I opened the window, and let it go free..."

Mother's voice trailed off, and the pain of loss clouded her eyes.

I SHALL ALWAYS REMEMBER MY brother through his music, as his heart sang when he played his violin. His love of music resonated through the strings of his instrument. His favorite pieces became my favorites, and for many years after the war, I could not bear hearing those melodies without grieving for him. Neither was I able to attend concert halls without looking for him in the orchestras, waiting for him to show up among the musicians.

Time is powerless to erase precious memories held in the heart.

Gyuri 1939 graduation photo

CHAPTER FIVE

Marriage

FROM THE FRYING PAN INTO THE FIRE

A week at a Catskill resort with Aunt and Uncle was a special treat, but trying to recapture any part of our stay there is like looking at a blank page in a book. I understand that even blank pages serve a purpose; they are breaks between chapters to ready the mind for what is yet to come. In my book of life, I later realized, the pause provided by my visit with Aunt and Uncle offered a chance to rest before the emotional taxation of all that was about to happen.

We arrived home on a Saturday. I still worked for Teddy Benjamin at the time, and a letter from her awaited my return. She expected me to report back on Monday. Surprisingly, I actually felt good about returning to that little under–ventilated workroom, where summers were absolutely sweltering. In those days, my co-worker Ilse and I could achieve a bit of comfort only when we stripped down to our underwear. Fortunately, the two of us worked out of the sightline of those entering the front door, and we did not have to grab for our clothes unless either of us were summoned to fit a rare off-season customer.

My first day at work was uneventful, except for Ilse's report that someone was looking for me while I was away.

"It was a young guy," she said, "puzzled that you were not back after having been away for a week. It seemed to upset him that we had no clue as to when you would return."

I knew at once that the visitor had to be Harry; he was the only person who knew where I worked. I wondered why he would track me down, as the two of us had broken up before I left for Toronto. Harry himself answered that question. As I left work at the end of the day, I discovered him waiting for me, pacing the sidewalk in front of the building. I barely had time to register his presence before he was at my side with arms around me so tightly I could barely catch my breath.

"Hey! What brings you here?" I asked, after I was able to collect myself. "Didn't I break up with you before I left?"

"Yes, but can't you give me another chance?"

After a moment of silence he quietly added, "I missed you, Babe! I don't want to lose you."

I could hardly say, "let's forget about it" and walk away. On the spot, head spinning, I did not quite know what to say. Finally, I agreed to talk things out. I accepted his offer of a ride home—on the condition that he not stay when he dropped me off.

The ride home was terrifying. Harry allowed his emotions to control him behind the wheel. His aggressive nature was never more apparent than when he was driving, and I was always ill at ease while sitting in the car with him. This time, however, was different. Jubilant over what he probably considered a conquest, he chose the side roads to avoid rush-hour traffic and drove like a fired-up cowboy. Even so, he could not understand why I nervously held onto the edge of my seat all the way home. He thought it was funny. I was relieved to get out of the car and call it a night.

"How about next Saturday?" he asked as I opened the car door. He apparently took it as a given that we were back on track.

"Oh no, not so fast" I blurted out. "I want to make sure how I feel about it before I can give you an answer." Eyes downcast, he turned his head slightly to conceal his disappointment and was about to challenge my decision, but I was resolute. "Please don't pressure me. I need time alone to think it over." After an awkward moment of silence, he looked up at me with a faint smile, reached out and pulled me close. He kissed me lightly before he got in the car and drove away. As I stood there watching his car fade out of sight, it took me by surprise to feel both relief and the pain of loss.

• • • •

OUR EVENING MEAL AROUND THE kitchen table was usually the most pleasant time spent together with Aunt and Uncle. Uncle always looked forward to my coming home, as I typically shared vivid tales of my daily activities. However, on that particular night, as we sat at dinner after Harry dropped me off, Uncle could tell something weighed on my mind. He asked if there was a problem, but I was in no mood to let my relatives in on what was happening. I had mixed feelings enough about what I wanted, and I was sure they would only continue pressuring me to get married.

I asked to be excused to the privacy of my room, where I stretched out on the bed, closed my eyes and tried to focus on the issues that were important to me if I were to have a lasting relationship with Harry. I wondered if my feelings for him had deeper roots than the obvious attraction to his masculine good looks and the mischievous twinkle in his eyes. And although his unpretentious, uninhibited American persona appealed to me, this was no time to rely on superficial magnetism alone. Destined to live by my feelings, I could not shake my sense that Harry was someone I had known all my life, and I allowed this sensation to cancel out my doubts about him. I was not sure I knew him well enough. Finally, in such moments, I had to rely on my intuition, as I could not speak English well enough for in-depth conversations. Unbeknownst to me at the time, such conversations did not interest Harry in the least anyway.

For me, America held the promise of a good life, the opportunity to make up for times lost during my formative years. My coming to America was to be a real life adventure, but not for the prospect of finding fame and fortune. I looked forward to exploring the richness of freedom and opportunity this country was known for. The one thing I had not counted on was the internal conflicts arising from living in service of two different cultures. For example, it was quite a shock for me to discover that my naturally courteous demeanor could tag me as a foreigner. Apparently, I stood out in the United States, where manners were far more lax than those in Hungary. In America, respect for authority, elders—, and even consideration for others— seemed to have little use. I found such offhand, casual interactions far less amusing in real life than they had been on the silver screen years before. In time, though, I came to appreciate the informality of such interactions, partly because I saw them as a sign that—in certain respects—social hierarchies in the United States were less stringent than those I had been accustomed to in Hungary.

Once I stopped being so judgmental, I started to find ways to bridge the gap between my two cultures without having to compromise my principles. Living with my relatives slowed my ability to close such gaps, however, because they constantly ridiculed me for my attempts to "advance" into the American mainstream. Fortunately, however, I had the opportunity to experience everyday American life in action away from their influence while at work... As I became more familiar with American customs, I was able to begin to come to terms with the differences between Harry and me. It would have been hard to predict how much these cultural differences would affect my relationship with Harry, but I was too naïve to worry about that then.

He was ambitious, but how honest, loyal or dependable he was, I could only guess. Was he the man of my dreams or wishful thinking? Either way, I was eager to escape my relatives' demeaning treatment, so I decided to move forward with the relationship.

I decided to wait for a while before letting Harry know of my decision. I needed some time to get comfortable with the idea of us as a couple, except that Harry got ahead of me. Without asking for my answer, he invited me to a family party.

"Saturday is my sister Elaine's birthday, and I would like you to come and help us celebrate it." His invitation took me off guard not only because it was totally unexpected, but also because his approach was so direct. He probably never guessed how easy he made it for me to give him my answer.

HARRY SUGGESTED THAT I MEET him at the movie house where he worked. Though it was a long trip, Harry had made the trip to my house many times, so it seemed only fair for me to make the journey this time. When I got to the movies, the last feature was almost over.

At the end of the show, we walked the short distance to his home hand-in-hand, as if it was the most natural thing for us to do.

The Kottlers' (as Harry's family originally spelled my surname) house on Larchwood Avenue was somber-looking—of masonry construction with a little open porch at the side of the entry door. I was more curious than excited as Harry ushered me inside, where family members bustled about in preparation for dinner. With all the chaos, my presence was casually acknowledged, but without the slightest measure of welcome. I began to think my being there at that exact moment was a big mistake. It was an awkward situation, far from anything I expected. Feeling like an intruder, I turned to Harry and asked if he had secured his family's permission to invite me.

"I didn't have to ask," he answered. "I only told them to expect you." I figured that was Harry's way of saying: I wanted you to be here and that is good enough for me. Perhaps it was then that he inadvertently got me off to the wrong start with his elders.

Without a doubt, Father Kottler was the uncontested ruler of his household. The man was in charge of everything, including cooking and serving the food. It was not what he did but how he did it that upset me. That day at Elaine's birthday dinner, he was crude and insensitive as he dictated his wife leave the kitchen.

"Get out of here!" he bellowed. "You can't do nott'n", you are only in my way! Go! Get out!" He had no qualms with humiliating her in my presence.

No such exchange would ever have happened between my parents. I felt embarrassed for Harry's mother as she left the kitchen without as much as a look or sound of protest.

"Okay, dinner is ready, let's eat!" Mr. Kottler's voice was strong and commanding, but this time he was not unkind. It was the voice of a shepherd gathering his flock. Standing at the head of the table Mr. Kottler—Izidor—was ready to serve the meal. Once he was ready, there was no dallying around. Six feet tall, a little on the hefty side, and sporting his few remaining strands of hair carefully spread across his shiny head, he wielded his authority with self-importance and a no-nonsense attitude. His children never second-guessed him; his rules were unquestionable, but so was his love for them. They trusted and admired him.

Izidor (or Izzi, as he was called in family circles) immigrated to America as a young man. From a rural Jewish settlement in Russia called Ruziner, he followed his older brother Benny, who was already settled in Pittsburgh with his family. While growing up, Benny and Izzi could not afford more than basic educations, but they acquired the sort of life skills one could not gain in any school. Ready to weather the storm of life, each man in his own way managed to support his family. Benny was amiable and mild-mannered, Izzi boisterous and domineering. The two men's wives were not on the best of terms—a strain never to be reconciled.

Of Izzi's children, Ruthie, the oldest, was her father's favorite. She inherited a lot of his personality and looks. Harry, a year younger, was expected to be his father's right hand. Elaine came three years later. When I met Elaine on her birthday that year, she was a young bride with her husband Dave—home on a short furlough from the service—at her side. Elaine resembled Mrs. Kottler, but she was more engaging than her mother. On Elaine, the features she shared with her mother bore a lively sparkle. She had been the baby of the family until Herbie, the youngest, arrived on the scene twelve years later. Ruthie and Elaine both admired their father, and he seemed to favor them.

Mrs. Kottler—Selma—was short and stout. Her height measured less than five feet, and her full head of beautiful hair was still dark brown when I first met her. She was a handsome woman with high cheekbones, but her less than inviting demeanor chilled me. She barely spoke, and her scornful stare in my direction suggested she did not approve. Selma hailed from the part of Russia that became Poland after World War I. Her father was an affluent logging contractor, and she was very young when her mother died. The only mother she remembered was the aunt her father took for his second wife.

The story passed around the family was that Selma had studied to be a pharmacist. She was eighteen when she came to the U.S. to be united with Izzi, to whom she had become engaged in the old country. Before coming here, Selma had been accustomed to a life of luxury. In contrast, she and Izzi struggled to make ends meet. It was a difficult adjustment, a transition only made all the harder by Izzi's tyrannical household government. When the pressures of her marriage—including three pregnancies that followed in such short succession—became too much for her to bear, she suffered two severe breakdowns. I do not know what triggered her first breakdown, but the second one happened following Herbie's birth. I met Selma after both those episodes, so how exactly they changed her I can never be sure.

SERVINGS WERE ABOUT TO BEGIN, but not before Mr. Kottler settled a lively dispute over seating arrangements. The meal was simple: pot-roast, potatoes, carrots, and peas. As I learned later, on other days the main fare might have been a meatloaf, chicken or steak, but with hardly any variation in the vegetable department.

It was somewhat strange for me to sit at the table with people whose table manners defied all that I had been taught was proper. Whether fingering food in the common bowl that they never intended to take or holding their forks as though they were daggers, it all seemed foreign to me. I am sure that, to them, I seemed fussy—even a bit snooty. Such differences in table manners seemed to set me apart from the rest of Harry's family from the start.

DISHES, DISHES, AND MORE DISHES. Looking at the seemingly endless number of them piled on the Kottlers' kitchen counter after Elaine's birthday meal; I remembered how I used to hate to be assigned dishes as my chore when I was growing up. There was no hot water coming out of the spigot then, and the only available dishwashing detergent was "kopor"—a rough, sand-like substance which was neither able to cut the grease nor kind to the hand. Although Mother tried hard to convince me that the greasy dishwater kept hands nice and soft, I wished there was someone else in my place to be granted that cosmetic advantage. In fact, I have dreaded washing dishes ever since. So as I looked at the pile of dishes at the Kottlers' that evening, I silently thanked the good Lord that I was not the one on duty this time, even with hot water and without the burden of kopor.

Ruthie and Elaine

Regardless, nobody even made a move to clean up the mess before the birthday cake took center stage on the table in front of Elaine. Elaine made her wish and blew out all the candles with one courageous puff, and together we all burst into a discordant and thunderous rendition of "Happy Birthday." Adding more dishes to the pile, our feast had a sweet ending with cake and ice cream. Afterwards, Ruth and Elaine took to the kitchen to clean up the mess, while Harry remained with his brother -in-laws as Mr. and Mrs. Kottler invited me to join them in the living room.

I figured Harry's parents were about to have a warming-up session with me.

"Come, come," said Mr. Kottler, gesturing for me to take my spot in a stately old cushioned chair. As he pulled up two dining room chairs and placed them across from me, he appeared affable, unlike Mrs. Kottler, whose unsympathetic gaze continued to make me self-conscious. I started talking to shake off my uneasiness.

"Thanks for having me. We never celebrated anyone's birthday like this. Everything is so different here in this country. It will take a while for me to get used to living here."

Mr. Kottler picked up my thread and ran with it. "You are right; the customs are different in this country, just as you are very different from us."

I looked at him quizzically, waiting for him to back up his claim, but surprisingly, it was Mrs. Kottler who jumped in, barely able to contain her disdain. Her words spewed out like spittle.

"You Hungarians Jews are not at all like us."

Mrs. Kottler's outburst strangely echoed Ruzina's sentiments in the Malmo hospital ward. Mr. Kottler, meanwhile, put down his wife's biting remark with a short wave of a hand and a little giggle, as if to say, "don't pay attention to her.' But his insinuation that Hungarians Jews like me did not measure up to "real Jews" was not really any different from the beliefs his wife expressed.

I was beginning to feel the blood rush to my face. The Nazis had not questioned my legitimacy as a Jew, I thought to myself, and, though mortified, I managed to make the same statement aloud. As if he had not heard me, Mr. Kottler went on:

"And another thing. What do you know from Jewish customs and holy days? What makes you different from the Goyim [people outside the faith]?" Not only did he completely sidestep the Holocaust as an event; Mr. Kottler represented himself as the sole authority on what a Jew was supposed to be like, and I detected that the Kottlers' prejudice against secular religious observers (which for example, Budapest Jews were known to be) was based on nothing more than ignorant assumptions.

If the Kottlers wanted to know so much about my background, why could they not have asked their questions without making such a special effort to intimidate me? Tiring of their interrogation, I asked them what the point of the conversation was.

"Well, we wanted to know what your expectations were where Harry is concerned. Maybe he is giving you the wrong impression, but he is not ready to get married. Besides...you are very different from us," they repeated. At that moment, I knew immediately why they had kept Harry out of this little parley.

I wondered if Harry's parents had any inkling as to how much this conversation hurt me—or if they cared at all.

How was I to react to such indignities when my past scars had not yet healed? What kind of people could attack me so callously, especially knowing all I had been through? Selma's own family had been decimated in Poland during the Holocaust, a fact that made their insensitivity to my history all the more absurd.

I do not know how I did it, but I braved the storm brewing inside me and managed to remain calm and civil on the surface. Their actions were driven by fear of appearing inferior in the face of an invented opponent, but I only figured this out much later. At the time, I mostly wondered how much Harry knew about the way his parents felt and what he had to say about it.

I glanced at my watch and decided to end the conversation.

"It is getting late, and I need to be going."

There was nothing more to say.

With that, I got up and went to ask Harry to take me home. I found him deeply engrossed in a Pinochle game with his sisters and brothers -in-law. When I interrupted him, the vague expression on his face revealed that his mind was preoccupied. He had barely uttered a "Wait, I'll drive you home" before the game stole his attention away once more. When the game finally ended, I bid everyone farewell and could hardly wait to step outside. I appreciated the chance to breathe fresh air. The cool evening breeze helped wash away my anxiety before we got into the car and began rolling. We were both absorbed in our own thoughts until Harry broke the silence.

"So, you got a chance to meet my folks. What was it you and my parents were talking about?" I was glad he asked. But did it mean he was unaware of how his parents felt about me?

"Well, actually they only took advantage of the opportunity to tell me why they felt that I was too different to be the right match for you—and that I should not have any expectations because you are not ready for marriage."

"I knew how they felt, but that is why I wanted them to meet you. You are very different not only from us, but from anyone I ever met before, and that is one of the things I like so much about you. As for my parents, they resent that, and my mother may never be able to get over it, but I made my choice, and I am resolute."

"What about you not being ready for marriage?"

"Well, in defense of my father's remarks about that, you should know that it has not been long since I got divorced, ending a very short-lived, ill-fated marriage. He probably wanted to leave that for me to tell, and I am glad he did, because coming from me you can get it straight. Actually, I was forced into that marriage when the girl I dated a few times claimed I got her pregnant. Shortly after the wedding I found out that she used that ploy to get her parents after me. I was not going to be tied to a loveless marriage and filed for divorce. End of the story."

Hearing about the marriage did not upset me as much as the fact that his father neglected to tell me what he meant by Harry not being ready. Perhaps he was waiting for me to ask, or maybe he was just waiting for Harry to tell me, just as Harry said. I guess Mr. Kottler was trying to protect his son from making another mistake—and to alert me to be on the defensive. Regardless, this early experience programmed me to expect nothing but offenses coming from the two people who had the audacity to cast such judgments over me.

AFTER COMING TO THIS COUNTRY, I found I loved the picnic part of the Fourth of July. I did not, however, like the fireworks, even though they were lovely to look at. They sounded too much like the bombs as they whistled before they reached their target with earthshaking explosions.

Harry's family planned a Fourth of July picnic gathering in Parvin State Park, and he took it for granted that I would join them. The park, a very popular multi-purpose outdoor recreation area near Vineland, New Jersey, was a little over an hour's ride from where I lived. The road leading there was a little tricky; for the unfamiliar traveler, it was easy to get lost on your way.

On a beautiful, clear day, Harry came for me in his father's car somewhere around 8:30 am. We were to meet the rest of the family in the park by 10:00 am. What I did not know then was that Harry's dad clocked the time at all family gatherings and if you were running late, you got an earful of stern reprimand. Well, as luck had it, somewhere along the way Harry must have made a wrong turn. We got hopelessly lost. At one point, I got exasperated and suggested that we stop and ask for directions, but Harry stubbornly drove on without any idea of where the road was leading. That my pleas fell on deaf ears was not so much the problem; rather, I was more concerned about how the prolonged journey caused Harry to become increasingly agitated until he neared the point of explosion. He was angry with himself, and reasoning no longer did any good. The wisest thing I could do was stay still. I did not know where all his extreme frustration was coming from. All I knew was it scared me. I did not care if we ever got to our destination as long as he calmed down. But that was not to be—at least not until we finally reached the park and endured the old man's ranting.

In time, I came to recognize what I thought was the root of Harry's internal struggle. He was conflicted. He wanted to rebel against his powerful father, but he also wanted to please him. Harry believed he had to emulate his father in order to win his approval, but Harry was not his father, and never could be. As a result, Harry became a bully, always trying to demonstrate his prowess.

I had no idea what or where Coney Island was, but one Saturday morning Harry wanted to take me there, so we climbed in the tired old Packard for the journey to the amusement park. I was excited about what promised to be a fun adventure, and indeed the day turned out to be one of the first life-altering outings of my time in America.

We were about half way to Coney Island when Harry suddenly stopped on the shoulder of the road. Much to my surprise, when the car came to a full stop, he turned off the motor, turned to me and took my hands in his.

"I love you and want to be your husband and take care of you," he began. "I want you to be the mother of my children. Would you marry me?"

Seeing the love in his eyes, I felt my heart swell. I had thought maybe this proposal would happen soon, but I had not expected it on that particular day. I was on the verge of saying yes, but I could not shake the memories of his terrible temper, and my common sense kicked in. It was not easy for me to confront him about my fears, but he had to know how I felt.

"You know I love you," I assured, "but I don't know if I could live with your angry outbursts. They frighten me."

His smile gone, he somberly drew back and flatly stated that his anger would vanish once he was free of his father's domination. The magic of the moment slipped away. In one respect, I understood how he felt because I was in a similar situation under my Aunt's control. The big difference was that I had found ways to assert my own agenda more aggressively while still appearing compliant with my Aunt's expectations. Obviously, Harry and I had contrasting dispositions, but I was confident that together we would be able to find a way to resolve the problems tormenting him. I agreed to marry him, to be his partner in life.

When we reached Coney Island, it was near midday. I got dizzy just looking at the crowded park. Attractions spread over what seemed like an infinite expanse. Harry looked rather pleased with himself as he held my arm and we merged into the crowd. Like a little kid, he wanted to be everywhere at the same time and sample all the stuff that looked edible, from pretzels to hot dogs to cotton candy. We rode rides, watched sideshows, and enjoyed every minute. As the close of our night drew nearer, an eager vendor stopped us in front of his souvenir photo booth. He fast-talked Harry into having our picture taken with our faces peeking through the openings of a life-size rendering of a Hawaiian costume-clad couple. The whole thing took no more than a few minutes, but then the unexpected happened. When Harry was about to pay, the vendor—quicker than lightning—pulled the twenty-dollar bill from Harry's hand and refused to return the change. In a flash, I saw Harry's face turn red. Without a word, fists clenched, Harry was ready to pounce on the man. The vendor backed up, white as ash from fright, and swiftly extended his hand, trembling as it held out Harry's ten dollars change.

By that time, I, too, was shaking, for fear of a violent ending to our otherwise happy outing. Harry's nonchalant mood returned as if nothing has happened. He had his money and his photo, and that was that. The incident was over.

Well, it was nothing like that for me. The slightest indication of upcoming violence makes me absolutely paralyzed with fear. It took me a bit to regain my composure, but when I did, I told him how upset I was about the way he had behaved.

"I am sorry," he replied, "but I was not going to let that bum get away with that switch-and-bait trick. It was enough to make me mad as hell! But let's forget about it, okay?"

I thought maybe he was right. Perhaps that was the only way for him to get results when dealing with a person like that. I tried to put the incident behind me.

We had not eaten a decent meal all day, and with the sun settling down on the horizon, it was too late to get on the road to make it home safely. We decided to find a restaurant and stay over for the night. We found a good meal, but the only motel available turned out to be a real dive where sailors brought their girls for one-night stands. We heard a lot going on through the walls that evening, making the

Our wedding portrait. Phila. Dec. 1951

place not the most conducive atmosphere for our first night together, but after a while, it did not seem to matter at all.

Six months later, we got married in a service at the Beth Shalom Synagogue chapel in Philadelphia. A reception followed at my relatives' home. Aunt Elisabeth and Uncle Alex provided and arranged everything. Besides Harry's immediate family and close relatives, the small guest list included my cousins Bobby and Theresa with her husband Mort, his parents Mr. and Mrs. Smith, my co-sponsors Mr. and Mrs. Molnar, and my friend Inge. Unfortunately, my parents could not be there. They were still in Canada and on the waiting list for permanent visas, which prevented the immigration service from issuing them visitors' permits.

The animosity between the Kottlers and the Wengers flared early on in Harry's and my relationship, when Aunt and Uncle sidestepped the custom of inviting the Kottlers' participation in planning the wedding. It especially ticked the Kottlers off when my relatives did not give them the correct time for the ceremony and caused them to arrive at the synagogue far too early, way ahead of schedule. Neither Harry nor I were aware of this power play, and the Kottlers burned with humiliation as they were forced to linger for over an hour in the synagogue's hallway until we arrived.

This incident unfortunately set the mood that carried over for the entire wedding reception. The reception provided an opportunity for Uncle Alex and Aunt Elisabeth to flaunt their modest financial successes. They had little regard for people whose fiscal status did not at least measure up to their own. Neither Aunt nor Uncle could boast of more than the minimum required education in the old country, and their intelligence was no higher than average, yet they looked down on the Kottlers, avoiding conversation with them whenever possible. When social circumstances like the wedding forced my relatives to speak with the Kottlers, their tone was unmistakably patronizing. I am sure it did not occur to Mr. and Mrs. Kottler that they were actually being served with their own medicine.

Izidor responded to my family's condescension by propelling himself to the center of attention, his manner suddenly more bellicose than usual. His booming voice and haughty laughter reverberated off the walls. After all, this was his son's wedding too, and why should he not make merry? My relatives considered such public behavior unre-

Mother, Dad and I in Toronto, Canada (Dec.1951)

fined, but Izzi had no qualms with getting under the Wengers' skin to let them know there was no intimidating the intimidator. Meanwhile, Selma, whose small frame brimmed with envy and resentment, seemed to feel outnumbered. Neither of Harry's sisters nor their respective spouses caught wind of this unsavory interplay, and little Herbie was too busy filling himself with sweets.

Fortunately, I was sufficiently wrapped up in myself to allow the adults' indulgence in such snobbery and overall stupidity to ruin my good mood. These petty conflicts, however, would have a lasting and caustic effect on the relations between the two families joined by marriage that day.

Harry and I with Mother and Dad in Toronto

COMPENSATING MY PARENTS FOR MISSING out on our wedding, Harry and I went to Toronto on our honeymoon. He wanted to meet my parents, and they looked forward to meeting him, too. Harry later confessed that he was concerned that my parents might be anything like Aunt and Uncle. He was greatly relieved to find my mother very different from her sister and my father an amicable fellow.

A week later, we returned to Philadelphia—and to our modest three-room apartment on the second floor of a privately owned building. The owners, Mr. and Mrs. Pecter, had two daughters: fifteen year-old Roz, who lived with them on the third floor, and Pearl, who lived with her husband Irv and Mutzi, their black cat, in the ground floor apartment. A corner brick house in walking distance to public transportation and shopping, our building was well kept, much like the other row-homes in the middle-class neighborhood. We were not more than fifteen minutes away from my relatives, but the Kottlers had to travel across the city to see us. Yet, as time went on, weekend clan gatherings at the Kottlers' would become part of our routine, even as we grew in numbers with children of our own.

Shortly after we returned from our honeymoon, Harry got a wonderful position as project manager with a growing building firm. He dropped out of school, narrowly missing his graduation. I kept my job working in the alteration department of a neighborhood specialty shop where the owners were two wonderful women. Everything was going well until my father-in-law's first (uninvited) visit. I can still see him; merely one-step over the threshold, casually flipping his hat over my ceramic candy dish on the dresser. His offhand disregard for the value of my property was only the first stunning example of what turned out to be his inspection tour through the apartment. His entry dramatically changed the atmosphere in our home, particularly when he started opening cupboards—and wiping his finger across the clothes rod looking for dirt like a staff sergeant. His intimidation of me reached its most intolerable point when he pulled the trash can out from the kitchen closet and turned to me, as if I were a servant, and scolded that it should have been emptied.

I was too angry to respond to the jolly chuckle that accompanied his "Oh, I just wanted to see what kind of housekeeper my son married." And just when I did not think he could possibly add more insult to injury, he thoughtlessly retrieved his hat from the candy dish, snagging the lid caught inside it on his way out. I gasped as I saw my parents' precious European gift shattered on the floor, but the big oaf just stood there looking surprised, and mumbling something like "well, no big deal."

He left without showing the least sign of remorse. I was humiliated—and furious that my husband had allowed his father to barge in and imply he had the right to evaluate my worth and skill as a wife. When I asked Harry why he said nothing, first he tried to convince me that I took his father too seriously and that this was just a laughing matter. Nevertheless, when I maintained how offended I was, within moments his demeanor changed completely. He claimed it was I who was to blame.

"Why didn't you take out the trash?" he yelled. "The can filled to the brim was enough for him to see the kind of housekeeper you turned out to be!" He blasted loud enough for everyone else in the house to hear. Then, with a final burst of energy, he kicked the bathroom door off the hinge. It suddenly and powerfully hit me that Harry might never be free from trying to win his father's approval. When Harry finally calmed down, he ruefully admitted that it was his father he was angry at, though that was little consolation to me.

Except when I saw Harry pitifully spent, physically and emotionally depleted—I suddenly forgot my own anger and turned to comfort him instead. Deep down inside, I wanted to believe that in time this would change, but my faith only opened the door for more painful things to follow.

WHEN HARRY HAD SIMILAR OUTBURSTS later, I had no one to turn to for moral and emotional support because I did not really trust anyone enough to share my woes. Consequently, I turned inward to seek the help and guidance of a Higher Power.

A YEAR LATER, I GAVE birth to our first child, a son. My wish to have a boy—to fill the void my brother left behind—was granted. We called him Gary, with George as his middle name in my brother's honor. He made us a family. According to my hospital roommate, she never saw a man looking at his wife as lovingly as she caught Harry watching over me while I slept after Gary was born. The miracle of Gary's birth overwhelmed me. Seeing that beautiful warm little creature filled me with awe and gratitude, and I know I was glowing with happiness.

The only place we could find room for the bassinet and changing table in our small apartment was the kitchen. The arrangement worked out well, since we had the sink on hand to double as the baby's tub. Truth be told, I doubt that it made any difference to Gary where he was as long as his needs were met.

As for myself, if I had enough food and clothes, a roof over my head, people to love me, and people I could love, I was satisfied. Everything over and above that I considered luxury. I had learned to be a frugal manager from my mother, and I would have been perfectly happy to stay in that apartment until we were more financially stable. But not Harry. Once we had Gary, he grew impatient. As a new father, he took his role seriously and insisted that we find a place to live that was better for raising children. However, as he was not about to settle for a row house, our search took us way out to the Northeast city limits to an in-progress development of starter-size family homes constructed from prefabricated materials.

The ones we saw and liked were wood-framed, with wood-paneled interior walls and stucco exterior finish. Their price made them attainable for people in our position, but my aunt failed to see it that way. The idea of us moving so far from my relatives provoked her ire. She accused Harry of scheming to put a distance between my family, and me and she claimed I was ungrateful. She gave this same sort of performance each time it appeared as though I might make an independent move. She hoped to keep a hold over me with accusations of disloyalty, asking how I could make the choices I was making "after all they'd done for me." Whatever drove her to make me feel guilty and inadequate, her effort to control me put a strain on our relationship. The more I tried to please, the more I empowered her to inhibit me. More often than not, I allowed her to control me because I did not know what else to do. I wanted desperately to believe that whatever my relatives did was out of love for me, and this belief in them would lead me to a regrettable mistake.

Uncle Alex proposed what he thought was a solution for all parties involved:

"Aunt and I really don't want you to move so far out to such an undeveloped area, particularly with your parents coming. Because the banks would allow you only a limited mortgage in your present financial situation, we decided that if you find a piece of property in the city near us and come up with a building plan we can agree on, I will give you the mortgage to build a house where both you and your parents can live."

Elated by the idea of living side by side with my parents, I, like a fool, wanted to accept the offer without a second thought of the possible consequences. As for Harry, while the prospects of building his own home in the city appealed to him, he resented Uncle's proposal. If it had been up to him we would have followed through with our original plan, but he did not want to be the bad guy who denied me the chance to live close to my parents—especially after everything we had all been through, so he agreed to go along with the arrangement.

I know now that even if Harry had been willing and able to communicate how he felt, I am sure that I would have managed to convince him to see things my way. Maybe that was why he never really even tried to fight against the idea.

FROM THE TIME I WAS fifteen years-old, I lived with "unfit" labels stamped onto my consciousness by those bent on destroying me. Those labels were hard to erase. After being treated scornfully for so many years, I began to see myself through the eyes of those who defamed me. When I decided to come to the United States for a fresh start, my self-esteem was at its lowest. I was timid and dependent, in need of encouragement, love and nurturing. I never expected to run into a situation where I would find my feelings of unworthiness reinforced, and certainly not by the very people from whom I anticipated moral support. It soon became obvious that Aunt and Uncle were not too interested in finding out who I really was; they were content to see me always as the poor little dependent relative. Judging by their standards, I was not "smart" because I was too obvious and did not spend my time trying to out-maneuver others in order to gain the upper hand. Because such game playing was not in my nature, I failed to detect the more obvious motive behind Uncle's seemingly caring, generous offer to help us with the house. By the time we realized that their proposal was designed to make us surrender our autonomy, backing out was no longer an option.

We settled on a corner acre lot at 65th Avenue and 3rdStreet, near the Philadelphia city limits and only about five minutes away from Aunt and Uncle. With plenty of open air, good schools nearby, and transportation and shopping in walking distance, the location could hardly have been more desirable. I was flying high, looking forward to a kind of dream come true.

As regards the building process, Harry had the knowledge, but Aunt and Uncle held the purse and the right to have the last word. This power arrangement led to a string of nasty confrontations between them. The escalating friction increased the frequency of Harry's outbursts. The constant presence of tension in the air dramatically changed our every-day life. There was no telling anymore what would set off Harry's rage, but often it seemed to coincide with a visit to his parents' house, where Harry took his complaints and from which he often came back ready to turn his anger on me.

Each episode drained Harry. As I am writing this, I cannot help but wonder if the military training he had received as a paratrooper in World War II—and the severe spinal injury he sustained when his parachutes failed to open in time—did not at least partially cause his erratic behavior. Harry had been laid up in the hospital in a cast from the chest down for six months but was able to work himself free of paralysis with rigorous swimming exercises and strong determination. Still, such experiences were bound to have taken a toll.

Regardless, by the time my parents came, his hostility had already reached the point that it soured their welcome.

In the middle of all this—the pressures from my relatives and the strain caused by Harry's behavior—I began to feel as if I was in quicksand, sinking, and unable to save myself.

GARY WAS SIX MONTHS OLD by the time my parents could settle in the United States. Our house, a one-story brick ranch, included my parents' apartment separated from our living quarters by a sliding door. From the time they arrived, Mother and Dad were happy and active grandparents. Gary was a novelty, as first-born grandchildren always are. He did not like to be held by anyone but me. When someone else would raise him on their arm, his body would stiffen as his arms swung out in a balancing position like a high-wire performer.

My wish for a son granted the first time, I again turned to the Giver of Life during my second pregnancy and said, "If you are sending me another boy, please send me a mischievous one." I guess it was an easy enough wish to grant because, two years after Gary was born, I gave birth to another little boy. We were going to name him Ron because we had great affection for Harry's cousin with that name. Luckily, Ron agreed to share his name with our second son. (It is contrary to Jewish custom to name a newborn for a living relative without that relative's permission.)

When we took our Ron home from the hospital and placed the

new arrival into my mother's embrace, I remember her saying softly, "This one is a sweet and cuddly child. He melts right into your arms." Funny how she sensed from the start the sweetness that became one of Ronny's trademarks.

Two years passed, and, when ready to give birth to my third child, I looked to the heavens and pleaded, "Thanks for granting two of my wishes. Would you please send me a little girl this time to even the family score with an ally on my side?" God must have listened, as Debra-Joy came into our lives. My new baby seemed to have come to this world bearing some sort of baggage because she screamed more than she slept. The doctor insisted that she was not a colicky child, yet the screaming continued. As she got older, she would awaken me with blood-curdling howls, but when I would rush to her room I would find her sleeping deeply and would have to shake her to wake her before she could be calmed down. These episodes—as it later unfolded—were triggered by recurring nightmares and continued into Debbie's adulthood.

With my parents there, I was not housebound, and though the children became the center of my life, a growing urge to be involved with the world outside of my own little circle led me to join the League of Women Voters. Through the League, I learned how to become a well-informed, active participant in the country's democratic process without the hindrance of party affiliation. I flourished in the League. Encouraged by an exceptional group of women, I discovered some of my innate talents. When I happened to mention my love of drawing, I agreed, at the insistence of some fellow League members, to give a try with illustrating our monthly Philadelphia newsletter. The reviews were so favorable that I got stuck doing it for several years. The experience encouraged me to cultivate my dormant artistic talent. Later on, I was asked to be editor for the same newsletter, something I was hesitant to take on, as I never had formal schooling in English. I gave it a try and after about three years, I had to beg out of the job. The League taught me not to be afraid to speak freely. I learned that my thoughts and opinions mattered. My relationships with some of those exceptional women matured into life-long friendships. Feeling validated by people of high standards for the first time in my life profoundly impacted my self-image.

Meanwhile, however, my relationship with my parents began to erode due to Harry's conduct. Aunt Elisabeth, resenting my growing awareness and independent thinking, used Harry's behavior as a way to drive a wedge between my parents and me. Aunt Elisabeth acted as if my courage to venture out on my own without seeking her advice was an attempt to insult her authority. What I found incredible, though, was Mother's neutrality towards Elisabeth's manipulations, especially considering Mother had sworn never to forgive her sister for refusing the help that could have saved Gyuri and me. It pained me most of all that Mother permitted Elisabeth's self-righteous chastising. Father also remained silent, but he and I were cut out of the same mold; we chose compliance to avoid altercation. Eventually, however, Mother finally did lose her cool with Uncle and Aunt. She vowed never to lay eyes on them ever again. It was then that I finally had a chance to have a heart-to-heart talk with my mom. We cleared the air between us, and I finally learned about how the final rift between my mother and Aunt and Uncle came to be.

"I know" Mom began, "that you didn't understand what made me go along with Elisabeth, but we came here without any idea of what we were going to walk into. It was not fair for you to keep us in the dark about your eroding relationship with the Wengers. We were not only angry, but we felt betrayed by you, and that made me side with Elisabeth."

"But why," I asked, "why did you allow your sister to keep punishing me for her invented offences? How could you ever believe her claims that I would be disrespectful and ungrateful?"

"After living under the same roof with Harry and getting to know what he was like, we believed everything Elisabeth told us, and could not help but blame you for allowing him to behave the way he did toward them and, later, toward us. It was I, more than Father, who felt betrayed. He was more sympathetic towards your predicament, but, not wanting to stir things up, he went along with me."

"I still can't believe you chose your sister over me after all that we have been through," I countered.

"Well my dear, all I wanted was to get away from Harry, and where else could I go? But now I can tell you that when I found out that my sister's machinations were directed to hurt me and not you, it changed everything."

I had no idea what my mother was saying.

"The reason came from her own mouth," Mother continued, "when she carelessly admitted to her long-standing resentment of me. She thought I was prettier, wittier, and more popular than her, none of which was actually true. As soon as she said that, I could not help but relate that to her relentless effort to distance us, and I instantly understood her revengeful behavior. She tried to hurt me through you. Actually, if I had any inclination of all this, we would have stayed on in Canada."

I was floored! This was the wonderful sister my mother adored? But then I asked, "How about the children, anyukam (Hungarian for mother)? Are they not your greatest pleasure? Are they not worth you being here?"

This was a tough question for her to answer.

HARRY WAS AMBITIOUS AND DID well in his construction work. His dedication stemmed from a desire to provide for his growing family. Before long, he decided to start his own small construction business, and he was soon recognized for his exceptional knowledge in the field of historical building restoration. His work ethics and quality performance attracted prominent customers, particularly from the field of art during the peak of Philadelphia's Society Hill area redevelopment. Harry enjoyed his work and business associations, through which people found him amenable and well mannered. He treated his employees as equals, so his business associates never witnessed the less admirable behavior he displayed in more personal settings, behavior which in time alienated his closest, if not only, friend, Ben Sauber. Always trying to impress, Harry got into the habit of fabricating "facts" about things he knew nothing of, and he became indignant and angry when proven wrong. I found this to be true on several occasions when I publicly repeated things he had said to me, only to be embarrassed to find his information was incorrect. After that, I made sure to double-check most everything he said. My confidence in him shaken, I eventually realized that I had better not rely on him as my primary source of information.

My EXPECTATIONS OF MY HUSBAND as a father fell short soon after Ronny was born. From the time Ronny was a toddler, the little boy became the target of Harry's frustration, his punching bag. The poor child came to me for shelter, which angered Harry even more. Family life grew increasingly dysfunctional under his management, while the business thrived. Harry's idea of record keeping, however, consisted only of holding everything in his head, which made for difficult communication with clients and authorities. Unfortunately, because we had no money to hire a qualified person to take charge of administrative work, Harry wanted me to go to school and learn bookkeeping and office management. I had no intention of being stuck behind a desk doing something I was not cut out for, but knowing how important it was to assist him, I gave up my work and began organizing files, keeping records, and typing specifications and contracts with two fingers (like my father used to do).

Technically untrained for these jobs, I drew on my common sense to get them done. The toughest part of the bargain was prying information out of Harry's secret file compartment: his mind. By the time we were in the position to open an office in town, the children were old enough for me to be there during school hours. As the business increased and the workload became too much for me to handle, we hired part-time office help to take over the bulk of recordkeeping. As our children grew into their teens, everything seemed to be on track and we were financially solvent, with only five more years to pay off our mortgage (which had been transferred from Aunt and Uncle to our bank).

Over the years, several unscrupulous clients and major financial debacles pushed Harry over the edge. He turned sour and disillusioned. To prove himself undefeated, he began to venture into uncharted territories. For example, his efforts to become a franchising agent for swimming pool constructions consumed all our resources as he tried to build a sample pool against the side of our house. We found ourselves knee-deep in basement floods—and neck-deep in debt. The pool company withdrew its support.

The ground was slipping from underneath us, but my husband did not heed my warning. He was right, and I was wrong. "You are crazy!" he would yell. "Why do you make things up? You don't know what you are talking about!!"

In the meantime, never intending to make good on his promises, he kept taking deposits from prospective clients. Each time he came upon a new opportunity, he approached my parents to finance his ventures, none of which ever materialized. Finally, desperately trying to remain on top, he re-mortgaged our home and used up the children's savings accounts and his paid-up, dividend-earning VA insurance—along with all other assets we had accumulated. He became obsessed with being a powerful businessman and lost sight of almost all else. My parents realized this when the money they loaned him twice was not repaid. When they refused to give him any more to squander away, he cursed them out, sent them to hell, and at one point, he threatened to punch my father out. Frightened, Mother and Dad moved out of the house.

Harry continued not to make good on his debts. Soon, despite the fact that paying off our mortgage completely was only a few years down the road, the bank repossessed the house and we lost everything we owned.

It was then that I could no longer be loyal to my vows. I left my husband. I told him that, unless he was willing to pull himself together by seeking medical intervention, our relationship was over.

I had nowhere to go for help but to my parents. Never expecting me to leave Harry, they were in shock to hear how desperate I was. Father no longer worked, due to his advanced Parkinson's disease, but their frugal lifestyle made it possible for them to help me. At first, we entertained the possibility of moving together into a house large enough for all of us. Mother and Dad finally decided that the needs of my children took precedence over my father's condition, and they decided to buy a home for us. The money they could afford to give me was enough to pay for a fifty-year-old brick row-home a few blocks away from my parents.

Harry did not want to believe that I was actually going through with my plan, but when I moved out with the children and any furniture I could transport, he started to take me more seriously. It was one of the most heart-wrenching decisions I had to make in my life. The on-going emotional turbulence, coupled with the financial struggle, had taken its toll on me. Unfortunately, the situation had damaged the children most of all in the long run, depriving them of security and the assurance that love and a spirit of guidance would rule our home. Missing out on those most essential requirements for healthy mental and emotional development, those turbulent years left them with indelible scars. It is a miracle that they would eventually grow into responsible, wonderful, loving beings after all.

IT TOOK ME TWENTY YEARS, most of which was a high-wire performance more than a blissful marriage, to stand up to the man who had put me in such a difficult situation.

No, I am sorry—he did not put me there. I put me there. And it was I who, like a dutiful wife, supported his every whim against my own judgment, and it was on account of me that the entire mess with the house situation exploded into a major disaster. Why did I spend all the time helping him in the business when it would have served better purpose if I was out doing what I knew best and developing my own resources? WHY? Because that is what HE wanted me to do. As a result, when I found myself on my own to support myself and three teenage children, I did not know where to begin.

Harry was lost in his own chaotic reality. Out of desperation, he moved in with his older sister. It did not take long before Ruth got tired of his antics and urged him to move elsewhere. Ruthie and I grew to be friends through the years. She was instrumental in getting me a job at the dress factory where she worked as payroll clerk, and somehow I managed to keep our relationship going. Ruth never took sides. She was a fair, kind, and understanding ally. We did not live far from each other, so we got together frequently, and our children were close.

Unlike Ruth, Harry's parents never come forward to see if they could help while their grandkids and I faced such uncertainties. On the contrary, my in-laws actually insinuated that I was the cause of all the problems. Elaine suggested the same thing; despite the fact that she had moved to California by then, that did not stop her from siding with her brother.

Harry wanted nothing more than for me to take him back. He pleaded with me daily until I told him that he would have to shape up, get on his feet and seek medical help before I would ever consider living with him again. By some miracle, Harry got a job as project manager with a large firm, which moved him to rural Pennsylvania. His performance appreciated once more, his confidence returned.

After eight months of separation, we reconciled, under the condition that he seek medical help. The mental health clinic at the University of Philadelphia Hospital offered a program that included the use of Lithium as treatment for sufferers of manic depression. Harry participated in the program. While the treatment's success was not instantaneous, it saved our marriage in the long run.

OUR FINANCIAL DISASTER STILL UNRESOLVED, we desperately needed legal help. We could not pay our lawyer's fees, and few lawyers would have wanted to tackle our mess even if we had had the money. Quite unexpectedly, Max Mandel, a distant friend and a fine, distinguished gentleman, came to our rescue. We knew Max socially but never realized that he was a prominent, highly respected attorney. Hearing of our predicament, he volunteered to help us. It took that amazing man three years of hard work to untangle the mess Harry had managed to create, but Max took on the task out of the goodness of his heart. He did it because he wanted to help us salvage our finances—and our marriage.

CHAPTER SIX

Children

FROM DREAMS TO REALITY

And He said: your children are not your children. They are the sons and daughters of life's longing for itself. They come through you but not from you, and though they are with you, they belong not to you. You may give them your love, but not your thoughts. You may house their bodies but not their souls, for their souls dwell in the house of tomorrow, which you cannot visit, not even in your dreams. You may strive to be like them, but seek not to make them like you. For life goes not backward nor tarries with yesterday. You are the bow from which your children as living arrows are sent forth.

—Kahlil Gibran

Harry and I had three children before I realized how little I knew about the man I married and how absolutely incompatible we were. Now I find it strange how blindly I put my trust into a man when I knew little about his principles and values. Because of my upbringing, I believed that in marriage, two people merged their own sets of ideas and ideals to form a united front and children were to be an extension of that blessed union. In Harry's mind, marriage seemed to mean that man had the uncontested right to direct all matters according to what pleased him. My attempts to be included in his decision-making pro-

photo of our three little angels

cess met strong and often angry rebuttal. Protecting what I believed to be the children's best interests became a battle that I usually lost.

Harry's priorities were so clear in his decisions. He indulged the children with expensive clothing and gifts, at the same time denying them an updated edition of encyclopedias. Our values were at extreme odds. To make matters worse, his wild spending sprees depleted all our savings for the children's education. Where the children were concerned, Harry and I saw eye to eye on virtually nothing, but the Holocaust destroyed whatever confident self-image I may have had, and I was no match for Harry's aggression.

Though I tried desperately to be an advocate for my children's welfare, I was plagued by self-doubt. I tried to encourage my children to "be themselves," but when there was any conflict with either Harry or the children themselves, I backed off, insecure and rejected. Sometimes I questioned even the wisdom of having had children in the first place.

In different ways, we were both sadly lacking as parents. Harry was ego driven and I was unsure, in over my head. Though we both loved all three of our children in our own ways, our conflicting but equally wrong approach to parenting made us ultimately both responsible for creating a dysfunctional environment and its effects.

"I cannot wait to get away from this family! I do not belong here!" Gary exclaimed heatedly when he was just fifteen years old. What I took then for a rebellious teen outburst came back to haunt me. It happened later when Gary, at 23, turned to follow the ways of the Christ Family, a loosely woven nomadic cult. We only learned about it from his landlord in the Florida Keys when we called to check why a package I sent him was returned. He vanished without a word and we heard nothing from him for weeks Not until he heard that we sent out a search through the FBI did he call to let us know he was on his way to leaving all worldly things and attachments behind.

Harry took Gary's choice with relative calm, insisting it was a passing phase. I, however, was devastated for I knew what he did not: Gary had always wanted to get away from us.

My son disappeared at the same time Mother lost her long battle with cancer. I was glad she was spared of the grief of knowing what had befallen her daughter and first born grandson. For me, the pain of losing both a mother and a son at the same time was unbearable. As usual, Harry lacked empathy or understanding.

Gary, however, had always been a very sensitive soul. His outer appearance had fooled me into believing he was well adjusted and strong, and I had often counted on him for emotional support when I should have realized he needed a parent even more than I did. It was an unfair burden that, in the end, he could not handle very well. Instead of confronting me, he tried to live up to what he thought were my expectations, and since those expectations were not grounded in reality but rather in my dreams, it was destined to not work. To save himself, he chose to leave.

Years later, he told me that distancing himself from me was the most difficult thing he had to endure but that, in order to survive, he felt he had to cut all earthly family ties and follow what he felt was his calling.

"I always love you mom, but I do not belong to you" were the terms I had to accept to have him back in my life many years later. Finding and keeping Gibran's profound words eventually helped me strike the right balance, but as any parent knows, we relinquish our hopes and dreams for our children at a heavy price.

Ronny's life turned into a rollercoaster ride until he settled into marriage and became a parent himself. His quick wit allowed him to diffuse tense moments with humor. He was a giving, helpful friend to everyone. When I once commented how lucky he was to have so many friends, he soberly responded: "The truth is, Mom, that I am a friend to many but nearly none of them are my friends." He was a clown with tears in his eyes.

The basis for our mutual devotion was trust, and the unconditional acceptance of each other. Instead of being hung up on each other's shortcomings, we openly discussed them. Ronny often sought my guidance, but one time, when I offered my unsolicited opinion on an issue that weighed on his conscience, I was quick to ask if I had overstepped my bounds.

"You are my mom," Ronny replied. "You are never out of line when you care to make your point on my behalf. If what you say makes sense to me, Ill keep it in mind. Otherwise I'll forget it." Ronny was a remarkable man—a remarkable son. His premature death at age 35 darkened my sky. His wife and child remain my connection to a much-loved son.

The kind of relationship I had with Ron was one I hoped to develop with Debbie, but her anger towards me made it impossible. Trying to make her understand my woes only fueled that anger. Her response that "Everything is always about you!" sparked many of our emotional battles. Both of us suffered, but I never gave up trying to bridge the gap between us. My attempts at verbal communication turned sour, as we seemed not to speak the same language; in her interpretation, my words took on different meaning than I had assigned to them.

Debbie was both exceptionally bright and strong-willed. Her desire to enter academia took her to try three different colleges before she chose to escape into marriage with Bruce. Marked with failure from the start, the union ended in divorce after five years. Followed by an attempt to live in a communal setting in upstate New York, Debbie moved to Florida to be near Ronny and built a successful massage therapy practice there. Ron's death was a crushing blow. Not until she found solace in embracing Jesus as her savior and remarried (this time to Guy, with whom she was to share a devout Christian life) could my daughter come to peace.

Nonetheless, after a while, the debilitating effects of fibromyalgia would come to permeate Debbie's being, and when she was no longer able to continue practicing as a therapist, she headed back to school. She earned her Masters degree to teach English as a second language.

Debbie received her Masters diploma, along with an award for her writing. After the ceremony, she handed me the certificate. "This is for you, Mom," she told me. She made me proud and she knew it.

Ronny's Bar Mitzvah composit

Nine years into Debbie's marriage, her husband's sudden death from an unfortunate accident left behind a physically afflicted, but spiritually strong woman guided by her faith in God.

When I moved to Florida seven years ago, I followed my intuition's powerful lead. God only knows that, had it not been for the strong feeling that I needed to be near my daughter, granddaughter Haley, and her mother Laurie, I would not have moved to Florida. Only after Guy died did I fully understand why fate had directed me here. I was meant to be near my daughter when she was in need.

The tremendous irony that the two surviving children of a Holocaust survivor have both embraced Christianity has not escaped me. Much has been written on the subject of children of survivors, and I am sure other people in other books have explored this. From my perspective, I can only say it took many years of "mothering" for me to understand the real meaning of unconditional love. It requires not tolerating but rather *accepting* others' differences from you, even (and perhaps especially) the differences between you and those who are as near and dear to you as your own children. It was not always easy for me to learn to practice acceptance in this way. It was often quite painful. Nevertheless, I found it is entirely possible to adore even those whose worldviews seem entirely different from yours.

SPARKS FROM THE FIRE

· · · · · · · · ·

CHAPTER SEVEN

Having a Life Worth Living

I am certain that my life's journey was not routed by happenstance. So many things have happened to me that some might call coincidences, but I know a divine power ordained them. Each crossroad has required me to make a choice, and I did so, letting my intuition be my guide. I had two primary goals. In terms of my career, I had longed to complete my formal education in fashion design and technology. But I also believed passionately that I had a social obligation to make use of my Holocaust experiences, not for myself but for future generations. Even decisions that some of my closest observers called sheer insanity led me closer to those goals, though I did not always know they would at the time.

IT WAS DURING GARY's BAR Mitzvah service—the Jewish observation to acknowledge a boy's coming of age at thirteen—that we recognized the first symptoms of my father's illness, Parkinson's disease. As the condition progressed, it transformed my vigorous, courageous father into a frightened shadow of his former self. He died not long before his 80th birthday. To make matters worse, during the last painful stages of my father's life, Harry had triple by-pass surgery. He recovered, but was unemployed for more than a year. When he finally found a job, he had to commute to the Pocono Mountains, three hours away. Traveling there daily was too much; he came home only on weekends.

By that time, Debbie was the only child who still lived at home. I was forty-eight then, and I decided to enroll in a private two-year

program to learn the technical aspects of fashion and accessory designing. Upon graduating, I walked away with an associate degree and
five awards, one in every category. Harry and Ronny celebrated with
me at the school, and then I was delighted to be surprised with a party
thrown in my honor by some of my friends and their children. Unfortunately, my mother, who was suffering the debilitating effects of
a long battle with cancer, was unable to join in the celebration of my
long-delayed accomplishment.

Diploma in hand, I continued catering to a loyal clientele at home
in my garage-turned-workshop, even as I fostered more ambitious
plans for the future. Although my school specialized in training students to enter the garment production industry, I consciously decided
not to become a party to industrial mass production. I stubbornly remained loyal to my belief that overpriced mass products left little to
individual imagination. Driven to make clothes that suited individual
taste, including my own, I dreamed of having an opportunity to work
closely with a designer similar to Grete, with whom I had completed
my apprenticeship in Budapest. It was a long shot because there were
far fewer custom designers in this country than in Hungary. Remarkably, however, just the sort of opportunity I was looking for came to
me in the most unusual way.

It came in the form of a conversation with Fanny, another Czech-
Hungarian Holocaust survivor I had met while working at Teddy
Benjamin's specialty clothes shop where I had started my dressmaking career in the U.S. An excellent seamstress, Fanny had moved on
from Benjamin's shop to new employment quickly, but our friendship
endured for many years thereafter. One day not long after graduation,
I happened to mention to Fanny my desire to work with a custom
designer.

"Well, I might just have a lead for you," said Fanny. Fanny had
a sister, Dori, who was also a dressmaker, and Dori's son Max drove
taxis. One day a passenger he was to pick up at the airport turned out
to be an elderly British gentleman, who said he was a fashion designer.
He asked Maxi if he knew of any experienced dressmakers who might
want to work at his new design studio in Philadelphia. Some weeks
passed, and Max was summoned to pick up a passenger in center city

en route to the airport, and by sheer "coincidence," it was the very same designer. Greeting Max with the warmth of an old friend, he asked if he found any dressmakers for him. At this point, Max told him that both his mother and aunt were dressmakers and he would ask if either of them were interested. Neither of them were, and Fanny suggested I follow up on the lead.

How could I *not* follow up on it? Just what I had been looking for had fallen into my lap.

WHEN I FIRST MET TED Tinling, I was taken aback. His peculiar towering figure was always partially bent over, making his large, shiny, egg-shaped head all the more prominent. As his immense, powerful hands gingerly examined the samples and photographs of my work, my eyes were drawn to the strangely oversized beads of the turquoise necklace (his trademark, I would later learn) dangling from his permanently outstretched neck.

His intense blue eyes resting on the photos of my work, he commented, "Your hemlines are the best I have seen for some time. That is, you know, the sign of excellence."

I did not know that. However, coming from someone of his caliber, it was quite a compliment. Following a lengthy interview, I was hired to begin my new position as dressmaker and second assistant at his center-city headquarters. It was to be the highlight of my career.

As a prominent designer who dressed Britain's upper crust throughout the 1930s, Mr. T. owned an old-world European haute couture salon in London. He was known particularly for his designs for tennis clothes. The lace panties he created for Gertrude "Gussy" Moran to wear at Wimbledon in a 1949 match caused uproar—and Teddy's temporary fall from grace in Wimbledon's most elite circles. He went on to design clothes for Hollywood stars and to an appointment as the official designer for the Virginia Slims tennis series. Ted saw the tennis court as a stage upon which stars deserved to play in dazzling costumes, and eccentricity was a signature of his design.

We shared a similar work ethic and design language. Neither of us conformed to trends or accepted anything but the highest quality craftsmanship. Teddy was the missing link in my dressmaking education. Only when working side by side with him did I truly refine my technique. He was inspiring, and I grew strong and confident under his tutelage.

Nevertheless, even as I admired Teddy so, he was a chameleon. He knew all too well how to protect his self-interest; perhaps such skill reflected his training as a British Intelligence officer in World War II. At one point, Teddy feared Margaret, his first assistant, might leave following her impending marriage. The two went a long way back. He had groomed her into her position right after she finished school, twenty-two years before his relocation to the U.S. He was observant enough to realize she had a competitive side. He offered me her job, and I declined, but I do not think that is the version of the story he told Margaret. Rather, I am sure he led her to believe that I could hardly wait for her to leave so I could step into her place. After that, Margaret's distrust of me was palpable. Mr. T. was quite cunning; he continued to cultivate the silent feud between us to secure Margaret's loyalty. In the process, work became a very hostile place to be.

After a while, my toleration of Margaret finally reached its limit. I once overheard a conversation between her and another worker in which Margaret referred to someone having "Jewed her down."

I turned and looked her squarely in the eye.

"I am a Jew, and I don't appreciate your denigrating comment."

"Sorry," she mumbled, barely audible, and walked away.

I am certain that the incident did not pass by Mr. T. unnoticed. I imagine a sly smile of satisfaction might have flickered across his face, but I will never really know. Margaret stayed with him until the end.

I, on the other hand, stayed with Mr. T. for two years before leaving the studio. But even after my departure, I continued to help him with special orders for another year. Acknowledging me for my professional talent, he always compensated me generously for my work.

Mr. T. often declared his plan was to live in the United States and die in England. He got his wish. Ted Tinling died in his homeland on May 24, 1990, at the age of seventy-nine. To this day, I frequently recall the amusing anecdotes he shared about his eclectic life. He once, for example, owned a pantaloon that had belonged to Queen Victoria, though I cannot recall how he ever managed to find such a thing! His obvious love for his craft was contagious.

To this day, I often find his wonderful tidbits of advice creeping into my head, guiding me as I work:

- "When you press a garment, you must give it shape," he instructed. "Mold it as if it was clay; imagine there is a body inside."
- "Organdy [a very fine, transparent cotton] is to be handled as if with fairy fingers."
- "Don't think too much. Just do it."

And when I made a mistake, he knew just what to say: "Nobody will know the difference—only you and I."

Thank you, Mr. T.

IT WAS A VERY HOT day in the summer of 1987 when, on my way home from work, I felt like stopping for a breather at the home of my friend Shirley. I took a chance because I never knew when Shirley would be home, but I got lucky.

"Hi Eva! How wonderful that you decided to stop in. I was about to call you. Come, let's sit in the kitchen. Have a cup of tea with me while we talk." Her Mona Lisa smile played on her lips.

"You sound like you have something special in mind," I replied.

"As a matter of fact, I do," said my friend, her speech softly measured, emphasizing each word as if to signal its significance. Shirley was not much for small talk, so I figured whatever she had to say must be important.

"Okay," I said, by then quite curious. "I am all ears."

As we sat there sipping tea in her kitchen's cozy little nook, Shirley began to reveal an exciting scheme:

"Not so long ago you mentioned that after two years with Ted Tinling you are ready to make a change. Did you ever think of starting your own business?"

The question caught me off guard.

Eva Cutler

"It is quite true," I said, "that while I love working for Ted, without a chance for future advancement, I am locked into a dead-end job. It is time I investigated what other options are out there. Why are you asking?'

"I think you ought to open a shop on Oak Lane Avenue."

"You must be kidding!" I exclaimed. "A shop for me? What gave you that idea? Can you imagine me as a shopkeeper?"

After a brief but thoughtful pause, Shirley sat up straight, exhibiting for a moment her typical quiet authority.

"Yes, I can," she pronounced, deliberate and certain. Capturing my full attention, she went on: "Wouldn't it be great to have your own place with the freedom to express your creative ideas and idealistic approach? Isn't that what you really want?"

In a conspirator's tone, she added demurely, "Having a high-standard shop in the area would also be a boost to the community—and I have just the right place in mind for you."

"Is there more to this that you're not saying?"

"I'm serious. The building I'm thinking of is located on a strip of businesses, and its current occupant is generating a lot of controversy. First, he let the place become overrun with vermin, which began to invade nearby shops and homes. But now the parents in the neighborhood have become increasingly concerned because kids have begun to congregate there. The site is dimly lit, and this occupant has installed vending machines—possibly to purposely attract local youth. Regardless, no one is quite sure what's going on, and many community members want him removed. I figured that, if he does go, the store and location would be an ideal place for you."

Over the years, I had gotten to know Charlie and Shirley well enough to understand why people held them in high esteem. While some people may be long on words and short on action, Shirley and Charlie are the exact opposite. They can always be counted on, whether it concerns the welfare of an individual or the whole community. Therefore, I took Shirley's word that her proposed solution just might benefit everyone.

"It sounds like quite a challenge!" I reflected. "If I were to give it a try," I hedged, "where do you suggest I start?"

"Talk to the landlord first. The owner of the property has been trying to evict the occupant, who happens to be drawing welfare. So the owner's hands are tied by the system, which protects welfare recipients against eviction."

It took a year of dogged tenacity and legal action by the community to have the tenant relocated. I made a deal with the property owner. I agreed to restore the premises in exchange for a low monthly rent. When I finally had a chance to inspect the empty structure, I was in for a shock. It was in deplorable shape, completely filthy. When I started to remove the marble chips covering the floor of the display windows, the stench of cat urine permeated the room. I felt as though I would vomit. The middle room was stacked with supplies left by a plumber who had sublet from the previous resident. When the plumber finally came to remove those supplies, only then did I discover that the clutter of his belongings had been offering rats an ideal place to nest. Between that and a massive flea infestation, all other renovations halted until I fumigated the entire area.

It took a lot of scrubbing, scraping, and painting before I could fully appreciate the interior's spacious, straight-through layout. There was plenty of room for all my needs. The store and design area fit comfortably into the first room, and our generous friend Ben Wexler constructed an attractive window-box divider to separate the two sections. An open entry to the middle room made for easy communication to the future sewing room and office. But what really made the place complete was its kitchen and little powder room in the back. It so happened that Lit Brothers department store (one of Philadelphia's landmarks) was closing its doors and offered their store furnishings at nominal prices just when I was ready to furnish the shop. As a result, I could purchase high quality fixtures within my budget.

Little by little, as the character of the interior became clear, I became more inclined to see how the shop could serve both the community and my ideal to promote artisans who made wearable creations. Although some of my well-meaning critics considered my idea to start that sort of an atelier a foolhardy, frivolous endeavor, I remained strong in my conviction that the shop was an opportunity for me not to embark on a conventional business venture but to follow my heart's desire. When I found out that my timing coincided with a nationwide artisan renaissance, becoming part of that movement altered my professional direction. My instincts vindicated, I was confident.

I placed an ad in the *Crafts Report* and a call to the Philadelphia Weavers Guild to invite artisans to display their wearable creations in my showroom. My public relations produced results. Of all the crafters who responded, the one who made the most memorable impression on me was Myra, a twenty-something budding fiber artist. Our first meeting turned out to be anything but ordinary. She came in, looked around, and after a few cordial words hesitantly proceeded to show me her finely woven natural cotton camisoles. I was not the least impressed by them, but before I had a chance to comment, she surprised me.

"I really don't think I want to put my things in your shop," she declared.

I was not insulted. I was curious.

"What makes you feel that way?"

"Oh, I like you, but I don't like your shop. I don't think your arrangement would complement my work."

Attracted by the young girl's brazenness, I was not about to let her off the hook that easily. Instead, I asked her what she might suggest I do differently. My willingness to elicit her thoughts worked wonders. The air between us thawed immediately, giving way to a friendly exchange of ideas and negotiation for a mutually agreeable working arrangement. Myra and I often chuckle as we recall that first encounter. We went on to develop a strong, close relationship, one always based on the same sort of openness with which it began.

When my shop, "Ava's Clothes Garden," opened on the last Saturday in October 1977, it proudly showcased my former teacher Maggi's jewelry, the works of other weavers besides Myra, and a leather crafter's decorative practical wares. In addition, the shop hosted an informal modeling of my one-of-a-kind fashions as well as fashions by two other designers. For the event, invited guests, relatives, and curiosity seekers from the community filled the space. Among those who attended the festivities was Ted Tinling, whose presence highlighted the occasion for me. When he handed me an original watercolor painting of a cat and said, "I named it Felix to bring you good luck," the sentiment in his voice belied his usually more reserved British demeanor. His gift now hangs in my home as a constant reminder of a dear man whose brief presence in my life richly contributed to the development of my professional identity.

IN PHILADELPHIA, OAK LANE AVENUE is a diagonal two-way traffic run from Cheltenham Avenue to Old York Road. The sparsely populated street would amount to little more than an insignificant thoroughfare without the small shopping strip at its heart. Although people dotting the sidewalk were mostly from the area even during the busiest hours of the day, others passed through on their way to either Murray's Deli, Mr. Simons' barbershop, the butcher at the corner of 8th St., or Mr. Gallelli, whose reputable cleaning and tailoring establishment attracted people from near and far.

Mamma Lombardi's little Italian restaurant further down the street was somewhat disconnected from the cluster of stores and easy to miss during the day when the red neon sign displayed in its window was not alight. When Harry came home on Fridays hungry and tired after a three-hour commute, he was usually only up to "grab a bite" somewhere and unwind. After a while, to break the monotony of our usual eateries, we decided to try Mamma Lombardi's because it looked like a homey little place and was in short walking distance. Once inside the restaurant with my eyes adjusted to the dimly lit interior, we discovered a peculiarly over-decorated room teeming with ornamental streamers cascading down from the entire ceiling. I felt as if we had stepped through a looking glass into Alice's land of wonder. It was not exactly what we bargained for, but being tired and hungry, we decided to stay. Leading to our table, the waitress navigated with ease through the streamers, with us awkwardly ducking all the way behind her.

"How about a cocktail?" asked the waitress, handing us the menu.

"No thanks, but could you please see that we get our food without much delay?" Harry answered. She nodded in agreement, and when we placed our order, she left. I ordered ravioli. Not much time passed before the waitress returned with our order, but the large lump with red sauce on my plate in no way resembled what I had asked for. Turning my attention away from the "thing" I turned to the waitress, "I think you made a mistake. I ordered ravioli."

"But this IS ravioli," she said with indignation. "This is how WE serve it here." As far as she was concerned, I was ignorant in the ravioli department. I left the place convinced that the experience at Mamma Lombardi's wonderland would be remembered not for the food but for the color it brought into our otherwise un-eventful weekend dining-out routine.

The memory still makes me chuckle.

As it turned out, running my store was a novelty but was not my forte. Designing and problem solving was. Coming up with suitable suggestions for a customer to express her personality was a tall order, but doing so often gave me the chance to dream up daring ideas to satisfy the frivolous side of my otherwise restrained personality. When I let my imagination run free, the results usually turned out more sophisticated than something I would wear. Sometimes it became difficult to translate my most outlandish ideas into workable patterns without compromising their looks, but I thrived most when faced with such challenges.

One of the advantages to having a store was that I had a place where I could work on design ideas and resolve problems uninterrupted after business hours. With Harry away on his job during the week, I could often be found engrossed in my thoughts, with pattern paper rolled out on the cutting table in front of me.

One night, the sound of someone fiddling with the door handle startled me. It was eight o'clock. Who could it be? Startled and annoyed by the interruption, I cautiously peeked past the divider to the front of the store to see my friend Joan's smiling face looking back at me through the window. I hurried to let her in. As one of my staunch supporters, Joan visited fairly often, but her appearance at a late hour alarmed me.

"Sorry I startled you. I called you at home," she started, "but when I got no answer I figured you were still at the shop."

"What brought you here at this hour? Is something wrong?"

"Not at all," she replied with a cheerful smile. "As a matter of fact, I came to talk to you about something Walter and I thought might interest you."

The distance from the door to the worktable might have been no more than twenty steps, but it seemed an eternity until Joan and I positioned ourselves facing one another on either side of it. As her tall, square-boned figure leaned against the table, a mischievous gleam danced in her eyes, all the more highlighted by her sassy little nose and usual cheerful grin.

"How would you like to meet up with us in Budapest?" she asked. My chin dropped, and I did not quite know what to say. My reaction caused an even wider smile to spread across her face.

"I don't know..." I started, and then went silent for a few moments. "What's the deal?"

"Well, you know about Walter's Hungarian family background. Ever since he discovered that his cousin in Hungary was the only surviving member of his family left from the Holocaust, he wanted to look him up. In September he is scheduled to present a research paper in Switzerland [Walter was a globally sought-after research scientist], and so he decided to combine that trip with a visit to his cousin. As we were making plans, we thought it would be fun to meet up with you and Harry in Budapest."

"Hmm ...I doubt if Harry would go for it."

"How about you?" asked Joan. "Are you comfortable with the thought of facing your past?"

"Living in America for thirty years gave me a chance to distance myself from the past enough not to let that influence my decision. Nevertheless", I admitted, "something might come up to trigger underlying feelings of fear and resentment."

"Give it some thought," said Joan. "This is only June and we are not going until sometime in September." That is how we left it, but the idea started to stir up memories and the yearning for old friends.

I no longer knew if any of those friends were around to be found. The mind's eye keeps things as they were, and I was not certain I was ready to trade those memories for a new reality. Harry was willing, even eager, which surprised me. What surprised me even more was my reaction. It suddenly hit me that I secretly hoped he would decline and I would be off the hook.

Nevertheless, the idea of the trip began to sound intriguing. I decided to go along on what promised to be an unusual journey into the past. Harry never said it, but I believe he saw this as an opportunity both to do something meaningful for me and to satisfy his own curiosity about the place he heard so much about. Having Joan and Walter for company helped tip his decision toward going.

As the day of our departure drew near, some of my friends decided to send me off with a bon voyage gathering. Most were curious to know if I was emotionally prepared to take this journey. Except for one friend, who questioned my rationale for returning to the country that brutally cast me out and designed to bring about my demise.

"How could you remain patriotic to them?" she asked in an unusually irritated tone. The question floored me. "Patriotic? This isn't a fair question." I replied. "What does my going there have to do with patriotism? How I feel about the regime responsible for those atrocities has nothing to do with what ties me to the country of my birth. That heritage is just as much the fiber of my being as being Jewish. I chose neither, but I treasure both." I was amazed how those words rolled off my tongue without a chance to think. Deafening silence followed my passionate response.

Under Soviet control in 1980, Hungary's ruling party conceded to ease restrictions on tourism and commerce with the West in order to stimulate their economy. This was not by any means a sign to abandon caution. When I applied for a visa to enter Hungary, the political realities in the region prompted me to question Hungarian Embassy authorities about whether it was safe for me to go, as I was anxious they might find reason to detain me. The Embassy promised me that as an American citizen I had no reason to be concerned. Still looking for more assurance, I visited a highly recommended psychic reader, as I had had positive experiences with her on a previous occasion. All I said was that I was planning to go on a trip, and she went on to insist that the trip would be safe, that I would find a friend (with the initial **S**), and that I would meet my uncle.

"I have no uncle left in Hungary," I had protested, but she had insisted that there *was* one and that I was going to see him. From that point on, I began to look forward to my trip abroad relatively confidently, especially as I had an American passport and an American husband at my side.

ONCE WE MADE THE CHOICE to go to Hungary, some friends gave me a journal. But being a terribly inconsistent person by nature, I rarely follow through on anything with regularity. Although I would try to write while there, the pages would remain empty beyond the first couple of entries, but my heart would fill with unforgettable memories.

DURING THE HEAT OF TRIP preparation I could think only of what I wanted to do once I got there. Our group elected me to find a place to stay. While I was growing up, we considered restaurants, hotels, and nightclubs luxuries intended for the privileged few. The only hotel name I had ever heard mentioned in our household was the Metropol, where my father met some of his chess partners on occasion. I knew it was located somewhere in the heart of the city, which is where we wanted to be, so I went ahead and reserved two rooms without actually knowing anything of the place's current condition. Our flight to Europe was long but uneventful until the plane landed in Prague. At that point, only those of us continuing on to Budapest remained on board, having been advised that for our own safety we should remain seated and keep away from the door. A look through the window revealed the none-too-comforting sight of a group of armed soldiers on guard. With the air circulation off, heat built up inside the cabin, and the time we were grounded seemed endless. With not even a drop of water available, I started to get paranoid. Fortunately, the delay ended before my fear would overtake my senses, but by the time we landed in Budapest's Ferihegy airport, I was frazzled. The Prague interlude put me on alert.

My mind positioned itself to ward off any real or imagined offense. When the customs officer questioned my reason for coming, an edge crept into my voice: "Because I wanted." Eventually, however, the familiarity of hearing Hungarian spoken all around me softened my uneasiness. Harry, meanwhile, had no idea of my emotional rollercoaster. He passed through the gates looking almost cocky, secure in his unquestionable American identity.

Harry and I hailed a taxi. On the way to the hotel, something inside me began to stir. My eyes glued themselves to the window, looking for familiar signs along the way, but the ride from the airport rolled through unfamiliar districts outside the city. Besides street signs, only an occasional billboard with Hungarian slogans came into view.

It was easy to tell we were getting closer to the city when the scenery began to change from near desolate roads dotted with industrial sites to more populated but relatively low profile residential areas. Once inside the city, the taxi driver dodged other cars on roads not built to accommodate their traffic. With no room for parallel parking, cars parked on sidewalks and door-to-door delivery was taken literally, as drivers had no choice but to let their passengers out directly at the building's entry. Yes, this was the very first impression of the Budapest I left behind thirty-two years ago under very different circumstances.

Words are inadequate to describe my first response to the sound and sight of yellow trolleys as they whizzed by on their tracks between the rows of grey, timeworn buildings. An odd nostalgia crept upward from my heart. Still, it was not until we passed by the old Radius movie-house did my excitement accelerate to the point that I could not contain it. I rapidly chattered to Harry that I was five years old when my cousins Ica and Klara (who would later end up in Israel) took me there to see a Jackie Cooper film. Incredible as it may sound, as much of a sensation as it was for me to see the little blond kid performing on the screen, what left me with a lasting impression was the bar of chocolate they gave to each child at the entrance. Goodies like that were a rare treat in those days.

When Harry and I finally arrived at Hotel Metropol, we found a depressed exterior that could hardly be mistaken for a Hilton. To our relief, however, we found a welcoming lobby and a courteous clerk at the registration desk.

"May I have your passports?" requested the clerk. What seemed a reasonable request at first began to raise my suspicion when he examined them and, instead of returning our only identifying documents, he set them aside in a folder. Feeling the cold hands of fear clutching at my heart once again, I nearly lost it! My God! Was this not what my past dreams were all about? Seeing panic written all over my face, the clerk went on to explain: "There is no reason for fear. This is a necessary formality. The current political system requires foreign visitors to be registered at the police department. Your passports will be returned tomorrow."

His sympathetic words helped restore my composure, but not until I held the passport in my hands again did I feel completely at ease. The clerk spoke only Hungarian, and the words of my native language did not roll freely for me because I had rarely had a chance to speak them since my parents died. Judging from the clerk's expression, my way of speaking the language must have sounded strange. At the side of an English (only) speaking husband for nearly thirty years, it was a wonder I had retained as much of my mother-tongue as I had.

We found our room clean and spacious, furnished with a large solid wood wardrobe, chairs and a desk, a decent bed with fresh linen waiting for us. The bathroom, though seemingly ancient in style, served us well. Through the wide French window, we came face-to-face with the Atheneum Press directly across the street. Not until we turned in the first night did we come to understand that the press operated around the clock. Its steady rumbling, pounding beat invaded our time for rest. In a way, I was lucky for having only one good ear under the circumstances, as I was able to block most of the noise out. Harry, on the other hand, decided to put up with the inconvenience of having trouble sleeping rather than scout for another place to stay. (So would Joan and Walter when they arrived with their younger daughter Rebecca two days later.)

When we woke up after our first night in Budapest, I could hardly wait to get a hold of a phone book to locate my friends and my father's cousin Uncle Eugene or "Jeno" (we always addressed our elders as uncle and aunt) and his daughter Judit.

I looked first for my friend Zsuzsa's married family name and found only two listed: one for Peter, the other for Laszlo. I had learned from my parents that she had a son Peter and I knew her husband's name was Laszlo. For some reason, I chose Peter's number.

When I heard a woman's voice answer with a "hallo," I was so choked up that I could barely find the words to say "I am looking for Mrs Kunos (ne Gero Zsuzsa)." All the while, I was trying my best to sound Hungarian. I could sense from the sound of the woman's voice on the other end of the line that she was suspicious.

"And who wants to know?" she responded sharply. Her unexpected attitude made it even harder for me to find the right words to explain that I was there from America and trying to locate my girlfriend, but I managed to get the words out. Then I asked, "With whom do I speak?"

After some hesitation the women responded by throwing the same question back to me. When I answered, "I am Eva, Zsuzsa's girlfriend," she let out a squeal loud enough to crack the phone.

"Friedrich Eva?" she cried, using my maiden name. "It can't be true! It is incredible! I am your girlfriend, my dear and shining star, I am Zsuzsa! I can't believe it is happening! I was thinking of you only yesterday, wondering what might've become of you, and here you are!" The warmth floated through the ether as we talked.

"When can you come to see me? I can hardly wait!"

"Is tomorrow alright for you?" I asked.

"Come, come, my sweet … I'll be here waiting."

Our meeting decided, I hesitantly asked about her brother Steve, my friend Feri, and his sister Kati. They were all still there, all still around, she said. "I'll try to call them and see if they could come to meet you here," she volunteered.

"Tell me, how come you answered the phone at Peter's residence?"

"Oh," she said, "We recently traded apartments, and, when you move out of your district, you can't take your phone number with you. That is how our numbers got switched."

Wow! Was that a coincidence, or what?!

Zsuzsa and Laci lived on the Buda side of the city. We could get there by public transportation. Following Zsuzsa's instructions, it did not take much for Harry and me to find our way. She lived in a cluster of three-story matchbox houses. When we arrived, she stood on her balcony, wearing a red housecoat, anxiously looking out for me. I practically flew up the stairs to meet her. Laughing and crying, we crossed the bridge of time.

After we gave each other a long look, she reported, "I called Steve. Feri is out of town, and Kati went nuts when I told her you were here. She cannot come today, but this is her phone number. She hopes you can meet her in town tomorrow."

"You think Steve will come?"

"I don't know," she answered, knowing well what prompted my question.

"He is happily married now and so much water rolled down the Danube since we were kids, but we shall see."

I had been sixteen when twenty-one year old Steve had asked me to marry him.

My answer: "I am too young to think of marrying anyone."

His response: "I'll wait for you."

I did not have the guts to tell him that he need not bother, and thoughtless as I was, I asked Zsuzsa to tell him for me. Deeply hurt, he avoided any contact with me thereafter. All those years later, I was afraid that even the war had not cleared the slate between us. I was proved wrong, however, when Steve came with his wife Klara, carrying a box of pastries.

He remembered, but not with bitterness. Our reunion was like waking from a deep sleep where nothing but the time has changed. We sat and talked for hours, but there was much, too much to tell within such a short time. It all seemed incredible—our own experiences of detainment and survival. It was as though we relived a bad dream in common, as we sat around the table nibbling on pastry and sipping coffee in the comfort of my friend's home. Much was said about what we had gone through in order to pick up our interrupted lives. Steve and Laci, for example, had escaped removal to a concentration camp by finding refuge in a hospital morgue. I was astounded!

For some of my friends, that process of trying to regain their lives was further complicated by having to adjust to the rules of Communist Soviet occupation. Admirably, my comrades had risen above it. Steve worked in a shoe factory under the Nazi regime but became a highly esteemed building engineer/city planner. Feri, a former knitting mill coolie, became a prominent mining engineer. Laci's expertise took him to work with communication systems, and I was told that one of the girls from our Synagogue youth group, after returning from the camps, became the first female to join the Budapest police force. She eventually became a Judge. Harry just stood there dumbfounded by all he heard as we talked. He kept repeating: "I can't believe it…I just can't believe it." It must have been something to witness a small group of friends reunite after so many years with so much tragedy behind them. Even harder to believe, so much of what we had shared in common had remained intact.

At the time of my visit, Zsuzsa worked at the parliament's police security department. Her job forbade foreign correspondence. Steve's wife Klara offered to keep the line open between us. Our correspondence through Klara would fill the gap between us until Zsuzsa retired.

Later, when I met with my friend Kati on that Budapest trip of so many reunions, I found myself in the company of a severely depressed person. Before the war had broken out, she was a registered nurse and married to the man she dearly loved. His death in the camps was a devastating blow to this emotionally fragile woman. She married again and had a child who died of heart failure at an early age. Kati never got over it and lived only with a wish to die.

During much of the time I spent with my friends in Hungary, Harry went to the Gellert health spa, where he enjoyed swimming and the healing affects of artesian mineral baths to ease the pain of his injured back. Our activities took on a different orientation when Joan, Walter, and their young daughter Rebecca arrived. We set out to explore the authentic riches of the country. We could go far with the American dollar in those days, in a country hungry for tourists. Merchants and restaurants bent over backward to please. We dined at the most elegant places, where a full course dinner included soup and a luscious dessert prepared and served with great savvy. All this for no more than ten dollars a head! Not even the smallest eatery lacked a gypsy band, and a variety of beautiful authentic crafts could be purchased for a song anywhere we traveled.

When I found out that the farmers' market my mother had frequented on Fridays was still there, I suggested we go check it out. What we saw there was well worth the trip! September is the height of Paprika season in Hungary. Never and nowhere else have I seen the likes of large, fresh paprika piled high on farmers' stands brimming with colors ranging from green to orange and red. We just stood there in awe. Mushrooms of several variety, fruits, vegetables galore, fish, meat ...

We spent a fun, dizzying day there, eating in the market. Not only do peasants bring their livestock and produce, women also bring their linens and embroidered finery.

On a day in the "Alfold" (the plains), we were welcomed in the setting of a "Magyar Csarda," where goulash was served country-style. After the feast, horsemen (csikos) dressed in authentic regalia entertained us with daring acts. We even had a chance to ride an ox-driven cart. It amazed me how there was so much of my country that I had never had a chance to see while I had lived there. And although these things were staged for tourists, they offered a glimpse into the nation's identifying features, the spirit which survived a thousand years of struggle.

At last, Harry and I sought out my one remaining relative, father's cousin Eugene and daughter Judit. I found their address in the phone book, but their phone was out of order. I did not want to leave without attempting to look them up, so we took a chance and went there, hoping to find them at home. They lived in an old building in Kalvin Korut, but I didn't have any idea which apartment was theirs until the janitor directed us to their door. A tall, slim, wide-eyed young woman answered my knock.

"Who are you looking for?" she asked from the slit she dared to open.

"I am looking for Eugene Breyer and his daughter Judit. I am Eva from America." My answer seemed to confuse her. She opened the door a bit wider and inched closer.

"But Eva is in America," she said, eying us, not sure whether to believe me. She was about to close the door in my face when suddenly the man sitting at the table with his back to the door called out "Eva, come in," as if he was waiting for me.

The man was "Uncle" Eugene. How was he to know I was coming? I was bowled over! So was Judit, who still stood holding on to the door. When we asked to go in "Uncle" turned around, wide, almost-silly grin written on his wrinkled face.

He did not waste time with greeting or overture. "You didn't know it," he blurted out, "but I am not your father's cousin; I am his half brother and your uncle." Waiting for the floor to give way under my feet, I stood in front of him completely stunned. The psychic had been right about my uncle after all.

So, here I was facing the man I have known as my second cousin all my life, when in fact he was my uncle. It took my return to Hungary for him to let the skeleton out of our family's closet. It made no difference to me that a man I did not know fathered both him and my father. The people involved in that family secret were long gone, and the information had no affect on my life. Obviously, however, it must have meant a lot to Uncle Eugene for him to blurt it out the very moment he laid eyes on me!

The psychic was right after all!

My first trip to Hungary was far from mundane ... It was miraculous.

HARRY DIED A YEAR LATER. Zsuzsa lost her Laci a few years after Harry died. When I returned to Hungary again in 1983, the Soviets were still there, but nearly out of the loop. Feri, my brother's closest friend, greeted me at the airport. He still carried Gyuri's and Vicki's picture in the inside pocket of his jacket.

I continued to visit my home country about every three years to be with my friends. Some years ago, I took my daughter Debbie along, and in 2005 I asked my granddaughter Haley to accompany me so that I could acquaint her with the country of my origin.

At the time of this writing only Zsuzsa, Klara (Steve's widow), and myself are left from the old gang of days gone by.

CHAPTER EIGHT

The Cup Runneth Over

In 1981, Harry still commuted to Hawley in the Poconos, where he rented a room and came home on weekends. Meanwhile, I remained in Philadelphia, to run my shop.

One day a client's husband walked into my shop to get his wife's garments. I was about to take them off the rack when the phone rang.

"Please excuse me, Richard, I'll only be a moment," I assured him as I hurried to answer the call.

"Good afternoon, Ava Creations, can I help you?"

"Can I speak with Mrs. Cutler, please?"

"This is she. May I ask who is calling?"

"The Coroner's office from Hawley, ma'am. Sorry to inform you. I am calling to let you know that your husband passed away."

"Oh, no! My God!" I gasped. "When did that happen?"

"His landlord found him this morning. Apparently he died in his sleep." He sounded like a news reporter. After a brief pause, he added, "His remains are at the funeral parlor to be embalmed."

"Embalmed?" I asked, feeling the blood rushing to my head. "Who gave you permission to do that? He is an organ donor! Why didn't you call me before you assumed authority? You were not dealing with an unidentifiable body!" I shouted into the phone. "You must immediately stop that procedure!"

Regaining my composure to a degree, I tried to strike a conciliatory tone. I requested that they wait for further instructions.

The anger, frustration, and pain I felt were too much to bear. I slammed the phone down and began to sob. In the midst of all the excitement, I forgot about Richard, who patiently waited until I calmed enough to call Rabbi Levin to summon his help.

Rabbi Levin was always there for me whenever I turned to him for help and advice. He never chastised me in any way for my unconventional Jewish attitude. He was wise, accepting, and for the most part, caring. I had great respect for him and so did my children, but for some reason I could not find comfort in religion itself.

The Rabbi was also familiar with the state of Harry's and my troubled marriage.

"Why now?" I asked him after Harry's death. "Why now, when we just began to breathe new life into our marriage?"

"God in His wisdom takes care of all His children when it is time to do so. It is only to the faithful that the Lord is just." That was all he said, leaving me to contemplate his answer.

The Rabbi intervened to help resolve the problem with the funeral parlor and the donor registry. We honored Harry's wish to be a donor and then held a memorial service at our home.

Family and friends filled the house. Ronny, Debbie, and Debbie's fiancé Bruce were there, along with Harry's youngest sibling Herb and his wife Jan. I moved about in a daze, with incredible sadness in my heart. I wrestled with thoughts of my brother somewhere in a makeshift grave with anonymous others, of my parents whose death was anything but peaceful, and of Harry gone just as things had begun to look up for us. In a house full of caring people, I felt alone and dejected, uncertain of how to face the world on my own.

Herb's welcome voice interrupted my dark meanderings. He put his arms around me.

"You are not alone, you have us. We are your family."

It was as if he knew just what I was feeling. Herb cared. He was sympathetic. He had been the only person on Harry's side of the family who was interested in knowing about my Holocaust experience. Looking at the handsome, distinguished young man at my side, I found it hard to imagine that he was the little twelve-year-old boy

I had met so long ago. Though he was a respected physicist in an important position with good financial standing, Herb did not think of himself in terms of his professional stature. He reached prominence because he loved his work, but as far as he was concerned, that status had little to do with who he was. I loved the way he downplayed his success and how he made his riches available to those of us in need. In an ironic twist, Herb, the family's youngest sibling, took on the role of patriarch. He walked into those shoes as though someone had made them just for him. The welfare of his family, extended members included, topped his list of priorities. More than a brother-in-law, Herb filled much of the void created by the loss of my own brother.

Herb

CLEANING OUT HARRY'S CAR AFTER he died was not easy. It was new when we bought it, but it had been a "lemon" from the start, and I was set to trade it in, but I was not looking forward to getting it ready. The surprise waiting for me in the glove compartment more than made up for the task. There, amidst other belongs, I found an unsigned anniversary card.

No other card he had given me through the years, and there were many, came anywhere close to the sentiments expressed in the one he could not live long enough to give me. For a man who angered so easily, a man never gentle or soft with either words or action, he found a way to reveal a different side of him through the narrative of this card.

"To My Wife, the joy of my life;
Love is for all seasons,
It buds in the spring,
Blossoms in the summer sun,
blows gracefully in autumn's wind, and like the winter's
snow
falls gently on a welcome heart
BECAUSE OF YOU I HAVE KNOWN ALL THE
SEASONS OF LOVE"

Harry must have been frightened all his life. It took him thirty years to learn he could trust me enough to let his guard down. I was sad that I had to settle for the card to give me what fate deprived me of: the pleasure of experiencing the gentle side of him. What really matters in the end, however, is that he reached that plateau, where he was no longer afraid to reveal the feelings of his heart.

My discovery of this card was perhaps what Rabbi Levin had in mind when he spoke of the wisdom in God's timing.

DEBBIE MARRIED BRUCE THE SPRING after Harry died. Rabbi Levin officiated at the ceremony, held at the Fairmount Park arboretum. Ronny, Herb, and Bruce's brothers held the chuppah, the wedding canopy, over the couple.

RON AND HIS BRIDE-TO-BE LAURIE tied the knot on a beautiful November day in 1984.

The wedding took place on the sprawling green behind the Florida home where the pair would live. Excitement filled the air. We had a whole day to take care of last minute preparations like checking wardrobes, testing lights, welcoming out-of-town guests, and snapping cameras.

Because the ceremony would happen at sundown, I had plenty of time to worry. To add a little more spice to the growing tension, I called to my son:

"Ronny, what if it rains?"

"Oh, Mom! There is no rain in the forecast, so don't worry!"

"Weather forecasters are not infallible, son, and it is better to be safe than sorry." I persisted with my motherly worrying. "So, how about getting a tent, just in case?"

To keep me from nagging, Ron summoned a tent. When erected, it took on the look of a reception hall. The set was complete. Shortly after the sun set on the horizon, the garden turned into a magical place with the turn of a switch. As if little fairies had waved their magic wand, a towering tree flashed vividly into sight, its draping branches streamed with tiny bulbs to light the sky. The splendid sight made a heavenly canopy for the wedding ceremony.

LIKE SO MANY OTHERS, I grew up in a world where organized religions each, in their own way, stressed the importance of paying homage, of exulting God. These religions suggested that praying for blessing and forgiveness was necessary for alliance with God. I did not feel that such belief systems valued individual intuition. I had difficulty relating to God portrayed as someone outside of us in the "Heavens," a person who stood in judgment over all of our deeds. I did not believe that wrath had anything to do with what God was really about. Each time I attempted to follow ancient religious rituals and practices that left little room for mention of intuition, it did not feel right to me. I was searching for something elusive, something that refused the kind of clarity or certainty that I sometimes felt religion tried to push onto me.

Though Rabbi Levin could relate to some of my religious questions, I still could not sit through his services without feeling detached. I hungered for something I could not name, something to fill the loneliness I felt deep inside but I could not explain.

Fear
Intimidates,
Debilitates,
And within a short time
It brings you to your knees, hopelessly defeated.

1986

My children had dispersed. Harry and my parents were dead. I felt deserted and forsaken. While attending a support group for widows and widowers, I met a man from Iran at a time when American prejudice against Iranians was at its peak. Because of my own experiences with prejudice, I was sympathetic toward him, and we became romantically involved. But within a matter of months we parted ways. In the end, my time with him had only emphasized my loneliness. I was so vulnerable that the last thing I needed was what happened next. One night, shortly after my ill-fated relationship drew to a close, I was mugged—right in front of my house. This offense pushed me to the edge, and my nerves could take no more.

My breakdown was a curious experience. It brought me frightful images seemingly ordained by paranormal forces, even as I felt I had a keen sense of reality. It was difficult for me to distinguish between the two, as hysteria ruled my entire being. I had no one at my side to quiet my fears lovingly, and the businesslike officials who attended me so systematically made me feel as if my dignity and rights were being violated once again. The amazing thing is that I was lucid enough to take note of every person's response to my irrational behavior, and I remember clearly every nuance of each episode that occurred during that period. I learned so many things from that experience that I began referring to it as a breakthrough instead of a breakdown. One of the most valuable insights I gained is that our mental health system is more concerned with efficiency than the sensitivity and consideration needed by someone under emotional duress.

• • • •

WHEN I WAS A YOUNG child, I remember the adults talking about Mrs. Eibenschutz, the neighborhood grocer's wife. She suffered a "nervous breakdown," the grownups said. I went to school with her daughter Edith, and we were friends, but I felt funny asking her about her mother's illness; everyone spoke in whispers about it, and I had no idea what the term meant.

Later, much later, during my first years in the U.S., Estelle, a friend who was my age, suffered a breakdown. When I called to arrange a visit with her, her mother said that Estelle would not leave her room, nor have anything to do with anyone; she just sat staring at the walls in the darkness. I was puzzled as to what had caused such a drastic change in her behavior, but there were no answers. Nobody was able or willing to discuss it. In those days, psychiatry offered some answers, but the field did not have the same legitimacy it does today. It was far easier to get someone out of the way by institutionalizing them than it was to probe the causes of their emotional suffering. I saw that trend changing after World War II, with so many veterans returning from combat emotionally scarred. Only then did the medical doctors begin to cooperate with psychiatrists.

While such collaborative efforts to understand the delicate nature of the human mind and its frailty were the first steps toward a new way of thinking, stigmas associated with mental illness persisted (and in some ways, still do). When one was suspected of seeing a psychiatrist, that person was considered a mental "case," and who in their right mind was willing to subject themselves to that label? Not until people began to realize how the pressures of everyday life could drive one to the breaking point did the general public come to terms with the enormous value of psychiatric therapy.

MOST PEOPLE I KNOW, INCLUDING myself, tend to think they are in full command of their emotions. I believe we find it hard to accept our vulnerability. I think that comes partly from the fact that we are not generally encouraged to know ourselves and respect our instincts. Everyone attempts to convince us that they know what is best for us. My aunt and uncle, for example, encouraged me to swallow how vulnerable I felt, to simply forget the horrors of my experiences during the war. It was their idea of a quick fix, but asking me to deny the seriousness of the physical and emotional damages I had endured was like expecting a temporary poultice to suffice as a cure for a festering gunshot wound. Regardless, neither they nor I ever considered therapy as an option.

And then the walls caved in.

Demons began to haunt me. Invisible entities kept me awake night after night, and pursued me during waking hours, telling me how worthless I was. They frightened me, and I was convinced they had the power to destroy me if I did not obey their never-ending stream of instructions. My resistance weakened, I did as I was told. On their command, I lit candles and recited prayers for the dead.

One night, they beckoned me from my bed.

"Remove all your shoes from the closet," they ordered, "because they represent bad omens." Wearily, as if in a trance, I acquiesced.

Then they instructed me to repeat the performance. They told me God wanted me to do it before the demons could release me. So I restored the shoes to the closet only to remove them once more.

But as I began to extract them for the third time, my mind cleared suddenly, as if struck by lightning.

"Nonsense!" I yelled out, anguished. "My God has nothing to do with this!"

The ring of truth brought a sudden calm over me, but only for a moment, before I again heard the voice of my invisible demons.

"Hostile entities want you dead," they warned. "Follow our command and burn every shred of physical evidence of your past to conceal your identity."

Gripped by the cold hands of fear, I rushed down the stairway and into the kitchen, returning upstairs with two butcher knives and the largest available stainless steel stockpot.

As I carried out these instructions, a strange balancing act took place inside me. My tormentors compelled me to do their bidding, yet I still had the presence of mind to take precautions to avoid a major calamity. I put the pot on the beveled glass surface of the dresser.

In it, I put letters, documents, and my precious autograph book to be torched. When the flames began to rise, I placed the lid on to extinguish the fire. The glass cracked under the heat and the room was filled with smoke, but there was no time to waste; I had to get out of the house. I believed murderous invaders were on their way to kill me.

Shaking beyond control, I grabbed the knives and hurried downstairs to go outside, but the door was locked and the key was nowhere to be found. I ran to the window, but it did not open. Hopelessly trapped and panic-driven, I ran back upstairs. In a last desperate effort, I pried open the window to set off the house alarm.

Stepping out on to the extended roof, I stood there in my nightclothes, a knife in each hand, screaming for help. It was two o'clock in the morning. Neighbors who had rushed out of their home were terrified at the sight of me. The police arrived and tried to convince me to come inside, but I resisted, insisting there was a plot against my life. With no sign of invasion, they were convinced I was out of my gourd and trying to set the house on fire. I told them, quite rationally, that I had put the lid on the pot to prevent just such a thing from happening, but they refused to listen.

All the while, my invisible tormentors kept on. This time they warned me that if I touched anything other than wood I would be electrocuted. Alarmed by my unorthodox behavior, the police asked me on the spot if I would agree to sign myself into a psychiatric facility, which I promptly refused. Therefore, they considered me a ward of the state and drove me to the nearest police station.

When I got there, I sat for several hours, denied the right of a call to summon a friend. These officials treated me as if my feelings were of no consequence.

At the crack of dawn, the police took me to the Philadelphia Psychiatric Center. As I waited to be called into the admissions office, a nurse passed. I approached her, hoping she would help me make a phone call, but she retreated. I shuddered when I saw the alarm that crossed her face.

"I have neither a weapon, nor do I intend to harm anyone," I reasoned. "Do I look dangerous to you in my frightened state?" Averting her eyes, she scurried away without a word. Abandoned again, I worried about what was in store for me.

Once I entered the admissions office, the clerk began to follow the ordinary registration protocol, asking for personal data. I responded calmly to these queries, until she asked about my religious affiliation.

The question touched a nerve.

"I don't think that is any of your business!" I retorted. Feeling increasingly uncomfortable about being stuck without an advocate, I again asked the woman at the desk to allow me to make a call.

"Later!" she barked, marking her authority. At that moment, I decided hers was the last denial I was going to tolerate. All the impersonal treatment and callousness I had encountered in the last three hours had tried my patience to the limit. I had not gotten anywhere with asking, but then my rational mind kicked in:

"You are in America now! You have rights, use them!" I reminded myself.

Encouraged, I opted for action. I slowly took my address book out of my purse and looked up my friend, Max Weiner. I reached for the phone on the desk, pulled it over, and dialed his number. The receptionist was dumbfounded.

"What do you think you are doing?" she demanded, her voiced hushed by astonishment.

"Something I have every right to," I replied, and nobody stopped me.

It was about 5 o'clock in the morning, but I knew that, under the circumstances, the Weiners would understand. Max, founder of Philadelphia's Consumer Education and Protection Agency and the founder of the Consumer Party, was the only person I wanted at my side for protection.

His wife Bess answered the phone. At the sound of my voice, she summoned Max, who was astounded to hear where I was.

"What in heaven's name are you doing there?" he asked

"Please Max, just come and I will explain. I need you."

Max showed up a couple of hours later with Dan Berger, a mutual friend. Both men had always perceived me as someone who took everything in stride. I was the last person they ever would have expected to be wrecked by nervous collapse. I was grateful that they responded. It was amazing how the mere presence of my friend changed the hospital personnel's attitude towards me! This was the preamble of a very interesting learning experience, for which I had not volunteered.

I AM SUCH AN ANTI-DRUG person that I refused to take any medication until Max assured me it was to my benefit.

"Give yourself the chance to calm down, and take it from there," he advised. I relented, but only temporarily.

Unbeknownst to me, the doctor called Ronny and told him I was "mentally ill."

Ronny was shocked, and immediately arranged to travel from Florida to be at my side. Debbie, who lived in Arizona with her first husband, called to speak with me. Making contact only increased her apprehension, however, when I was reluctant to hold the phone in my hand to speak with her. Debbie took it as a sign of resentment on my part, but, in actuality, the demons were warning me not to touch the phone. If I did, they threatened, Debbie would be electrocuted. How was I to explain the reason for my strange behavior to her without confirming the doctor's diagnosis?

My poor kids! They had no idea what was happening. Ron arrived the next day expecting the worst. He found me frightened out of my wits. We sat and talked, and when I told him what happened, he reassuringly put his arms around me.

"Mom, I am here. I love you. You are not alone. Debbie and I will take care of you. You'll be A-OK."

Ronny was always able of showing affection and warmth. He never forgot to remind me how much I meant to him. In that moment, my children's love gave me the incentive to fight the demons whose comings and goings needed to be confronted.

During Ron's visit, a nurse came in with my daily dose of medication.

"These pills are making me jittery and anxious," I told her. "I prefer not to take them until I have a chance to speak with the doctor,"

"But you HAVE to take it," she responded, her voice intolerant.

When she persisted, Ronny intervened. After all these years, I still chuckle when I recall how my little boy stood up for me with all his 5'7". He stood, put his arms around me protectively, and addressed the bullying nurse in a commanding manner I had never seen before.

"If my mother doesn't want to, she doesn't have to!"

The nurse left, and no one approached me with that medication again.

After a few days, Ronny had to leave, but he arranged for Debbie to come and take over. My daughter dazzled me with her remarkable efficiency and authoritative composure. In retrospect, I have found it interesting to reflect on the different responses of my two children to such an unusually demanding situation: two different personalities united for a common cause, two different ways of expressing love ideally balanced. Ronny with his affectionate, emotional support, Debbie with fortitude and discipline, enabling her to take matters in hand so that I felt secure. My daughter guarded herself from feeling too much. I now realize it was the only way for her to stay strong.

I remained in the hospital for a month and a half. The psychiatrist in charge saw me only twice during that period. When I was admitted, I had expressed a need to be counseled by someone from Temple University's department of metaphysics, for I felt that heightened spiritual awareness would improve my mental equilibrium. The doctor dismissed the idea with the wave of a hand, invalidating un-conventional "mumbo-jumbo." Instead, he prescribed Xanax and Haldol. Even if the medications worked at the start, they became counterproductive very quickly. After a few weeks of taking the prescriptions, my regular personality dulled. In its place came more hallucinations. I approached the good doctor to ask that he take me off the medications for my remaining days there—or at least for a trial period. He refused.

"That is absolutely out of the question," he answered, prompting me to probe further.

"So how long do you suggest I have to be on these drugs?"

"For the rest of your life."

That was enough for me to understand where he stood as far as my well-being was concerned. I decided to take matters into my own hands once more. Since I was not planning to circle the corridor indefinitely like the other zombies, I resorted to deception. We lined up every morning at the nurse's station to receive our daily medication. We were to ingest it under their careful eyes. I was pretty good at pretending without arousing suspicion, and after a few days of removing the pills from under my tongue on the way to my room, I was back to normal.

The doctor never knew about it, and I believe he could not have cared less.

We were required to attend group therapy sessions several times a week. There we sat in a circle without a clue as to what we were supposed to do. We waited for some direction and/or motivation from the therapist, who stared at us without a word. The awkward silence was so ridiculously unproductive that I could not understand what the staff expected to accomplish, unless they were trying to make us feel even more vacant and lost. Many people were not actually being cured; they were just being heavily medicated. During my relatively short stay, I saw several people released from the hospital only to be back again in what seemed like no time.

I needed to distance myself, so I looked for something that would occupy my mind and stimulate my creativity. The answer waited for me in the hospital's craft studio workshops, where I produced a ceramic frame and a leather belt. It was the first time I had worked in either medium, and I found both thoroughly therapeutic.

My caring friends were also a delightful diversion, and I took comfort in the string of visitors who poured in to see me. One day a balloon bouquet arrived from a dear friend, Gwen. Its strings attached to a tooled brass box, made in India. Curious to see what made it so heavy, I opened it. Finding a mass of clear glass marbles inside, I squealed,

"Now, here is a real friend! She found my marbles."

Everybody around me burst into laughter.

WHEN THE TIME CAME TO leave the hospital, my release was contingent upon a commitment to seek further treatments. My doctor wanted to assign me to one of the staff psychiatrists, a condition I was not about to accept. I knew I had to search for someone able to help me walk the difficult journey up the steep incline to complete recovery. I aimed to become a fully functioning person in the real world once again.

My daughter screened several professionals and interviewed them on the phone until she hit the bull's eye. I sought someone spiritually oriented and committed more to the Hippocratic Oath than monetary compensation. And, as Debbie added, he or she had to be someone familiar with the history and treatment of Holocaust survivors. *That Debbie thought to include that on her list of requirements revealed her understanding and deep concern for me.*

I was in no position to afford the steep fees psychiatrists usually charged, but I believed that the right person for me was out there. Dr. Robert Dreyfus, a psychiatric associate at Jefferson Hospital and Medical School, answered my prayers. Following an in-depth interview, we agreed to begin therapy at $25.00 a session, and I started to see Bob three times a week. He generously gave me access to his private phone to call day or night.

Bob's first suggestion was that I read *Hope and Help for Your Nerves* by Claire Weekes as soon as possible. During the months that followed, the book became my bible. It helped me survive immensely traumatic anxiety attacks. I have lost count as to how many people I passed that book on to for problems they encountered in their lives.

As time went on and my condition improved, my sessions with Bob gradually became less frequent. I continued my therapy for three and a half years, and I owe Dr. Bob more than money could ever pay. I am indebted to his humanity and professional integrity. He helped me achieve a total clarity of mind, fuller self-appreciation, and a renewed faith in the existence of human decency.

MY TIME IN THERAPY HELPED me understand that a trauma does not go away. If you do not address it, it remains deep inside you. For me and so many others who survived the Nazi atrocities, it is impossible to erase every memory of that treacherous era. Some traces remain intact in the subconscious mind and inevitably surface. My journey in therapy illuminated not only my own condition but also the traumas my parents relived before they died. As their respective illnesses reached final stages, Mother and Dad began to hallucinate. Haunted by tormentors from Nazi-occupied Hungary, they could not shake the feeling that they were being plotted against. Fear reinvaded their bodies, every bit as real and paralyzing as it had been so many years before. It was devastating to watch them live their last days plagued by such horrific delusions.

ONCE OUT OF THE HOSPITAL, I realized how ill prepared I was to face the world beyond its protecting walls. I barely had a chance to rejoice that the worst of my mental breakdown was behind me. For no apparent reason, unnerving feelings surfaced and gave way to a full-blown anxiety attack. It was the first of many along the bumpy road to full recovery. The episodes demoralized me and increased the burden of my already overstressed daughter, on whom I leaned heavily for security and protection selfishly, like a child. Incapable to think beyond my own needs, I readily accepted the misshapen reversal of roles as if it were in the right order of things. I never once thought that she might buckle under the weight of the responsibility thrust upon her. It never crossed my mind to consider her feelings. After all these years, I still find it difficult to account for my mind during that time.

Lost in a timeless zone I paid no attention to the passing of time and did not realize that Debbie was with me for six weeks until she called it to my attention over breakfast one morning.

"I have to go home, Mom, but I am worried about leaving you alone in this house. I have been here long enough to see you through the critical times, but you are still not well enough to stay here after what happened. You have to move out of this house."

I knew she could not stay indefinitely, but for her to suggest that I move…

"Move where? Oh, no! I am not ready to take such a drastic step!"

"Please mom, call a realtor and put the house on the market."

"What if the house sells before I find what is right for me? A decent place in a better location is out of my reach. I checked it out before I got ill. This is hardly the time to gamble the odds with my only measure of security at stake. Are you are asking me to take a *leap of faith?*"

"Don't panic, Mom," she pressed forward, "you will probably have enough time to find what is right for you before you have a buyer. I understand how you feel. A realtor could tell you how sales move in this area."

"Okay, if that will make you feel better, I'll go as far as to call a realtor for information. But I tell you right now, I will not let anyone pressure me into making a decision."

Our call to a local agency produced quick results. The agent who showed up the next day was a woman (I will call her Mrs. A.) with businesslike conduct but without a trace of the dreaded salesmanship pushiness. She relaxed me. It was to her credit that I felt comfortable walking her through the house and explaining my predicament. I wanted to trust her and for her to say what I wanted to hear, but somehow I had the feeling that even as Mrs. A. listened thoughtfully to every word I said without interrupting, she was counting the moments to when she could reassure me:

"Sales are sluggish in this area. We have several properties listed on this street. Granted, they are not nearly in the condition of yours, but frankly, since some have been on the market for as long as a year, I don't anticipate finding a buyer for yours very quickly."

She geared up to offer a proposal.

"A short time commitment would not be much of a risk."

"What do you mean by a short time?"

"Six months."

I closed my eyes, took a deep breath, and did what I was least prepared to do. *I took a leap of faith.* I agreed to a six-month contract with Mrs. A. As soon as I had, I felt as if a ton of bricks lifted from my shoulder.

"You feel better now?" I asked Debbie when Mrs. A. left.

"I will as soon as you find someone to stay with you. I can't leave you here alone, Mom."

At first I could not think of anyone, but then I remembered May

Li, a young Chinese student I had met recently at a friend's. It was a long shot, since I had not kept in touch with her, but that did not faze May Li one bit when I called. She sounded genuinely happy to hear from me. When I explained my situation and asked for her help, she said "no problem" and moved in soon enough to ease Debbie's concern. My daughter could head home with a lighter heart.

I felt comfortable with May Li around me. I admired her dignified demeanor. She was in her early twenties at the time and had only been in this country a couple of years. She knew how to give as well as to demand respect. I could not have found anyone more levelheaded, dependable, and caring even if I tried. May Li, sponsored by her uncle, a science professor, attained her provisional entry to study at his University with the stipulation that she hone her English language skills to qualify for the entrance examination.

Sometimes May Li and I experienced communication problems. It was not only that the distinctive Chinese pronunciation of her English was hard to decode; we of course had cultural disparities as well. I soon realized that if I cared to relate to her on mutual terms rather than mine alone, I had to understand where she was coming from. My common sense suggested that I pay attention to her body language instead of spoken words. Any time we would run into a dispute, inevitably she would shrug her shoulders and mutter a "whatever," indicating that she either did not get it or she did not think the matter worth discussion.

I changed my strategy. Any time I would find it necessary to acknowledge one of her admirable deeds, she would fall back on her mantra: "had to be done, that's all!" As far as I could tell, she found compliments unnecessary. I learned quickly not to negate her matter-of-fact attitude. Probing her mind would only lead me to a blank, impenetrable wall. Done with the past, she lived in the present: "What was, was ... That's all." She built a shell around her emotions. The only thing May Li had in common with the legendary Chinese women fashioned in Pearl Buck's popular and much-loved tales was her hard-to-read façade.

• • • •

BEFORE THE END OF THE first week of Mrs. A.'s contract, she had already found a prospective buyer interested in touring the house. My nerves were on edge as the realtor walked through my home with a woman who seemed very pleased with what she saw. Indeed! What I feared most was happening. She was ready to buy it. Pronto! When the realtor called to let me know, I nearly hit the floor, not the ceiling, for I was sitting on a chair, ready to faint. Had I been anxious to sell, I would have been delighted and flattered that the very first person who came to see my home was smitten enough not to even negotiate the price. Instead, I was stunned that it had happened so soon—too soon. I began to panic, with visions of finding myself homeless for an indeterminate time.

At the time, May Li exuded a faint smile as if she knew something I did not. "Don't worry," she said confidently. "Everything will turn out fine." I could not imagine then what made her so confident, but I later realized that she handled all her own hurdles with the same confident philosophical approach.

After a week of sweating bullets, the prospective buyer did not qualify for mortgage! May Li confidently exclaimed, "You see, it was foolish to get all upset!" We agreed on that, but we differed on our explanations for the good news. I thought God answered my prayer to loosen the noose around my neck. My young friend had been born and raised in Maoist China, without any religious doctrine. With the idea of a so-called Higher Power lost on her, she just smiled, shrugged her shoulder, and turned away, her voice barely above a whisper:

"Whatever."

As time went on, May Li and I bonded as friends, concentrating on what we had in common, rather than all the ways we differed.

AFTER THAT FIRST POTENTIAL BUYER, the realtor graciously terminated our short-term contract. I was free again—another ton of weight off my shoulders. I did not realize it at the time, but just after those events, I would come to a pivotal moment in my life. From that point, my future would unfold in a remarkably connected series of challenging events, stepping stones I was to follow.

The fiasco of my house sale had nearly faded into oblivion when a faculty member from the neighboring Eye Institute came to see me. He seemed to know me, but I could not place him.

"I was upset to see the ad in the paper," he said. "Don't you remember? I came to ask that you contact me when you are ready to sell your house."

"I am really sorry, but only now that you mention it does it ring a bell." I asked if he would hold out until I found a suitable place I could afford.

"Absolutely," he said. He found the house in excellent condition and seemed willing to wait. I told him I would contact him when it became available.

When he left, I looked at May Li and began to laugh.

"Now, if this is not the most hilarious turn of all things ever, I dare say nothing is! This guy actually makes me feel like I am doing him a favor by letting him buy the house!"

If I had expected more than a knowing smile and a "whatever" from my friend, I would have been disappointed, but I knew better by then.

WHEN TIME CAME FOR MAY LI to leave, concerned friends suggested I consider renting a room to a college student. My friend Brunhild and her husband Joe, a Jewish medical research scientist at Temple University Hospital, had rented rooms for years. Frequently more students applied than they had room to offer. Coincidentally, or perhaps not so coincidentally, just as May Li was ready to move on, Brunhild called to tell me about a German student they could not accommodate and asked if I would consider renting to him. I told her to send him over. I wanted to meet him before I decided.

BRUNHILD CAME TO THE US soon after World War II—not the best time to be a German newcomer. Jews in particular had reason to be wary of anyone who had been a citizen of the Fatherland during the Nazi era, which made it especially difficult for Brunhild to take her place in society. Some people were downright hostile towards her. All that changed when she met and married Joe, who recognized and fell in love with her gentle, loving nature. Although she never converted, love for her Jewish husband inspired Brunhild to learn the history and tradition of people she had been taught to hate, only to discover her oneness with them. My mother, who had trouble warming to most people, felt an immediate kinship with Brunhild. Mother and I differed in many ways, but I am fortunate to have inherited her rather objective approach to perceiving someone's character. She maintained, despite the pain inflicted on us by a maligned German regime, that we should not forget the cost of generalizations, the cost of targeting groups of people based on blind hatred. To ostracize and punish someone for their place of birth or for a background they did not choose, stood diametrically opposed to our better nature.

A good number of decent, high-minded German citizens like Brunhild and her family found themselves entrapped in the Nazi web. Young girls and boys automatically enrolled in Hitler's Jugend—his youth movement. To do so was not a choice. The Nazis had revoked Brunhild's father's medical practice because he refused to join the Nazi party, a refusal that compromised the safety of the entire family. Unlike others, however, Brunhild never tried to apologize for Hitler's affect on the entire world; neither did she try to reason away the consequences of her countrymen's behavior under Nazi rule. Her gentle, loving, and caring personality and her devotion to her husband Joe spoke louder than words ever could.

Over the years, Brunhild and I frequently talked about our respective experiences on opposite sides of the war. The love that tied Brunhild and Joe together in marriage was genuine, and so was our friendship.

A COUPLE OF DAYS WENT by before Brunhild called to let me know that the young man was on his way to my house. When I opened the door to a tall, thin, pale-faced youth with dark hair and light blue eyes, my first thought was that he did not look German at all. What did I expect? Though I had consciously resolved not to make assumptions based on someone's background or heritage, past experiences with Germans sometimes made those assumptions feel hard to avoid. He met me with such a stiff, formal "Dirk Martin Grube here" and such a firm handshake that I almost expected him to click his heels as though a German ready to march. Of course, however, he did no such thing, and I quickly figured that he also must have felt somewhat self-conscious about meeting a Holocaust survivor, particularly under the odd circumstances.

Brushing my fleeting nerves aside, I invited him to join me for a cup of tea in my favorite comfort place: the kitchen, where I deliberately positioned myself directly across from him at the table. To break the ice, I casually asked if I could simply call him Dirk.

"Sure, sure" he said, and offered a genial smile when I added that I preferred he call me by my first name as well. Ice cracked, I felt comfortable laying my cards on the table:

"I know Brunhild told you that I am a concentration camp survivor. Before we go any further, I want you to know that the experience did not prejudice me against the German people as a whole. I believe the guilt for crimes committed by the Nazis belongs only to those responsible for that era's demoralizing national catastrophe and not to subsequent generations. With that in mind, I would like to know what you think about those crimes—what position you have in relation to them."

Looking me straight in the eye, he replied softly, carefully weighing his words.

"My father was also a victim. He nearly perished in a Russian prison camp. I am a theology student at Temple University. As far as my political views are concerned, my ideology falls in line with the Green Party's creed."

The English language rolled off his tongue with only a gentle touch of German accent. I liked him. He appeared to be a tender soul, cautious, perhaps somewhat self-conscious under the circumstances, but open and focused. It did not take long to shed our guards and embrace camaraderie. After a while, I thought of him more like a relative than a distant stranger.

I asked Dirk to recall our meeting, which he remembers a little differently.

DIRK'S RECOLLECTIONS

The first time I met you was in 1986. I was a student at Temple University looking for housing in Philadelphia. You had a room for rent and I got your address through friends.

When I came to look at your place, we started talking to each other. I still remember telling you that my dad was a prisoner of war in Russia. You responded immediately: "I was on the other side—I was imprisoned in a Concentration Camp." I was baffled. My first reaction was to ask you whether you had a problem with me being German. You rolled your eyes and said, "No, why should I?—in a tone of voice as if that were the strangest question in the world. It was only after I understood what you mean when you say that it is a human issue rather than a German issue that I understood your reaction fully.

In the first months after I moved in at your place, I watched you carefully as to whether you would hold it against me that I was German. But neither explicitly nor implicitly did I notice any resentments on your side.

Three small details of the time I spent at your place stick out in my memory:

First, the room I rented used to be a garage which was refurbished. It was awfully cold at winter! Once I caught a cold and you cooked a chicken soup for me that was like the chicken soup my mom used to cook for me when I still lived at my parent's place.

Second, I heated the place with an electric heater which wormed up oil—exactly the same model that we use in the Netherlands now.

Third, you used to clean your house with an intensely smelling cleaner. You said that you like the smell of things being freshly cleaned. But I thought not only that it smelled awfully but I also got miserable from the smell. I figured the fact that you used such an intensely smelling cleaner probably had something to do with your past experiences...

I spent only half a year at your place because after that time I went back to Germany. And when I returned to the U.S. the same year, I got an opportunity to do house sitting so I did not rent your place again. I remember a party I gave at that place and that we discussed existentialism. We did not meet on a regular basis anymore, although we did not lose touch with each other.

We picked up our relationship when you moved away from Philadelphia to the Poconos. I remember that I lived in Philadelphia but came to visit you quite frequently. I enjoyed the quiet and peace your place offered over the hectic city.

I still remember the coal-oven you had and the efforts you took to warm up the house in the morning. Furthermore, I remember that my friend Manuel and I used your place as a basis when we hiked in the area. On one of those occasions, I met Gary and a friend. Both were dressed all in white. We had some conversations on political matters, but we did not have much time to spend together because Manuel and I wanted to do some hiking and came home only at night.

I remember meeting Ron at your place in the Poconos, too. Although I had met him in Philadelphia beforehand, we were never particularly close. But when I spent a couple of days out in the Poconos with him and Haley, we started talking to each other seriously. And to our mutual surprise it turned out that we were excellent discussion-partners! Above all, we could discuss politics in a fashion so profound that I have hardly ever experienced it discussing politics in the U.S. We thus got closer and I remember visiting him and his wife in Florida. It was thus a great shock for me to hear that Ron had died!

There were other things I remember, e.g. the neighbour Adolf (whom we suspected to have been a Nazi but were apparently wrong) and the car I left in your garden for more than year…

But more important are probably two of our meetings that occurred when I was back in Europe. The first one is when I lived in Kiel, working on my Habilitation. You came over to Europe with a friend in 1996 and planned to visit Bergen-Belsen! I must confess that I was very nervous about it. I was afraid that exposing yourself to those memories in such a fashion might do damage to your health. Thus, I was glad that your friend, an American, joined us.

But what a surprise when we got there. Rather than being deeply shaken or emotionally stirred up, your first comment was "This is not Bergen-Belsen! What happened to the Concentration Camp?" Apparently, the look of the place had changed dramatically after you had been liberated. Frankly, I was somewhat relieved by that reaction because it showed that your reac*tions were not as dramatic as I had feared them to be.*

And indeed, the whole visit to Bergen-Belsen was very informative and, obviously, somewhat emotional—how could it be otherwise? But it had not such a serious impact on you as I had envisaged. At some point, I had the feeling that your friend and I were more emotionally shaken than you were. Afterwards, we spoke surprisingly little about it. I remember us sitting in the car and pondering on little things, e.g. we wondered whether the boss of the memorial whom we had spoken to was gay or not. But we did not go at great lengths into your feelings and memories. I was never sure whether you were disappointed about Bergen-Belsen or whether you were, probably implicitly, happy that things turned out the way they did rather than stirring up many emotions.

And I remember you giving a lecture to some of my students at Kiel about your experiences as a Hungarian Jew and being taken to a Concentration Camp. Although the turn-out was disappointing in terms of numbers, the sphere was very intense. After you had finished, there was a long period of silence.

Finally, I remember you coming over to Europe in 2005. By then I lived in the Netherlands, where I got a position as a chair in the Philosophy of Religion at Utrecht University. I was glad that you came because I had married in the meantime and we got a child, Jonathan. Thus, that was an excellent opportunity for you to meet my wife Christiane and Jonathan. Of the numerous activities we did in the Netherlands, I remember both of us going to visit the Anne-Frank museum in Amsterdam. But at that point, I was much more relaxed than when we went to Bergen-Belsen. And indeed, although the museum was fascinating in its own cruel way, you did not seem to be shaken much afterwards. I remember us musing about the question of why this funny little guy with his weird moustache could have fascinated millions of people—or how the Nazi-leaders, most of whom were neither strong, nor blue-eyed, nor "Nordic" in any way, could have maintained their particular 'Übermenschen' ideology.

REPLACING MAY LI WITH DIRK went beyond a mere "changing of the guard." It presented the next stepping-stone on the road I traveled. At an earlier time in my life, the idea to befriend someone all the way from China bordered on fantasy, and it was un-thinkable to welcome the friendship of a second generational German youth after the Holocaust. Yet they both happened to come my way in unexpected circumstances. Both May Li and Dirk were about the same age, set apart by their gender and cultural origin, but not by their human values. And while Dirk was much easier for me to relate to then May Li, we bonded with what we had in common. The way I looked at it, they both could have been my children. My mother instinct drew them close to me, and without their parents, they welcomed my caring. Artistic projects, bargain shopping, shared ethnic cooking, and May Li's need of my dressmaking skills built the foundation for the friendship we still enjoy. With a Masters degree to her credit, she occupies a valuable position at a school for the blind and deaf, where she offers the life-sustaining skills program she also helped develop in China.

Dirk earned himself two Doctorate degrees—one, which would help promote his career in America, the other on the European continent. At this writing, Professor Dirk is a great addition to one of Netherland's highly acclaimed universities.

THAT SAME YEAR, RONNY CALLED to announce the birth of his and Laurie's daughter—Haley. Thrilled to greet his first child, he proudly exclaimed that she was a number 10 on the health scale. When I traveled down to Florida to meet her, it was an exciting visit for all of us. Before Haley was born, I had never really been one of those people who were consistently eager for grandchildren. Nevertheless, I was very happy to have Haley. She was Ronny's, and I loved her. As she would grow into a young girl, Ronny would seize every opportunity to bring her to visit me.

CHAPTER NINE

Teaching Tolerance

THE MISSION FOR WHICH I WAS SPARED

I used to go for the wild rides in the amusement park when I was young; they were frightfully thrilling. Carefree and fool-hearted I also loved to free wheel my bike downhill on a bridge that led to a busy city intersection, fearlessly submitting to the possibility of dangerous consequences. As a child, I could well afford to take such foolish chances while secure and protected in my parents' custody, where they made major decisions *for* me until Nazis took charge of deciding my fate.

Because I had not had time to develop my own principles and values, when I arrived in the U.S. after liberation, I was in no position to challenge the principles and values of my relatives—or to challenge their demand that I submit to them. Consequently, it took me some time to learn that I needed to defend my right to weight their views on specific issues against *what felt right to me*. I began to realize that only by consciously taking the time to listen to my own nature could I ever really come to understand my beliefs. Balancing and probing my intuitive forces has been the way of life for me ever since.

I do not remember the exact time, but it was some years after Harry died that a friend called to ask if I would be open for an interview about my Holocaust experience. I was curious and cautious with my answer. *Curious* as to why would someone be interested in the subject others had avoided with me for years as if it were a plague. *Cautious* because it meant *opening the door to the ghosts locked behind it.* My friend told me that the recorded interview would be part of Nora

Levin's archive at Gratz College, an archive intended to authenticate one of the cruelest attacks against humanity for posterity by putting a face on history.[4] When I heard that, the fear of traumatic repercussion no longer mattered to me.

By the time Nora came to my home to audiotape my testimony, I knew I had to let my guard down to allow memories to surface after thirty years of silence. I was in for a surprise. Somehow, as I spoke, everything except for the loss of my brother seemed strangely distant, out of my realm. Memory served me well to the minutest detail, yet I felt like an objective observer of history, a scholar probing the reasons for humankind's senseless, hateful behavior.

After the interview, Nora said she would like me to speak with students attending the Holocaust symposium at Gratz College. I agreed without realizing that I sealed my contract with destiny.

FROM THE MOMENT I STEPPED into the small classroom and met a group of high school students eyeing me curiously, I had the strange feeling that I was on familiar ground. Even the moderator assigned to the session seemed to have been an old acquaintance. I had no given outline for this classroom appearance, but any trepidation I had was for naught. I relaxed completely by the time I introduced myself and started to lay out my agenda. My casual manner immediately engaged my listeners' attention, as I went on automatic pilot and let the words flow freely from the wellspring of my soul. Allowing the message to take on its own form, I offered myself as an example of trying to take an objective approach to what I had lived through—an example of attempting to learn lessons from my own experience. The kids, hanging on to my every word, could hardly wait for a most stimulating and gratifying interactive session, where their questions probed the minds of perpetrators. I was astounded by how well those youngsters related to what they heard.

4　The late Professor Nora Levin established the Holocaust Oral History Archive in 1979 at Gratz College in Melrose Park, Pennsylvania. For more information, see www.gratz.edu.

At the end of the session, one of the boys approached me, asking if I was a student of Dr. Frankl.[5]

"Who is Dr. Frankl, and why do you ask?" I wanted to know.

"Oh, I read his book *Man's Search for Meaning*, in which he accounts for the ways he survived years of ordeals in the concentration camp, and you sound like him." Intrigued by the youngster's comment, I set out to get the book and find out about Dr. Viktor Frankl, and the strangest thing happened. I realized that I had already heard Frankl speak; some friends who worked at the Albert Einstein Medical Center had once invited me there to hear a certain Viennese professor address the issue of survival as it related to his concentration camp experiences. As I recalled his talk and read the book, I appreciated how he took a philosophical view of the Holocaust rather than focusing on his own experiences. Both of us had the same idea that those events were more than just a personal experience, and as a result, we each in our own way have turned them into a learning process. .

I told my friends: "The man speaks my language."

I DID NOT KNOW THAT anyone in particular had been monitoring my session with the students until an interfaith organization contacted me to say they were impressed with my manner of presentation and would like to assign me to speak at various schools. Pleased as I was to hear their valuation, I told them that I did not like to think of myself as a *speaker*, as I did not feel qualified or deserving of that title. I explained that I felt more comfortable speaking informally than from a lectern, and they assured me they wanted me to participate *because* of my conversational nature, not in spite of it. In other words, "title-shmitle," they said, and asked me again "Are you willing to accept assignments from our speakers' bureau?"

---

5   Victor E. Frankl, M.D., Ph.D. (March 26, 1905-September 2, 1997), an Austrian neurologist, psychiatrist, and Holocaust survivor. He published *Man's Search for Meaning* in 1946. In it, he describes his concentration camp experiences and uses them as a basis for thinking about the process of identifying meaning even in the most terrible of situations.

In that moment, I decided I would do it. Above all, I wanted to serve a just purpose.

MY FIRST ASSIGNMENT WAS A private school for boys. A student greeted me at the entrance and ushered me to the auditorium, where, ironically, the school had set up a lectern from which they imagined I would address the large audience. Seeing this, I wasted no time before asking the teacher to introduce me as a visitor or guest. I offered apologetically that I was not a qualified speaker.

He just smiled and said, "You need not be one to tell your story," then warmly shook my hand. The usual lively chatter of young voices abruptly came to a halt at the first sound of their teacher's voice calling for their attention. As I stood by his side waiting to address my listeners, a surge of inspiration engulfed my senses in a way I had never experienced before. The lectern lost what might have been its negative effect on me, and natural, casual approach worked wonders. I don't quite know how I ever kept the entire audience entranced for nearly an hour without having to think of what to say next. The words just rolled off my tongue as my story took its own form. I did not know where the words came from, but they felt so right that I just let it happen.

The talkback session broke the physical barrier separating me from the audience. The students posed a seemingly unending list of questions, which I managed to answer with the same spirited ease. Afterwards, the teacher turned to thank me for my efforts.

His parting words:

"You are wrong to think that you are not a speaker, because you are, and an affecting one at that."

Some of what he said went right to my heart. That is when it dawned on me that this was the mission for which I was spared. "Ordained by destiny" might be a far-out way to put it, but that is exactly how I felt. And that feeling is what would keep me going for the next twenty-five years, as I urged *tolerance* and *acceptance* for the sake of peace.

CHAPTER TEN

Awareness

I met her in school. She was teacher. I was student. She, a bouncing twenty-something with an irresistible magnetism and wonderful teaching instincts, could stimulate even the most dormant of minds. I, at the ripe "old" age of 48, was back in school to make up for the higher education I had been denied in Hungary. I had a good foundation for what awaited me at school; after all, I had worked in the needle trade for years, and I had learned much about the intricacies of construction through altering clothing. Earning the degree, however, required that I take a variety of classes. Of those, costume history, fashion illustration, fabric design and application, and jewelry making happened to be Maggi's department. I loved the way she approached her subjects. I admired her technical skills and knowledge, but it was the spirit that made her irresistible. She was open, direct, and fair. I learned far more from her than curricular requirements; she instinctively led me to some important realizations.

"You have a way of complicating things," she told me. "Make it simple! Make it simple!" She would say it to me again and again with each assigned project. I tended to go overboard with every assignment. Once she assigned us to draw six uniform blocks and create a fabric design within each of those boundaries. All of my designs spilled way outside the lines. Maggi commented on that fact when she examined our assignments in front of the class.

"Someone in this room is not about to be fenced in."

Everybody laughed. The smile on Maggi's face, however, looked more thoughtful than jovial. The solemn expression, a momentary abandonment of her teacher's stance, may not have lasted more than a moment, but I noticed and understood immediately that she tapped into my subconscious rebellion. She signaled to me that I could harness those defiant impulses. She alone would have made that school worthwhile.

My respect and love for Maggi's straightforward manner and sympathetic nature was reason enough for me to seek her friendship. Nevertheless, had she not also felt a connection between us somewhere along the line, our alliance would not have blossomed into a lasting relationship. Our relationship confirmed for me once again that when you meet someone whose manner beautifully resonates with your own, such a meeting is not chance. It is preordained. I our case we turned out to be each other's catalysts in some extraordinary circumstances.

Leading busy but different lives, to keep our relationship alive, Maggi and I had to designate one day for an annual get-together. That gathering, however, had to be set aside for a mutually agreeable project, as Maggi was never one to just sit and talk. Since we both loved baking cookies around the end-of-the-year holidays, Maggi suggested we could do our baking together in time to give the sweets as gifts. We would honor the cookie date for years. At first, we limited ourselves to her favorite basic Italian anise wafers and my cookie press specials, but over the years, we expanded with the assistance of her two young daughters. We had lots of fun baking up a storm to her husband's delight. Cookies galore spread over her large dining room table by the end of the day. We produced more than enough goodies for ourselves—and to share with others.

Our cookie-baking sessions continued until my breakdown three years after Harry's death. Every one of my friends, even those I least expected, came to visit me in the hospital and assisted during my recovery. Every one of my friends except for Maggi, that is.

I was still in therapy when I decided to call her.

"Is everything all right?" I asked.

"Yes…And you, are you okay?" Her voice sounded uncomfortable.

"Well, at least I think I am over the worst. I missed you, Mag. Where were you?"

"So sorry, Eva, I just could not cope with it."

That was all. After that, we picked up our thread as if nothing happened. When Christmas rolled around, we resumed our annual baking feat with an early morning start. By lunchtime, a variety of scrumptious cookies topped trays on the dining room table. With the last batch out of the oven, I got a cramp in my back—right between my shoulder blades—from being on my feet so long.

"Mag, I need a break to rest my aching back," I said.

"I know how to fix it," she said. "After dinner I get us into the hot tub outside and put on the whirlpool to massage your back."

"You must be kidding! You can't expect me to go outside in this cold! Besides I don't even have a bathing suit."

"Never mind!" she insisted. "Don't start with me! It takes only seconds from the door and once you are in, I guarantee you will not be cold. I have an old stretched-out bathing suit to fit you, too."

My last hope to ditch the idea vanished with her digging up the "stretched out' bathing suit from some old forgotten heap. She lured me into the tub, and I never lived to regret it. We sat there for hours under a starlit sky in the dead of winter, with the whirlpool gently massaging my aching back. Our words cut into the crisp, cold air like smoke signals until we almost turned to prunes.

"What are your plans?" she wanted to know.

"One thing for sure," I began, "I must move from where I live now. Tried to continue on after Harry died, but the mugging was the last straw."

"What mugging? I didn't know you were mugged. When did that happen?"

"Right outside my house. I was about to get into the car on my way to a League [of Women Voters] meeting when a young black man called out to me from across the street with an engaging smile. I thought he wanted to ask direction or something, so I let him near, but as he approached, the alarm went off in my head, and I reached to shut the car door. It was not fast enough, and he got in the way. In a desperate move, I leaned on the horn, and he grabbed my purse and ran. The impulse to sound the horn saved me from further insult, but left me shaken. I wasn't the same after that."

"I guess that incident triggered your breakdown."

"Most likely so."

"Have you an idea of the kind of place you are looking for?"

"Oh, I made two lists, three years apart, and they were identical. I wish to be somewhere in the mountains near the woods in a small house surrounded by nature, where I could find peace. You know we loved camping. It had been our dream to move to the Pocono Mountains after Harry retired. The plan died with him, and I am left with financially limited options."

"Want to know something?" Maggie asked rhetorically. "You may just have a chance to revive that dream. Last summer I went to Jim Thorpe with some friends to do landscape painting and fell in love with that place. It fits your description to a tee. I bet you can get something there now. They are in the midst of a crisis fighting against a deal in which Hari Krishnas would buy a sizable piece of land for a permanent camp."

"Jim Thorpe?" I marveled. "Was he not a Native American Olympic Athlete? I never heard of a town with that name. Where is it?"

"It is a little hamlet in the foothills of the Pocono Mountains. The town has a Victorian feel. The terrain is reminiscent to the Swiss Alps. They actually call it Little Switzerland. If you wait till spring, I'll take you up there."

I was curious. I went home and looked up Jim Thorpe on the map and found it 75 miles North of where I lived in Philadelphia. The following day I inquired about the possibility of getting there by public transportation. I found that besides sparsely scheduled buses from the Central Philadelphia terminal, the only way to the little town was by car.

Something from my gut urged me not to wait until spring.

That night, I heard a voice say, "follow your heart," as if it came from someone sitting right at the edge of my bed. Jarred out of a deep sleep I jumped up, looked around, but even when I found no sign of another soul in the room, I remained too shaken to go back to sleep.

Wherever the voice came from, it sounded an awful lot like what I felt in my gut.

THE MASTER PLAN—COMING FULL CIRCLE (ALMOST)

I felt a strong drive to follow my intuition and investigate the attractive idea of Jim Thorpe without delay. For the first time in my life, I came into awareness. By that, I mean I was able to recognize—with more clarity than ever—the miracles connecting so-called coincidences.

Commonsense might have told me that moving to remote Jim Thorpe was a difficult, even impossible dream. If I had followed commonsense, I would have missed a plan that God had in store for me. More and more, I listened to my intuition, even when it seemed inopportune or inconvenient.

Driving to Jim Thorpe would have been most convenient and taken less time, but snow and ice covered the roads, making them less than ideal for traveling. Most sane people avoided driving them. I called the Carbon County Visitors' Bureau for referrals to local real estate agencies hoping to get an idea of property prices and availability. The response from realtors was unanimous: "Sorry ma'am, but with your kind of capital, we have nothing to offer you here."

I did not believe them because my inner voice said otherwise, so I called the visitor's bureau once again, but this time to ask for a list of places where I could spend the night. There were only two to chose from: a small motel on the highway and Bear Cupboard, a bed & breakfast in town. I decided to stay in town where I would have a chance to meet the people who lived there.

Planning to get an early start the next morning, I went to dig my car out from under the heavy snow plowed upon it and to warm up the motor. It was very cold outside, but I was ready to shed my clothes by the time I finished shoveling and the car had a clear path to the road. With a sigh of relief, I got behind the wheel to warm up the motor, but turning the ignition only yielded a couple of groaning sounds, and after several attempts, not even that much could be coaxed out of the engine. The emergency service I summoned had no more luck than I did, and the car had to be towed. Determined not to let that glitch ruin my plan, I rented a car from Ugly Duckling, the low budget rental agency known for their well-maintained-but-no-frills vehicles. I needed no more than four running wheels and a functioning heater, and that is about what I got. Driving on slippery city roads has never been more hazardous than when behind the wheel of a car with questionable maneuverability, but somehow I had no trouble navigating even as I slipped and slid on my way to the Pennsylvania Turnpike.

Snowflakes danced in the air, daring the rays of a rising sun. Thanks to seasonal high road maintenance, the Turnpike road was clear all the way from the Northeast Extension to the Lehigh tunnel. I never realized that the tunnel was actually the passage to the world of peaks and valleys until I saw the glistening white snow-covered vista ahead. Dazzled by the picture-perfect winter scene, I hurried the few miles to the Mahoning Valley exit where I left the turnpike and followed the road leading to Jim Thorpe. After passing through Lehighton and the two small towns of Parryville and Weissport, I came to a short but treacherous hill sloping downward—the kind of hill that you have to drive slowly on even in good weather. I had no choice but to hold my breath and approach the slope with trepidation and confidence.

The sight of the picturesque terrain surrounding the little village I was about to enter made up for every tension-filled second of the winter drive. Welcome to Jim Thorpe! Two large, impressive red brick buildings on either side of Broadway seemed like columns marking the town's unofficial front gate of sorts. Further down the street the eye-catching old railroad station housed the Visitors' Center. I would later learn that the only time those rails carried passengers anymore was in the fall, when scenic tours took travelers through the Lehigh Gorge to view the spectacle of autumn plant life in its golden splendor.

When I arrived, the town seemed deserted. Vacant shops and boarded-up houses did not look too inviting. If this was the center, what might the rest of this town look like? I wondered. Experience would prove that my judgment sprang from a city-dweller's ignorance.

Bear Cupboard, to be my home during my visit, stood down Broadway, across from the massive, stately structure of the community's Opera house. I parked the car next to the bed & breakfast and walked up the steps into what appeared to be a small gift shop.

A young woman came to greet me:

"Can I help you?" she asked. Her tone sounded friendly and inviting.

"I just got into town," I started. "I am looking for the Bear Cupboard. Is this it?"

"Oh, you must be Mrs. Cutler. Yes, you are at the right place. Please follow me. Let me show you to your room." Down we went, where to my greatest surprise she ushered me into a very cozy street-level suite with a door to the driveway.

Looking expectantly at me, she said, "This is it, I hope you will be comfortable here. If you need anything, please don't hesitate to call on me."

I was tired but exhilarated, and, although I tried, could not rest for a moment. Bundled warmly in my winter get-up, I went outside. The crisp clean air opened my nostrils and revived my senses. Suddenly, prompted by a tremendous surge of energy, I began to walk. At one point, I lost steam while climbing the slippery, uneven sidewalk, and I stopped to catch my breath. I realized that the signpost I was leaning against was actually there to show the way to a gift shop. The light inside indicated that the store was open, so I went to check it out. I could see nobody inside, although the sign on the door said, "We are open, please come in." I knocked. The shop was actually set up inside the enclosed front porch of a residential dwelling, and through the window I saw the massive wooden door to the house opened by a woman wearing an apron.

"Come in, come in please," she said, apologizing for her appearance and explaining that she was in the midst of preparing lunch. "Please excuse me, but I need to get back. Take your time and browse. I'll be with you shortly."

When she disappeared behind the heavy wood door, I felt very uncomfortable alone in the store. Trusting a stranger the way she had trusted me just did not happen where I was coming from. As I tried to acclimate myself, my eyes spied intricately handcrafted jewelry on a glass-enclosed display counter and a variety of mineral rocks (among other items) carefully and tastefully arranged in on shelves and on the floor. The unique but casual, tidy appearance of the place quickly began to grow on me.

Not much time passed before the woman returned. She no longer wore the apron, and she appeared to have freshened up her look. Moving with grace, her short curly blond hair neatly in place, Midge (as I would come to know her) was all smiles with measured geniality when I told her that I came to town to see if it was the right place for me to move.

"Well," she started, "we have lots of places here to choose from. It all depends on what you are looking for. Us 'Chunkers' have been working hard to keep our community intact and upstanding in the face of harsh conditions."

"Chunkers, you say? Where is that coming from?"

"Well, our town was called Mauch Chunk before the late Native American Olympian Jim Thorpe's remains were buried here."

"This is news to me! And when did that happen?"

"1954, when his widow got wind of the town's revitalization plan initiated by Joe Boyle, our local newspaper man. Our town's history goes back to the 1800s."

"You know," she told me before I left that day, "Mauch Chunk actually is the Indian phrase for sleeping bear."

Midge turned out to be a delightful introduction to the random trivia of Jim Thorpe.[6]

WHEN I LEFT MIDGE, I went back and talked to the proprietress of Bear Cupboard. I told her why I had come to town. In turn, she told me her story—how she and her husband had just returned to Jim Thorpe after having been gone for years. Because they had recently

---

6   Founded in 1818, Mauch Chunk became a busy coal transport center, a popular tourist attraction, and the seat of Carbon County. Located at the foot of the Poconos and on the banks of the Lehigh River, the town suffered economically as usage of petroleum and automobiles increased.

SPARKS FROM THE FIRE

SPARKS FROM THE FIRE

bought a house, she recommended her real estate agent, Carol. She assured me Carol would be interested in finding what I needed, and within my means.

I looked up Carol the following day and asked her to show me whatever she had on her list that I would be able to afford. I did not want to live in town, I explained. I wanted to be outside, not too far from people, but not too close, either. I dreamed of nature surrounding me.

In a funny way, Jim Thorpe felt a bit like a miniature Budapest, at least in the sense that a small river divided East Jim Thorpe from West Jim Thorpe, just like the Danube divided Budapest. Carol drove me along muddy roads to the East side of the river. There were not too many houses along the road, and at one spot Carol stopped and pointed down a very steep incline, saying that there was close to half an acre for sale there. Then she started to drive further up, but I stopped her. All of a sudden, I felt something so strong. I looked down. I looked up down. I looked up. And then I saw this mountain, and I just loved it.

"This is my place, this is my home, that's where I'm going to live." The owner was asking 4500 dollars for it, and I told her I would take it for 3500. To this day, I still don't know where that figure came from or why it came flying out of my mouth! I just blurted it out, and then I came home.

The next day Carol called to congratulate me. I was a landowner! When I heard her say that, all of a sudden, I panicked. I just panicked. I thought to myself: What am I doing here? So I called Herbie. He didn't necessarily know more than I did, but I still asked him what I should do. He supported my instincts. If nothing else, he reasoned, it would be a wise investment. He told me to grab it, once all the necessary inspections confirmed that the land conformed to the building codes.

Well, I bought it.

And then I called Maggi to tell her.

She let out such a scream. "Oh, my God, what have I done?"

"What do you mean?" I asked.

"My God, if you made a mistake, it's all my fault."

"No, Maggi, it's not your responsibility. It's mine." I reminded her that, for all we knew, her little suggestion might have been the best thing to happen to me at that point in my life.

CAROL RECOMMENDED A TRUSTWORTHY BUILDER. Therefore, in one way, I was ready to get started. In another way, I did not know how to begin, and I wanted more counsel. So I called on Tony, a former protégé of Harry's who had by then become a housing developer. Tony gave more than advice; he attached himself to me throughout the building process, beginning to end. We met with the builder to make a plan. Financial realities would mean I would have to compromise some of my dreams for the house. I had hoped to have two levels with a skylight, but when all was said and done, the results were amazing: a bi-level house built on the slope with one end partially underground and beautiful windows all around. I had light and nature all around me, and it was paradise.

Across the way from me, a man and his wife lived in a big log house. He amused me because, when my house was under construction, he constantly stepped over to give instructions to the builder. I eventually learned that his name was Adolf and he was German. I told him immediately that I was a survivor, and I found out that he and his family had watched as the Nazis confiscated their farm and everything they had. We would become close neighbors over my twelve

My haven in Jim Thorpe

years in Jim Thorpe, and I would benefit from the many magnificent samples from his garden.

When my friends in Philadelphia initially heard about my plan to move to Jim Thorpe, many of them thought I had flipped my lid. One friend in particular, also a Holocaust survivor, told me I was making a mistake to move up there as a woman alone. No matter how much he warned me not to do it; I told him that I had a strong instinct that I had to go. After I settled in, he came up to visit, and he admitted it was the best thing I could have done. No one could believe how well my home had turned out!

Ronny bringing me his precious cargo.

When the house was almost ready and moving time came, Maggi and Ronny both insisted on helping. I remember Ronny standing in front of my new home when it was completely finished. He marveled, "Mom, I can't believe this—that you got this for what you had in Philadelphia. It's unbelievable." He loved Jim Thorpe, and enjoyed it to its fullest. I never knew when he was going to show up. Sometimes he would appear at the door with Haley at midnight. She would run downstairs to my studio. It was heaven for her. She loved drawing, and she loved my materials. One year she asked me to use my fabrics to make her a costume that recalled a wonderful memory from years before. When all three of my kids were young, I had sewn them a set of Halloween costumes. Debbie was Little Red Riding Hood, Ronny was the Grandmother, and Gary the wolf. One year when Ronny and Haley came to visit, Ronny talked Haley into asking me to recreate the Red Riding Hood costume for her, too. The memory of little Haley coming up to me and making that request is among my fondest recollections from my time at the foot of the Poconos.

• • • •

Not long after I settled into Jim Thorpe, I met a woman named Gert, who's family founded the town's newspaper she developed further with her brother Joe. Gert wanted to introduce me to Joe because she was sure he would want to write an article about me. When I did meet Joe, I told him some of my story, and he immediately requested that I speak to a school he was affiliated with, a Catholic parochial school in the community. As I was happy to take him up on it, when he heard my talk, he insisted that I continue.

"You can make a name for yourself, and you can make money," he urged me. I told him that making money was not my intention, but that I did want to speak to students, if I had the opportunity. Word got around, and I started to receive invitations to different schools. I even ended up going way out in the boondocks, places that were hard to find, but the teachers there were interested and I had some fascinat-

FOLLOWING HER LARGE GROUP presentation at Tamaqua Area High School, Eva talks with a smaller group of students in the school's library. Students are drawn to her through her honest appraisal of the Holocaust and its lessons for modern times. *George Taylor*

Saturday, June 30th/1990 *The Times News, Lehighton, PA.*

Times News *photo*

Survivor of Holocaust urges world-unity effort

By CHRISTINA M. PARKER
Special to The Morning Call

Hours after Israeli Prime Minister Yitzhak Rabin was shot to death at a peace rally in Tel Aviv, Holocaust survivor Eva Cutler told a group of Carbon County veterans that Americans have a unique opportunity to follow his example of striving for unity in a diverse world.

Cutler spoke to veterans at a commemoration marking the end of World War II in 1945. "WWII . . . The County Remembers" was held Saturday by the Mauch Chunk Historical Society and the county Department of Veterans Affairs.

The event featured Carbon County commissioners Thomas Gerhard and John Mogilski. World War II veteran Boyd Kelly and Raymond Mazzerala, director of the Veterans Hospital in Wilkes Barre, also spoke.

County DVA Director Charles McHugh Jr. was master of ceremonies.

Cutler was visibly shaken by peace-

Please See **U.S. ROLE** Page B6 ▶

Nov. 4, 1995

U.S. ROLE

▶Continued From Page B1

maker Rabin's death at the hands of a Jewish extremist. "I stand before you with a heavy heart and a great deal of pain," she said. "The shock is too much to bear."

The peace process Rabin worked to establish can continue, but only if people "get to know each other, regardless of race or culture or religion," Cutler said.

America's mixed population offers a unique opportunity to know and understand diversity, she said.

"We have to know each other. We have so much to share. This country has everybody here — the whole world unites in this country.

"But even here there are divisions. Even our leadership is working, not for unity, but on putting up walls of separation. We need instead to build bridges, and do away with the walls," she said.

Cutler spoke of her experiences as a Hungarian Jew during the Holocaust. She was rescued from the infamous Nazi concentration camp Bergen-Belsen near Hamburg, Germany, on April 15, 1945 — two days after her 20th birthday.

Gerhard, a veteran of the Korean war, said that "war is ugly" but sometimes necessary to preserve freedom. He denounced those who burn American flags.

Mogilski, who served in the Air Force, said, "Peace is a commodity we all strive for, but it's elusive. In 4,000 years of recorded history, there have only been about 250 years of peace. It's scary."

He condemned Rabin's killer, saying assassins are " . . . dangerously stupid in their belief that their way is the only way . . . "

It's up to America to protect freedom, said Mogilski, who sported an American flag necktie. "We do wear the white hats in this world. We are the good guys."

He thanked the veterans in the audience, saying that were it not for them, America as we know it would not exist.

Veteran's day Newspaper article

#1. Contents of the 04-11/95 Morning Call newspaper. Article and photo by Christina Parker:

Hours after Israeli Prime Minister Yitzhak Rabin was shot to death at a peace rally in Tel Aviv, Holocaust survivor Eva Cutler told a group of Carbon County veterans that Americans have a unique opportunity to follow his example of striving for unity in a diverse world.

Cutler spoke to veterans at a commemoration marking the end of World War II.

In 1945, "WWII … The Country remembers" was held Saturd by the Mauch Chunk Historical Society and the county Department of Veterans Affairs.

The event featured Carbon County commissioners Thomas Gerhard and John Magilski . Raynond Mazzarella, director of Veterans Hospital in Wilkes Barre, also spoke.

County DVA Director Charles Mc. Hugh Jr. was master of ceremonies.

Cutler was visibly shaken by peacemaker Rabin's death at the hands of a Jewish extremist. " I stand before you with aheavy heart and a great deal of pain," she said " The shock is too much to bear." The peace process Rabin worked to establish can continue, but only if people "get to know each other, regardless of race or culture or religion." Cutler said.

America 's mixed population offers a unique opportunity to know and understand diversity, she said. " We have to know each other. We have so much to share. This country has everybody here—the whole world unites in this country. But even here there are divisions. Even our leadership is working not for unity, but putting up walls of separation. We need instead to build bridges, and do away with the walls," she said.

Cutler spoke of her experiences as a Hungarian Jew during the Holocaust. She was rescued from the infamous Nazi concentration camp Bergen Belsen near Hamburg, Germany, on April 15, 1945- two days after her 20th. Birthday.

Gerhard, a veteran of the Korean war, said that "war is ugly" bit sometimes necessary to preserve freedom. He denounced those who burn American flags.

Mogilski, who served in the Air Force, said " Peace is a commodity we all strive for, but it is elusive. In4,000 years of history, there have been about 250 years of peace. It's scary". He condemned Rabin's killer, saying "Assassins are … dangerously stupid in their belief that their way is the only way …"

It is up to America to protect freedom, said Mogilski, who sported an American flag necktie. "We do wear the white hats in this world. We are the good guys."

He thanked the veterans in the audience, saying that if not for them, America as we know it would not exist.

ing experiences. The students, curious and open-minded, welcomed me, too. These early school visits led to a standing invitation from Lehighton High School and its history teacher, Neil Millheim. My visit there became an annual one, as Neil continued to invite me back. He commented that the more he listened to me, the more amazed he was that I never repeated any one thing. For Neil, I gave the history a human face. I put a human face on history.

In the late 80s, I returned to Hungary because Zsuzsa's husband had recently died. I wanted us to spend a New Year together as we had when we were kids. My visit coincided with Hungary's transition to independence from Russian rule. I witnessed the emotional turbulence that resulted with the collapse of a system to which many Hungarians had become accustomed, for better and for worse. Many of those people were anxious about losing a system that they believed took care of all their needs. As a result, my visit helped me understand the human complexities of these political changes in a way that many people who lived elsewhere, the United States for example, did not.

When I came back to the U.S., I was emotionally fired up. People in the U.S tended to simplify the situation, suggesting: Now Hungary is going to be free! I wanted to caution people to understand what these power shifts meant on human terms. So I contacted the newspaper in Jim Thorpe to ask if they would be open to print my rendition of that experience. I met George Taylor, a section editor who suggested I share my perspective with one of their reporters, but I refused his offer, saying I was the only one who could convey my feelings on the subject. I convinced them to let me write an article myself. And my career as an occasional freelancer began! I wrote feature stories on eclectic subjects, from hearing aids to bird population counts to clothing alterations. Once I even wrote about my attempt to use less electricity by buying a dual wood/coal stove for my new house. The stove proved useful for wood burning and not so functional for coal. Figuring out that stove became an arduous adventure—one I turned to share with the newspaper readers, titled "Romancing the Stove."

• • • •

I BECAME MORE SPIRITUALLY AWARE in Jim Thorpe. I had a lot of time to collect myself in its peaceful environment—time to search inside, time to search for like-minded people. I joined a meditation circle, held in the Crystal Waterfall, a new-age store. Those meditation circles opened up a chance for me to see from different points of view. I became more sensitive to how much I could control events and how much they were controlled by higher sources.

One day, I was at the Waterfall, having a session. We always locked the store during those gatherings. We were surprised when someone knocked at the door. When we let the visitor in, I saw her as she entered the store, but I didn't have my glasses on, and it took me several moments before I realized it was Debbie.

"Mom, get your things and come with me."

"What's the matter?" I asked.

"Don't ask any questions," she urged.

I followed her outside, and to my astonishment, there I found Olga, Irv, Phyllis, and Ben—my closest friends from Philadelphia. Debbie had summoned them before driving up to Jim Thorpe. I knew there was something wrong from the way they all stood there. But Debbie would not say anything more, only: "Let's go home."

My first thought: Something is wrong with Ronny.

We got home. We sat down. Debbie offered me some tranquilizers.

"What happened to Ronny?" I demanded to know.

"Mom," she said. "Ronny is dead."

Ronny died. I could not believe it. He was just here, I thought to myself. Then Debbie told me what happened: an aneurysm. I was numb, dumbstruck. I did not feel anything. Next thing I knew, Herbie arrived, all prepared with flight arrangements. We would all fly down to Florida. I would have an open-ended ticket while we waited for Ronny's remains to be shipped back from Jamaica, where he had been vacationing when he died.

Down in Florida Herbie stayed by my side, and he was so wonderful. It took a long time before Ronnie's body was shipped and we could hold the service. At the funeral, when I went over to his casket everybody reached to grab me. Fearing I might collapse, they did not want me to go near it. In a sudden urge, I pushed them all away, for I wanted to bid him farewell. Reading the words that came to me before the funeral lightened the burden of my sorrow;

> *"You came to me, a flash of light into my darkness you came*
> *A precious gift of life, warm and glowing*
> *Permeating through all, to all*
> *Your love had no boundaries your caring was not in vain*
> *Your spirit soaring high, you left us with your essence*
> *As you were passing by*
> *You are free at last my son, in God's comforting light*
> *Free, and at peace.*
> *Life's precious gift I will miss you*
> *Even as I know that you are with me forever in my heart, and soul.*
> *Good-bye, for now."*

Part of my heart was gone. I never go to his grave.

IN THE SEVERAL TIMES I saw Ronny before he died, something had been speaking to him, warning him of what was to come. During one of my visits to Florida, he came to me one morning and said, "Mom, I don't know what happened. It wasn't a dream, but it was like a dream, and I dreamt that I was dying."

"Ronny, it might not mean that you are going to die," I told him.

"I can't die," my son responded, "because I have a family now."

Then he added: "A voice said to me, 'Don't worry, they'll be taken care of.'"

The next time I visited, he asked me out of nowhere "Are you still doing the automatic writing?" Ronny knew I had practiced automatic writing before—putting pen to paper while a force other than me spoke through my hands.

"Why?" I asked. He just shrugged.

Ronny came up to Jim Thorpe to ski with Haley the February before he died. On the day he left, he said he felt very funny, very strange, but I had to take him to the airport, so we had no time to talk about it. I told him to see the doctor right away when he got home. But instead of going to the doctor, he went to Jamaica, to meet a friend for snorkeling. He never snorkeled. His death happened exactly a year after he experienced his first premonition.

RON'S UN-TIMELY DEATH PREVENTED HIM from personally fulfilling his desire that I play an important role in the life of his child. Nonetheless, years later, I would move to Florida in time for Haley and me to develop a meaningful relationship. She was 13 when I made the transition to the warmer climate. I am grateful for the closeness we have been able to share, for the opportunity to see my son's branch blossom into a lovely, bright, socially conscious young woman. She has so many of her father's qualities. She is balsam to my heart.

Debbie and my first reunion with Gary after seven years.

NOT LONG AFTER RONNY DIED, I was very lonesome for him. I had not heard from Gary for seven years, so I decided to seek him out. I tracked him down through the grapevine of sorts. Over the years, I had tried to keep track of his cult and had met other members' parents in the process, and one of them offered me a lead on where to send mail. I wrote Gary a letter, and I asked him to come back into my life. He did. Through the years, we have revived our relationship. He lives according to his own belief, and I do not have any problem with that. He is a good person, and he does good things, for which he earned my respect.

WHEN I REACHED MY 70TH birthday, I decided it was time to celebrate. I had never really had a birthday party before, but it felt like an important plateau—one that I had not necessarily thought I would reach. Because it wasn't just the anniversary of my birth; it also happened to be exactly 50 years after I was liberated. I considered that liberation my second birthday and decided to host an open house. Herbie generously gave me money to cater the event. For that remarkable dual birthday celebration, I invited what felt like the whole world.

BY THE TIME OF THAT wonderful party, I was freelancing for a different newspaper, *The Morning Call*, based in Allentown. When the regional office manager heard of my plan, she asked me to write an article about the day I was liberated, and I reluctantly agreed. The piece appeared in the Sunday edition. That is how I met my friend Darree. One day I got a call from a woman who said she'd read my article and wanted to meet with me. Her two young children went to school in Kutztown, Pennsylvania, and she wanted me to speak to their classes. As a PTA member, she would arrange for me to come and offered hospitality for the two days visit. Of course, I did not refuse.

When I met Darree at the school, my first impression was that she was a little country bumpkin. She bounced in, talking, her big curly, light brown hair tied up in the back, she looked more like a student herself, than the mother of school age children. Then she invited me to stay with her family overnight in their guesthouse, a former stone mill house. I had a very pleasant time there and at the schools, where I spoke to junior high and high school students.

I did not have much of an opinion about her either way when I left without a clue that my contact with Darree was going to blossom into a relationship at all, but she went out of her way to cultivate a friendship. She wanted me to know about her life and her children, and she wanted to know about my life. She started visiting me in Jim Thorpe and traveling to hear when I would speak at other schools.

On one of her visits to my house, we were eating lunch, and I told her that I planned to go to Europe on what I was calling a "healing journey."

"It's time that I close the door on that issue, for myself to be free of it. You can only close something when you look at it and you say, okay, it *was*, but it is *no more*."

She asked me what I had in mind. I told her I wanted to go through from the beginning, starting in Budapest and then following the path the Nazis forced upon me, leaving through Austria and heading into Germany. I wanted to go to the concentration camp where I was liberated, then to visit Dirk, then on to Sweden where I left my heart.

She asked if she could come with me.

"Of course" I said. "Let's go together."

I could never have guessed before that conversation that she would want to make such a journey with me. I had no idea at the time what a godsend her company would be. In the end, I would have had a very difficult time making the trip alone. Another "coincidence"—Darree coming into my life. Though we were relative strangers and she had been warned about traveling with an older woman, we embarked on the trip I had planned.

In Budapest, we visited Zsuzsa, and my old friend Feri. When I took Darree around the city of my birth, for some odd reason, I felt very uneasy. Maybe I invited those uncomfortable feelings to surface so that I could confront them and work for closure. At one point, when a plain-clothes policeman stopped us and asked for our identification, suddenly I became very defensive. Unbeknownst to me, the police was on the lookout for people who had recently been putting bombs in trashcans in Budapest, and we happened to be standing right in front of one of those cans. But I was not at peace at the time, and the whole incident frightened me more.

When we departed from Hungary by train, headed for Austrian and then Germany, I found myself glued to the window.

"This is freedom," I kept on saying to myself, "because I am doing this of my free will. Now I'm in a compartment for passengers to travel comfortably, and I made the decision to do this." As the train moved on from stop to stop, I repeated it over and over. I was free.

We connected with Dirk and stayed with him in Kiel, where he was incredibly happy teaching at the University of Kiel. He arranged for me to talk with an English-speaking class. The students interested me a great deal; they were very receptive to my story.

Dirk journeyed with us to Bergen-Belsen, where I was surprised to learn that he called ahead to make an arrangement with the curator there. The curator was very helpful; he, too, was interested in hearing about my experiences during and after the war. The concentration camp I remembered no longer existed. In its place, we found a huge, beautifully landscaped memorial garden in honor of all the prisoners. The nameless memorial marked the mass grave on which we stood.

Strangely, I was not especially moved by the site of the former camp. But the weather seemed moved. We had enjoyed sunny, bright days on our visit to Germany until that moment, but on that day, on that dreary, cold day—it rained.

After Bergen-Belsen, we made our way to Sweden, where we had a glorious time.

I will leave it to Darree to fill in the details of the rest of our trip—to give an account of my healing journey from her unique perspective.

WHEN THE TRIP WAS OVER, Darree and I knew each other better, to say the least. We had managed to get through even those unusual difficult circumstances that tend to arise during travel. Those moments brought us closer, helped us understand and appreciate each other. When the trip was over, we parted—exhausted, without a word spoken about our continued relationship. However, we *did* continue, and I am forever grateful for the higher force that brought me the jewel of Darree.

I learned from Darree that a destined relationship needs only one person to pursue it. In our case, it was Darree who picked up the possibility of our friendship and ran with it. My feelings for her deepened as I got to know her better. I learned to admire and respect Darree's intelligence, wisdom, and curiosity. We feel related in the spirit, which sometimes can be stronger and truer than blood.

My Life with Eva

By Darree Robin Sicher

When someone asks about Eva, I say, "There's the family you're born to and the family you find. Eva is the family I found." I have yet to meet someone who doesn't understand what I mean. Mine was not a conscious search for a missing piece in my life but more an unconscious and involuntary recognition of a search fulfilled. Of course, I didn't even know I was searching. Memory strains for details or dates of when my heart seared loyalty to this woman who I met by following a newspaper article. Hearts are funny like that – sometimes you just wake up and say, "Gee, I really love that person and I'm glad they have touched my life." Initially, our relationship was based on her reaching out to share her Holocaust experience and on me reaching in to expand my own understanding of humanity.

The article in the local Sunday newspaper interviewed a woman who visited local schools, discussing her experience as a Holocaust survivor and her views on universal human nature—on fear, following, and forgiveness. Although I put the paper in the recycling several times, the mystery of someone who survived one of humanity's darkest times and in turn dedicated her energy to helping young people understand surviving the dark side was very exciting to me. I was intrigued that someone would turn such a personal suffering into a language of the struggle of being human. I persisted in tracking her down and invited her to speak at the school where my children attended.

Initially, I pursued Eva to have a relationship. We shared lunch and stories of our lives and the lessons we learned along the way. Sometimes, it's OK to care about someone because you want to, not because you expect anything in return. That's how it was with Eva and me.

What called me to a woman who was younger than my grandmother but older than my mother? Possibly it was her world view being so different from most of the people I knew. Her early life experience from another country, another culture, another time. It seemed to fill a void between the cynical and naive world I grew up in. Eva seemed to embody both view points comfortably, accepting room for both in the world. Rather than "this or that," it was "this *and* that." She seemed rounded in spirit, with room for firmness and fickleness, humor and anger, celebration and disappointment. I didn't view Eva as some lofty matriarch, dishing out wisdom to the unenlightened masses. She was someone who was real and accessible. She talked about constantly learning, evolving and coming to terms with issues. She was in a constant state of growth. She was alive. She didn't claim to know anything, yet shared her personal experiences in life as one person's journey that was, in fact, every person's journey.

In reflection, what called me to Eva was that she was a survivor, not of the crimes of the Holocaust, but of the challenges of life. We were different in many ways and yet we were the same. I knew that if she could survive what life threw at her, then I could also survive what life threw at me. Can it be that easy—that you admire someone because they are proof that the road of life stretches before you, through you, and after you? Yes, I think it can be that easy.

Retracing Steps with Eva on Her "Healing Journey"

By Darree Robin Sicher

When Eva decided to revisit and retrace her early life and Holocaust experience, I was thrilled that she would accept my offer to accompany her. I knew nothing about Hungary, with the exception of what I had heard at Eva's presentations of her pre-war life. We would return to the land of her birth and betrayal. From there we would enter and exit each country that was part of her war time experience. I would travel as a blank book with the goal of being a support system for a woman on her journey to shed light on the ghosts of her personal history. The position seemed more an honor than a weight. Could I handle the situation if something went wrong, if the ghosts were too strong? Without hesitation, I planned a two week trip with a virtual stranger to see what we might find at the precipice of the dark side. I chose to follow her lead and needs, to act as a witness and a sponge.

Our October travels would take us through Hungary, Austria, Germany, Denmark and Sweden. We would travel by plane, train, car, and boat to the physical locations of Eva's experience. We would visit friends and be guided by endless people who seemed to arrive like invisible helping hands. While maintaining the intended direction, the trip with Eva constantly morphed to include challenges for growth and celebration. Rather than a travelogue, my reflections will whisper of the "A-ha!" moments along the way.

An evening international flight landed us in Denmark bright and early, and a lengthy layover afforded us the opportunity to investigate a country neither of us knew. What we found at the Copenhagen visitors center were engaging, English-speaking guides who were happy to enlighten us about their country and, after hearing of our intended travels, Denmark's role in the War. As the Nazis invaded each country, they instructed the crushed leadership to mark their Jews with the now infamous "Star of David" on their clothing. The king of Denmark refused to mark his Jews for easy collection, insisting they were Danes first, not Jews for disposal. He had a Star attached to his clothing and declared that everyone wear a Star. Denmark had the least number of Jews taken during the War. Did everyone in Denmark love their Jewish neighbors? Hardly. Yet the leadership of the country did not offer a segment of its own people as a temporary sacrifice to the machine of hatred. The leaders showed leadership and strength under moral and physical fire. Humanity provided resistance during a trying time of terror and brutality. Where did this strength come from? The question rolled around in my mind like a smooth stone, heavy with weight and history. "United we stand" never seemed truer.

In Hungary, our travels took us to many of Eva's old friends who had returned to Budapest after the War. None spoke English, so I relied on Eva's translations of any information and pleasantries meant for me, but mostly I sat and listened to old friends catching up in a language familiar to their life and location. The universal language of the body—a smile, raised voices, a gentle touch, darting eyes, laughter—reflected life's challenges without a language that was familiar to the ear. We stayed with Eva's childhood friend, Suzie, in her small apartment built after the War. Determined to return to her homeland, Suzie had returned to Budapest after the War, her delicate hands gripping the outside of a train as it traveled through the wounded countryside. They were both strong willed—what else would have kept them alive in the camps—and neither wanted to be told what to do. They were sisters of the heart, often laughing, sometimes gritting their teeth or arguing, always forgiving and accepting. On our way to the museum, they linked arms and sang national songs learned as children. They talked in hushed tones late into the night, elbows on the kitchen table, steamy cups of chamomile scenting the air. They argued over who would pay for bus fare and bags of ruby colored sweet peppers at the market. And they loved each other unconditionally.

The only situation they really seemed disconnected on was a feeling of safety in a community accustomed to armed guards and security checks. A bomb scare at the Synagogue. Young men with cocked black berets poking the trash with the nose of their guns outside the grocery store. Guards requesting ID at the train station. Suzie's casual acceptance of the military presence seemed to come from her daily contact; it represented security and stability. For Eva, the constant infusion of police presence set off the red flags of repression, leaping from her childhood as the beginning of the end of rights and freedom. It represented danger and abuse of power. Sometimes they would argue on the spot with raised voices, gesturing arms. When a disheveled man in a park passed us and circled back, Eva spun on her heels and roared like a tiger as he missed my purse. Eva was shaken. Suzie was cavalier. The land of their birth had betrayed them in the first decades of their lives. Eva would leave. Suzie would stay. It seemed that disconnecting from the location of betrayal sealed in Eva's heart a distrust of the homeland, like having an abusive parent or partner that you love and hate at the same time. Even when she was happy while visiting Hungary, she couldn't let her guard down for fear that a casual infraction or unspoken change of rules might result in some sort of punishment. Suzie, like so many of Eva's friends who managed to survive the fighting and the camps, returned to Budapest after the War. They moved into or created positions of power and wealth, forcing the motherland to repent and pay for its sins. They punched the pendulum in the other direction, forcing respect. It seemed that each coping skill paid a price. 50 years later, Eva was still trying to exercise the ghosts of abuse, yet her softness left her open to soak in life, to explore and celebrate curiosity. She had the leeway to show love. Suzie fought to go home and never stopped fighting. She was hard as a rock, creating a shield so strong as never to risk a breath of spring air or the hug of humanity. Suzie couldn't understand why Eva would want to retrace her trials of survival.

We visited some tourist spots but also areas where tourists don't go:

neighborhoods tired from rebuilding after the War and now rebuilding after the fall of Communism in Hungary. We visited neighborhoods tired of fighting. One afternoon, we met with Feri, a childhood friend and former policeman, at a favorite spot for coffee and cakes. Filtered light from the tall windows pooled on the checkered tile floor. We had coffee in white cups and pretty pastries on delicate white plates. Eva remembered fetching her father from this place and his chess games, reminding him to come home for supper. Eva and Feri spoke in Hungarian. The place was grand, ornate and sleepy. It was also void of customers and seemed smoky, filled with ghosts. When we left, stepping onto the busy Budapest sidewalk, I spotted the orange and pink of a Dunkin' Donuts across the street. Hungary's grandeur will fall again to the invasion of America's bland commerce. I savored the flavor of real Hungarian pastries on my taste buds and said a little prayer for the impending cultural loss.

Our big evening out on the town was a planned concert at the symphony to enjoy the music and meet up with some young Hungarian artists that Eva had met years ago on their tour of America. The symphony building did not disappoint the senses, where an elbow to elbow crowd chattered under sparkling chandeliers. It seemed that Hungarians gleamed with pride over their love affair with music, and the symphony building was proof. Once in our seats, the crowd murmured in semi-darkness until the sudden burst of music washed over us. Eva physically shuddered and tears slowly trickled down her worn cheeks. She closed her eyes, giving in to the receding music. She whispered that the last time she had been in this building was to see her brother's graduation performance before he would pursue a musical career. This happy memory had slept quietly, high in the rafters of the symphony hall until now, when her brother's spirit and dreams could soar down to kiss his sister's heart. Eva's tears caught lightly on her trembling smile. Often, pain and joy reside at the same address.

We left Hungary by train. We would travel through Austria all night, arriving in Germany in the morning. Suzie, determined and controlled, packed a huge sack of food – sandwiches on thick hearty bread, fruit, sweet peppers and bottles of water. This time, on the train taking Eva to Germany, she would not go hungry. At the train station,

Suzie's eyes welled as we waved goodbye. We left Budapest because Eva wanted to, not because she had to.

The train rumbled deep into the night. An occasional and un-settling hammering on our locked sleeping cabin door (from transit police demanding to see our passports) added to an evening of fitful sleep and a feeling of escape. After long hours of travel, we reached Ulm—our first stop in Germany—early on a Sunday morning. Al-though Ulm was not connected to Eva's physical experience during the War, she had learned that it was the birthplace of a brother/sister team of German college students who had been instrumental in a resistance movement called "The White Rose." Eva wanted to see if there was a gravesite or monument where we could pay our respects to their heroic deeds. Hans and Sophie Scholl had rallied compassion and common sense against the war machine in their motherland, but their treasonous acts ended their lives early, as German communities buckled under the fear and repression of their own government.

Our first challenge was that Ulm was not a tourist mecca and, on a Sunday morning, we were stumped on where to change our money. While I waited with the luggage in the train station, Eva ventured into Germany for the first time since she had been rescued from the concentration camp 50 years earlier. When she returned, we stored the luggage in lockers at the train station, and she updated me on the details of her adventures over a much needed cup of coffee. After wandering the streets of Ulm for at least an hour, the one location she found help was—of all places—the police station. As she told me of entering this representation of German authority, I marveled at her ability to push past her hesitation with the focus of finding an answer. The young policemen were helpful in directing Eva to a local hotel to exchange money, but the more important questions about Hans and Sophie Scholl were answered only by an older policeman, Eva's age. The difference in Eva's reaction to the authority figures in Hungary and Germany seemed internal and external, and I thought of the times I had heard Eva say, "There was a difference between the Germans and the Nazis." Eva often reflected on the Germans who had helped her and others even while en route to the concentration camps. People, regardless of nationality, who had shown humanity in the face of cruelty. She also reflected on the communities who were happy to turn their Jewish neighbors over to the Nazis, to have a way to dispose of someone they didn't want. People, regardless of nationality, who had shown cruelty in the face of humanity.

Following the directions of the senior policeman, we wandered the streets of Ulm, past the school named after Hans and Sophie, and waited in the damp autumn morning outside of a church for a minister who might offer help on our quest. Muffled hymns and organ music seeped from the windows of the brown stone church until service finally ended and content churchgoers strolled from the mighty building toward home. The minister's body language was open as he listened to Eva's explanation of our mission. With apologies, he informed us that there was no burial place for Hans and Sophie Scholl. There was, however, a nice bronze bust of each somewhere near the town center, by the historic Ulm church, which boasted the tallest church spire in all of Germany.

The church spire disappeared into the low hanging clouds. The bronze busts offered little information about the founders of the White Rose resistance. The good people of Ulm walked with Sunday casualness from here to there. We boarded the train and headed for Hamburg. Sometimes heroes—people who are brave and true and follow their hearts—don't get a burial ground.

In Hamburg we would be meeting with Eva's friend Dirk, a young man who once rented a room from her when he was a university student in Philadelphia. Dirk would be offering his home in Kiel as a staging place for our visit to Bergen-Belsen, the concentration camp where Eva was held during the War. He had phoned ahead and arranged for us to meet the curator of the museum that was on site. We would spend our first night in Hamburg with Dirk's parents and tour the city with Dirk as our guide. Although we were unable to reach either Dirk or his parents by phone, we continued our train ride heading from south to north through the beautiful German countryside.

The landscape tumbled away from the train tracks that cut through the small towns dotting the lush fields and forests. Ribbons of roads connected urban and rural locations. The area was so similar to my own community in Pennsylvania that I immediately recognized why the German settlers of the 1700s stopped when they got to Berks county. It felt like home.

Eva spoke the tiniest amount of German, and I spoke none. Our lack of understanding of the language meant we were unsure of the train schedule and the workings of an obviously organized system. As riders entered the train, I quickly, and apologetically, gave up where I was sitting as they pointed to small signs above each seat. Eva and I kept an eye on each other, but also welcomed the time to try to communicate with others. Eventually a woman who spoke English sat next to me, providing me the opportunity to ask questions about her culture and life in Germany. Christine was very accommodating of my lack of her native language as we discussed the trip Eva and I were taking. Eva had spotted a phone on the train and asked Christine if she would phone Dirk's parents for us. Christine was more than happy to help, even refusing money to cover the cost of the call. When she phoned, there was no answer and no answering machine, and our transfer to a new train station was approaching soon. Christine insisted that we leave a copy of the phone number with her, and she would continue to try to reach Dirk's parents to let them know we would arrive at the Hamburg train station that evening. With great thanks and a feeling of lucky serendipity, we departed the train, waving to Christine as the train pulled away. We didn't know the language and we didn't know exactly where we were going, yet the kindness of a stranger and the promise to deliver a message of our arrival was the real fuel to celebrate our forward motion.

Finally, we reached Hamburg station. Throughout our travels, I often positioned myself to help Eva with her wheeled duffle bag, but making sure to resist the urge to over-help. She was determined to fully participate in our cross country travels, including hauling her own luggage. Only occasionally did I give the duffle bag a hefty kick from behind to get it through the doorway of a train as we struggled to exit promptly. When we arrived in Hamburg, our focus to exit the train temporarily distracted us from the sudden shock of the sheer size of the train station. Of course it would be huge, we later reasoned, being an intersecting hub of one of Germany's largest cities. We stood in dumbfounded contemplation, devising a plan of how to find people we didn't know in an echoing, bustling, and cavernous station. Hurried commuters parted around us, washing past like water moving past two stones in a river. Over the din of conversation, garbled announcements on the intercom, screeching metal and shuffling feet, Eva yelled her idea. She would try to find the office where the echoing announcements were coming from while I waited with the luggage. While we discussed the details of our plan, a spry older woman briskly past us, spun on her heels and faced us both. "Eva Cutler?" she asked, her heavy German accent and sudden confrontation startling us into silence. "Eva Cutler?" she again questioned. Eva snapped out of her stunned silence and said yes. It was Dirk's mother who, in dashing to see if she could spot two obviously foreign women exiting the train, had overheard us talking in English. She spoke no English yet we all laughed and hugged at the amazing intersection of our lives. We found Dirk's father, who spoke some English, searching other platforms of the seemingly endless train station, picked up some food at a deli stand, and headed back to their apartment.

Later, Dirk filled us in on the behind-the-scenes of our Hamburg rendezvous. Due to a misunderstanding of our arrival date, both Dirk and his parents where traveling with plans to return home in the evening. His parents entered their apartment and answered the ringing phone. A woman said she was calling for Eva Cutler, who would be arriving at the Hamburg train station that evening at … and then the other line went dead. They tossed their travel bags in a corner and headed out to find these mystery travelers, who they had never met. Dirk was not expected until later that evening. His mother and father split up at the station, unsure how they would find their son's visiting friends. The convergence of lost and found was quite marvelous.

Breakfast conversation included what life was like in Germany during the war. Regardless of personal view, anyone called into service was subject to serve punishment or death if they refused to fight. Dirk's father was forced to leave college to be sent to Denmark, where he translated, enjoying his stay and the people he met. He didn't act like a Nazi; he was not dedicated to the passion of war. His challenges of survival after the war were great, but ultimately he created a happy family, home and life. Around his kitchen table, with his wife of a lifetime and his only child by his side, this elderly German man who had been forced into military service welcomed this elderly Hungarian woman who had been forced into concentration camps. They talked, they laughed, they loved life. They enjoyed sausages, were members of Amnesty International, and hated war. They both moved forward from fear and pain, choosing to participate in life and the world.

Dirk's parents packed us sandwiches for the ride to his home. They checked to make sure our seatbelts were buckled and chided us not to lock the car doors (a recent news story about someone trapped in a car accident because the doors were locked had made a deep impression on them). Two survivors of life's brutal times joined their son in shattering any assumptions of guilt by association. They were no more responsible for being born in Germany than Eva was for being born in Hungary. The universalism of good people who survived hard times was the thread that knit everyone together. We pulled away from the curb as they waved goodbye.

Our visit to Kiel, where Dirk lived and worked as a university professor, was the anticipated "mid-point" of our travels, the hinge where we would swing from Eva's experience before the concentration camp to her experience as a survivor of the concentration camp. Dirk's home would act as the safe haven for our trip to Bergen-Belsen. Eva seemed prepared for the visit mentally and physically. I wondered if things would change when we got to the concentration camp. I felt an odd camaraderie with Dirk, like we were the chosen next generation to support Eva's venture into the darkness and to participate in the lightness that may be shed. Our opposites made the situation whole, like we were the chosen son and daughter to carry the torch of refusing to let the story end with sadness and hatred.

It rained the day we went to Bergen-Belsen. I pondered how the weeping, grey clouds set the tone of the day, wavelets of pooled water arching from our speeding car. The windshield wipers thumped like a heartbeat, heightening my mild anxiety. When we reached the Bergen-Belsen Memorial Museum, the rains had quieted to a dull mist. I could almost touch the floating memories and ghosts. Dirk found the curator, who greeted us warmly. He encouraged us to tour the grounds at our own pace, and he would meet us whenever we finished.

But it wasn't the place where Eva had been held, trapped in a limbo between life and death. It wasn't the place where she struggled to survive, wondering where humanity had slipped away to, where hope withered slowly, daily. The place where we now stood—clean and thoughtful—was not where she somehow resisted the death that surrounded her. The curator told her that after liberation the camp was burned to the ground because typhus, lice, and rats were so extreme that they posed a public health threat. Wouldn't that seem like a denial of what had happened without the original structures? The curator agreed, but expressed the deep concerns that rebuilding the physical structures could never replicate the gruesome conditions that people survived in, and their bigger concern was not to make it "Disney-like" for visitors. For this reason, they had designed the grounds as a museum to educate and inform visitors, with a strolling memorial garden acting as contemplation burial grounds. These honest and sincere explanations seemed to quiet any fears Eva may have had about the death of millions being dismissed as a non-event.

Poster-sized photos of the first key inmates highlighted the subtle, incremental shifts in policy and attitude that made thinking and feeling a crime. The early criminals were all professional men and women—doctors, professors, businessmen, artists—and their professional portraits showed them posed in handsome suits softened with studio lighting. The photos and displays enlightened the masses with multi-lingual information, but the most striking information for me was not written in words.

A white map of war-torn Europe, the size of a dining room table, hung on the wall. Black dots pocked Germany, naming the overwhelming and unfamiliar locations of hundreds of concentration camps. Some neighboring countries, like Austria and Poland, were also infected with death camp locations. Striking against the duality of the white map and black marks were smudges or blurs where thousands of visitors had reached out a finger to touch a location on the map—"There, that's where I was," "…that is where our family perished….," "….when they went there, I never saw them again." Whispers of fingerprints were decipherable. Thousands of visitors who leaned forward—involuntarily—to touch the name and the dot that had shifted their lives, the way some mourners touch the body of a loved one in a casket. This clean, clear map was a conduit between lives and dreams lost and living souls, right here and now. Even as we wandered through a building that respectfully marked where Eva had survived, it was the name and the location that we were called to. The name gave a location for the stories and the survival. The location, regardless of the physical changes, gave a place to stand, to stop, to reflect, to focus.

One photo that seized my heart was a black and white one of a dead man, splayed on the dirt with his arms outstretched and head tilted to the side, like Jesus on the cross. Encircling his quiet body was a halo of boot prints in the dried soil. At the edge of his arm length, just beyond his fingertips, were the black boots and legs of two soldiers standing over his lifeless form.

The removal of everything horribly familiar from Bergen-Belsen seemed to also remove any trigger points that may have been lurking at this location for Eva. With my goal to be attentive without crowding her experience, I saw no signs that visiting this place would unleash a darkness that Eva was unprepared for. We wandered separately, but within easy reach of each other.

After touring the museum, we wandered outside to walk the memorial gardens. Massive, sloping granite headstones simply stated the numbers—in thousands—of bodies buried. Dried, hibernating heather, a rosy colored groundcover during the summer months, refused any color to the autumn overcast mist that wrapped us as we walked the length of the park. At the far end of the park, written in many tongues, was a long wall covered with condolences from a world that didn't get "there" on time. Sometimes, "sorry" is all there is left to say.

We met with the curator, who maintained the balance between gathering any historical information Eva could offer and all-out excitement that a Bergen-Belsen survivor was sitting at his table. Even if other survivors had visited, I had the feeling that he treated each as a welcomed dignitary. As we left, I felt a certain relief that the weight of such a place of sorrow was behind us. We would not forget the dead, but we would not leave our hearts at the funeral. Life was waiting.

In the next few days, Eva would speak at Dirk's university, we would tour the area nearby, and eventually we would wave goodbye to Dirk from the train platform.

Next stop, Karlscoga, Sweden. Our adventures included a surprise transfer as we traveled from land to sea. Our train merely stopped at the German port along the North Sea, where a waiting ferry lowered its gate like the huge mouth of Jonah's whale. The entire train slowly chugged on board while Eva's face lit with the excitement of the novelty of it all. On board the deck, the salty sea sprayed us as we looked out over the vast waterscape. Maybe we both felt refreshed in our freedom to go wherever we wanted. We over-nighted in Denmark, then off to the town in Sweden closest to Loka Brunn, where Eva had spent a year in recovery before heading to America.

As the train chugged across the changing landscapes of Sweden, Eva approached a conductor to confirm that we were headed in the correct direction for Karlskoga. While the two of them stumbled through the language barrier, a man several seats away rose and introduced himself. Overhearing Eva's question, he offered that he was just returning home to Karlskoga from a business trip in America and would be happy to guide us to our destination. His English was clear, and his face was kind. Arnie not only helped us transfer trains but also phoned his wife to pick him up at the station with the big car so they could give us a ride into town. Unbeknownst to us, the last bus of the evening had already left the Karlskoga train station, and the youth hostel where we were planning on staying would be closed by the time we arrived. Arnie's wife Britt phoned the hostel to explain our situation and ask if they might let us check-in anyway. As luck would have it, they were celebrating a staff party that evening and the manager, slightly inebriated, agreed to have us check-in late.

Arnie and Britt were the true saviors of our trip in Sweden. As we revised our plans in the back seat of their car, Arnie and Britt glanced at each other and shared a quick conversation in Swedish. Loka Brunn was a considerable distance from Karlskoga and accessible by bus. As it turned out, the bus schedules had just changed with the change of seasons and the day Eva had planned to visit was the one day that the bus was discontinued. Arnie and Britt offered to drive us up to the sleepy resort. Besides, we could join them for a meal the next day, meet their children, and catch our breath while we wandered the town. The idea of someone being a god-send never seemed so relevant. We accepted their generous offer.

The revelry at the youth hostel celebrating the end of a good year encompassed the first floor, but the upstairs was quiet. We were the only guests. With the long day of travel weighing on us, we readied ourselves for bed. It was at that point that we realized every bed was a bunk bed. As we settled into sleep, Eva noted that it was the first time she'd slept in a bunk bed since the camps. We slept peacefully because we could.

The highlight of our day with Britt and Arnie was the meal with their family. Their daughter was particularly interested in talking with Eva since she had just finished her senior paper on the heroic work during WW2 of Swede Raul Wallenberg. Eva was the first Holocaust survivor their daughter had ever met. When Eva casually mentioned that she had met Raul Wallenberg, their daughter almost jumped from her seat and hung on every word. Eva apologized that the meeting with Wallenberg was very brief and mostly she remembered him as being well dressed and handsome. Arnie and Britt's daughter beamed. That was enough for her.

Our final leg of the journey owed much to the generosity of strangers. Riding in the back of Britt and Arnie's car, I marveled at the blessings we had throughout the trip, with the grand finale of strangers rearranging their schedule to fulfill Eva's dream. The Swedish landscape was marvelous, but it paled in comparison to the wonderful people we had met.

We wandered the grounds of Loka Brunn, tucked in the serene Swedish countryside. The cabins where Eva and the other female survivors spent the year recovering—physically and mentally—were still standing and in use. The lake was clear, the air was crisp, the trees strong and sturdy. We walked the grounds as Eva relayed stories of good food, skiing, skating, warming by the wood stove, songs and laughter. The extreme kindness of the people of Sweden helped sooth the scars of the extreme pain of Nazi Germany. The buildings, the names, the location all reconfirmed the memories that good had, in fact, conquered evil.

By the end of our travels, we were tired but also at peace. We were both ready to go home and move on to what was to happen next in our lives. Later, Eva would tell me that the trip didn't make anything better, it didn't heal anything. But she said it did put a positive layer over some part of life that had been so hard, so negative. Scars are a sign that something has healed, but the original cut—the original pain—will never be erased. Healing doesn't deny that the trauma has happened—healing proves that you keep moving forward in spite of the trauma that has happened. My relationship with Eva—both during our trip and in other moments—has taught me that.

CHAPTER ELEVEN

The Library

While living in Jim Thorpe, I had read in the paper about the Youth and Prejudice Conference, an ongoing program run by the Institute for Jewish-Christian Understanding at Muhlenberg College in Allentown. I wanted to become involved in the conference's efforts to teach students about the effects of prejudice, so I went to one of the training sessions for conference facilitators. After the organizers met me, they invited me to speak to the students at the conference. Participation in the conference became a regular event for me.

As I was becoming more involved in the conference, my friend Inge asked me to read *The Library*, her one-act play about her experience as a young girl in Nazi Germany. I read it, and I was overcome. I looked at her, and I said, "My God, something has to be done with this."

"Oh, you're too partial," she said in her peculiar manner, but I insisted that she give me a copy. That's how it all started. I shared the script with my friend Patty Carlis because I felt *The Library* deserved to be seen, as it offered a very powerful piece of evidence about what happened *before* the Holocaust, about the seemingly smaller events that led up to the atrocities. People have to know about these early signs to watch for; that's the only way we can work on preventing such horrific events. Here more of the story of *The Library* will be told by Inge and Patty, and then by some of the others who shaped the development of the play after it left my hands.

THE LIBRARY

The story of a Jewish girl
in Nazi Germany

By Inge Karo

It all started when opportunity knocked on my door and I decided to let it in. By chance I read that Beaver College was starting a Continuing Education Program for non-traditional, mature students who had never taken the courses usually required for college admission. I always wanted to go to college, so without considering all the pros and cons I applied and was accepted.

In my first course students had to write original stories that were read aloud and critiqued by the teacher and the class. Heeding the advice that you should write about something you know, I wrote a short story about a little German Jewish girl who had to turn in her library card. The only student who guessed what the end would be turned out to be Jewish.

Many years later, Theater Ariel announced a competition for plays only five minutes long, dealing with 20th Century Jewish experiences that needed minimal sets and very few actors. Even though I had not the slightest idea what a script should look like, I went to the library immediately, took out a book on how to write a play, and converted my story into a script in the required format. I submitted it to Theater Ariel, who just as promptly rejected it. Not sure whether opportunity struck out or dropped the ball, I put the play and the rejection slip into my file where they stayed until my good friend Eva Cutler visited me. Though I didn't realize it at the time, opportunity came in with her. Eva showed me some things she wrote, I showed her my play. Eva gave it to Patty Carlis, Patty and her students revised the play with additional material, and the rest is history.

Just as my play changed after Patty and her students worked on it, my perception about my experiences as a child in Nazi Germany also changed.[7] I considered myself a refugee, not a survivor, and never felt that what happened to me had anything to do with the Holocaust. Then Patty asked me to talk with the cast as well as the audience at the start of each season. The fear of facing the students with nothing to say motivated me to think about the connection between the events in the play and the atrocities that came later. It enabled me to connect the dots, to understand and explain that these incidents were part of a plan that made it possible not only to persecute Jews, but to make this persecution acceptable to the average German.

It is nice to know that my story was the catalyst which lead to the powerful and moving play *The Library* has become.

---

7   Inge was eleven years old when her family managed to escape Germany before being taken to a concentration camp.

By Patty Carlis

Art has the power to transform us. This concept has been at the core of my work in arts education for more than 30 years. I believe passionately that theatre is the most powerful learning medium because it engages us both intellectually and emotionally. Theatre explores the human condition. Actors become artists in action. They investigate what motivates characters to make choices in a given set of circumstances and how those characters will deal with conflicts. These are the theoretical constructs that guide my work in educational theatre. Putting this into practice in a very real way became the challenge that my friend Eva Cutler presented to me. I accepted that challenge, and it transformed my life.

It all began when Eva handed me an envelope that contained a short story written by her friend, Inge Karo. It was a simple story of a young Jewish girl growing up in Nazi Germany who was forced to give up her library card because she was Jewish. When she placed it in my hands, I remember her words, "Patty, I think you can do something with this." I had no idea that the journey of developing this story into a play would change my life and the lives of so many young people who have been a part of this project for the last eight years. Let me go back and explain how Eva and I came to know each other. When I was president of the Board of Directors of PA STAGE, a regional non-profit professional theatre company in Allentown, PA, the artistic director selected *The Diary of Anne Frank* as part of the 1993-94 season. Knowing that this text is often used in middle schools as part of the Holocaust curriculum, the educational outreach department of the theater company recognized that the play presented an opportunity to introduce students in the Lehigh Valley to theatre as a compelling learning medium. We would invite students to attend special matinee performances. I suggested that we go one step further and use the play as a springboard for dialogue about the lessons of the Holocaust and the dynamics of prejudice. I envisioned a symposium in which the play would be followed by discussions in which Holocaust survivors would share their accounts of tragedy and triumph, enabling students to touch history in a more profound way. Beyond that, students would be asked to confront prejudice and discrimination in their own lives. And finally, they would be asked to come up with their own action plans in order to become agents of change in their own schools and communities. An ambitious plan—but one I believed in and found support for in the Jewish community in the person of Jeanette Eichenwald, a daughter of survivors, and Dr. Franklin Sherman, then the director of the Institute for Jewish-Christian Understanding at Muhlenberg College.

Enter Eva. Eva was one of the survivors who volunteered to speak to the children at this first conference. I watched and listened as she shared her personal experiences as a young teenager growing up in Budapest, Hungary. Her focus was not on her personal pain but much more on what her experiences can teach us about the evils of prejudice and discrimination and where they can lead if allowed to poison hearts and minds. She emphasized that each one of us needs to take responsibility and purge these affronts to humanity in our own schools and communities. It was evident that Eva had an uncanny ability to touch the souls of these young students. They responded to her message of hope and optimism.

The conference was a success, and the Jewish Federation of the Lehigh Valley and the Institute for Jewish-Christian Understanding forged a partnership that continues today. The Youth and Prejudice Conference became an annual event that has reached more than 15,000 students since 1994. I became the coordinator of the event and we expanded to two conferences each year—one for middle school students and one for high school students. Without a live theatrical production to use as the springboard for dialogue, we began to use films like *Schindler's List* and other documentaries that tended to focus more on the atrocities of the Holocaust. After viewing one of these films at the conference, a middle school student raised her hand and asked a very simple but poignant question. "How could anyone let this happen?" What struck me in that moment is that when we teach the Holocaust we teach the facts, the dates, the numbers, man's inhumanity to man, but what we don't explore are the circumstances that led up to them. How were people taught to hate and to justify violence?

Enter Eva, again. I am a believer that people come into your life at a particular point in time for a reason. The year was 1999. I had just finished a master's degree in educational theatre at New York University and was bursting with enthusiasm when Eva handed me this large brown envelope. The timing couldn't have been more serendipitous. It contained a short story and a short play that Inge Karo had adapted from her original short story called *The Library*. The simple story is a flash-back that reflects on an episode in the life of Rachel, an eleven-year old Jewish girl growing up in Germany during the 1930s. Rachel must give up her library card because the Nuremburg Laws passed in 1935 won't permit Jews access to the libraries. I saw the potential for this story to be fleshed out by weaving together more accounts from survivors of their experiences as children growing up in such difficult and uncertain times. A well-developed play could put a human face on history—a face that other young students could relate to. I spoke with Inge, who agreed to allow me to use her short play as a basis for a longer dramatic presentation. She recommended that I speak with Josey Fisher, the director of the Holocaust Oral History Archive of Gratz College. Josey edited a book called *The Persistence of Youth: Oral Testimonies of the Holocaust*. She recommended that I focus on three particular stories of survivors, one Jewish, one non-Jewish, and one from a mixed marriage. Each one vividly recounts in his or her own words what it was like to grow up in pre-war Germany. Primary sources are so important when tackling a project like this because authenticity is critical for credibility.

Armed with the play and my research, I approached Charles Richter, then Chair of the Department of Theatre and Dance at Muhlenberg College, with a proposal. I wanted to use drama-in-education strategies to develop a play that could be used to teach middle school students how some of the events that led to the Holocaust were possible. I suggested that this project be a course I teach at Muhlenberg that would serve a dual purpose: 1) to engage college students in a play-making process that would require intensive research and stretch their acting skills, and 2) to develop a play that could tour in area middle schools and serve as a teaching vehicle. Charles endorsed the project wholeheartedly and I began to recruit the students. I felt it was important that each one understand the nature of the material we would be exploring and the creative approach we would be taking to make this vision a reality. I interviewed five freshman women who impressed me with their sincere interest in the subject matter and their willingness to use unique and perhaps unfamiliar theatre techniques in order to explore the primary source material and bring it to life.

Abby Mahone, Rebecca Eckard, Elizabeth Rogler, Kelly Howe, Shannon Lambert-Ryan and I were to embark on a journey that would leave all of us transformed and create a bond that would transcend this experience we shared. Nora Whittaker, then a senior at Muhlenberg who had done an independent research project on the Holocaust, signed on to observe our work as we improvised scenes based on testimony from survivors. We began by listening to Inge Karo, whose accounts of her experiences growing up would be the most critical to the play. She told us how her own parents struggled to cope with what was going on in Nazi Germany and how all of this affected her. Rachel, the main character based loosely on Inge, is a child for whom the library was a refuge when all else around her seemed to be crumbling. It became clear from her accounts and from those of other survivors from *The Persistence of Youth* that, for young Jewish children, the most profoundly hurtful experiences of prejudice happened at schools and on the playground.

I asked Eva, who had become my muse for this project, to come to speak to us about her experiences growing up in Budapest. It was a day I will never forget.

We were seated in a small conference room in the theatre department offices. Eva's engaging smile immediately made all of these young women who had signed on to this project feel comfortable enough to listen to Eva's recollections and ask questions. She recounted a story that she had never told anyone before—a story that came to her as we talked about what she remembered about her friends, school, and when it was apparent that life for her and her family was changing. She told us about the day she was sitting in her classroom in her school in Budapest, when her teacher, whom Eva had adored, focused her eyes on Eva and said, "Something smells in here." The teacher then directed someone to open a window, as Eva recounted, to "get rid of that Jew smell." Eva told us how horrified, betrayed, and humiliated she was by her teacher's words. She was so shocked that when she went home that day, she even asked her mother if she smelled. As we listened, we were horrified and angry that teachers had become tools of the Nazi propaganda effort and were indoctrinating students to eventually become collaborators and perpetrators. But on an even more human level, we responded to Eva with empathy, tears, and hugs. She had shared a moment with us when she had experienced such vulnerability. Nora wove that story into the play, and it became the pivotal moment when the theme (What does it mean to be made to feel different?) would strike an emotional chord with audiences.

The students first performed the play on a tiny stage in the auditorium of the Jewish Day School in Allentown. Our set was simple: blocks and one table used to designate the four locations of the play—Rachel's home, school, the playground, and the library. What became apparent in that first experience of sharing this play with an audience was its simplicity and power. The actors created compelling characters, and the students in the audience were riveted. Equally as compelling was the way in which the actors, following the performance, talked to the audience about the process of creating the play. Each actor was not just playing a role; each had given life to a complex character. As the actors engaged the audience in a dialogue about the issues the play explores and what each character represented, it was clear that the audience members were able to relate on a personal level. I remember one ten year old girl who raised her hand and told her own story. She said that she related to Rachel's experiences because she, too, had been the victim of anti-Semitism. It was clear that it was difficult for her to revisit this pain, but important for her to release it. Watching the play gave her the courage to express it. It was then that we sensed that with this play, we would have the opportunity to touch the lives of children in a profound way.

But how would non-Jewish audiences react? Would they make the same connections to the characters? Would they see themselves in Rachel, a victim of ridicule? In David, a non-Jew who comes to Rachel's defense? Would they relate to the courage of Rachel's mother, who tried to protect her? Would they understand Rachel's father, who denies that the world is caving in around them? Would they be able to confront their own prejudices when they watch Christa betray her best friend Rachel? Would they recognize the role that the teacher played in teaching the children to hate? Would they appreciate the courage of the librarian as she takes the risk to give Rachel books when Rachel is no longer allowed to use her library card? Would they understand that three books and a journal symbolize the hope that someday Rachel would record her own story, so that others can learn the lessons of history? As our tour continued that year to suburban and urban middle schools, we discovered by listening to the students' responses in the talk backs that the answer was a resounding yes. That was the year 2000. A new century had begun and perhaps in some small way our play, so specific in its story and yet so universal in its message, would change perceptions and inspire the student actors, as well as the students who saw the play, to be agents of change.

And how has this project affected each new ensemble of actors who bring this story to life? Each year as I do the audition/interview with prospective cast members, mostly freshman theatre majors at Muhlenberg, I am inspired by their level of commitment and passion to explore this emotionally challenging material and to use their acting skills to teach others the lessons we can learn from history. As the director of the play, my biggest challenge is to try to recreate the process that the original cast had experienced in giving birth to the play. I use the same readings of history and direct testimony from survivors in order to immerse each new cast in the world of the play before we even tackle the actual script. Each year, the ensemble travels to the Museum of Jewish Heritage in New York City in order to learn about the history and traditions of Judaism and to view the exhibits that explain how Hitler was able to indoctrinate a nation to believe the validity of racial anti-semitism. But the most powerful experience for the actors is the day they imagine themselves as survivors sharing their memories of what it was like to grow up in Nazi Germany. Using the stories from *Persistence of Youth* to ground them, the actors bring this direct survivor testimony to life by giving voice to their words as if they were their own. It is an incredibly respectful process that pays tribute to those who had experienced such humiliation and dehumanization. It is what actors do and do well, but the impact of this experience forever changes the way in which these young student actors perceive this period in history. Their journals and final papers are a testament to each of their personal transformations as a result of this challenging rehearsal process.

The closing line of a short film called *Camera of My Family*—a photographic essay depicting the lives of a Jewish family before, during, and after World War II—says it best. "The past must be linked to the present if there is to be a future." My work on this project for the past eight years and my friendship with Eva has transformed my life by grounding my work in educational theatre with a clear sense of purpose. She has taught us all by sharing her stories, and she continues to inspire each of us involved with this project with her sense of hope for the future. She reminds us that we must each take responsibility to be informed citizens, to be vigilant in order to preserve our democracy, and to fight injustices wherever and whenever we see them. Eva has taught me by her example that each of us has the power to be an agent of change. She has transformed her greatest challenges and tragedies into meaningful victories.

By Dr. Peter A. Pettit

A memoir such as Eva's compels us with its drama, the unflinching portrayal of humanity in its best and worst moments and, not least, the keen insights and deep commitments to which it has led its autobiographical heroine. Beyond the atrocity that was meted out to her in arbitrary fashion, beyond the good luck that helped her to survive, beyond the goodwill of those who rescued her and nursed her back to health, there lies still the life of the woman who has continued to grow and to give throughout the 60 years since she survived the dark night. This is the woman I have come to know and with whom I have been privileged to work, a woman whose embrace of life and its possibilities is all the more striking for the ease with which her persecutors would have thrown away her own.

I do not know when or how Eva met Patty Carlis, but both were committed volunteers with the Institute for Jewish-Christian Understanding when I came to Muhlenberg College in 1999. The Youth & Prejudice program had grown out of a collaboration between the

Institute, the local Jewish Federation, and PA Stage, a professional theatre company that Patty led. When they staged *The Diary of Anne Frank*, Patty and Jeanette Eichenwald and Frank Sherman created a workshop model for high school students and their teachers to engage more thoroughly the issues of prejudice, discrimination and bigotry. Volunteer facilitators from the community and local Shoa survivors were drawn into the work, which garnered a tremendous response from area schools.

Over several years, when the stage production was not available as the dramatic centerpiece of the workshop, Stephen Spielberg's film *Schindler's List* stood in. But it is a long film, and more and more students came to the workshop having already seen it. So it was a welcome development when Eva showed Patty a copy of a short story by a fellow survivor, Inge Karo. "The Library" was autobiographical and had been developed as a 5-minute radio play. It was about to take on new life.

This illustrates one of the more remarkable aspects of Eva's personality: A project was having difficulty accommodating a blockbuster film of more than three hours dealing with the Shoa. Well, here's a friend who has an unpublished 5-minute radio play. Isn't there something that could be done to make it serve the purpose? Imagine! Well, that's what Eva did, and what Patty did—they dared to imagine. Is such daring to believe that anything is possible, that just what one needs can be fashioned from whatever is at hand, a product of the survivor experience?

During the spring semester of 2000, Patty and a truly remarkable band of first-year students took themselves and "The Library" through a transforming encounter. They studied the Shoa, the National Socialist period leading up to it, the Nuremberg Laws, and the lives of individual Jews, especially children, during the 1930s in Germany. They met with Inge and Eva and Josey Fisher, who had written a book on the resilience of young people faced with unspeakable terror and loss. They worked their way through theatre exercises to find the words and movements and conflicts and conundrums and truths of that time. In the end, they created a one-act play, also titled *The Library*, that a Muhlenberg College senior, Nora Whittaker, scripted brilliantly.

Here, too, lies some of the essence of what Eva has brought from her experience. Survival of the atrocities perpetrated in ghettos and at forced labor camps and in death camps was as much a matter of luck and caprice as anything. From such experiences, Eva knew, there was little to be learned that could be applied more broadly. But seeing the daily choices made by people during the1930s, before the atrocities began, when it was "only" restrictions and reclassifications and small indignities that were being administered, she knew that the important time to act comes early. The crucial time to stand for principle and for people is in the first moment of discrimination and dehumanization. It is then that single step might turn us away from the long road to the gas chambers.

The personal contact that Eva offered and has maintained, even after leaving the area for a retirement in Florida, has been vital to the ongoing success of the project. She has given of herself in sharing her own story, reliving the living hell of Bergen-Belsen, and extending the lessons of her own early years through the lens of her whole life. Attentive to community and political issues, she is unhesitating about voicing her concern when she sees anyone at risk of being treated in a way that remotely resembles what she once suffered. The earnestness of her witness unfailingly helps to shape and motivate the students who create the play each spring and who, as theatre educators under Patty's tutelage, carry it out to middle schools and engage their audiences in talk-back sessions about the issues it raises. When Eva arrives for the Youth & Prejudice conference, those college students are drawn to her as to one who has given them life. And rightly so: the life of their characters is as much her gift to the next generation as any other legacy she will leave.

Yet there will be a further legacy, too. One of the bright young stars of the first production, Kelly Howe, took up the challenge, again with Patty's mentoring, of creating a curriculum unit that will allow the play to carry its message into individual classrooms anywhere. As a five-session unit, the curriculum helps teachers and students, even those with no background in theatre, take up the play, enter its world through imaginative exercises, and explore its insidious dynamics. Even before the first copy of the unit had come from the press, Eva insisted on taking a prototype with her on a trip to her native Budapest. There she met with teachers with similar concerns and convictions, who are trying to bring the lessons of the Shoa to their students in a fresh and compelling way as well. As I write this, we wait to see what new fruit will come from the seed that Eva has planted—both in Budapest and in potential collaboration with the Institute. It is not the sort of initiative on which I would customarily recommend that we invest a great deal. The obstacles are considerable. The odds are long, at best. The cost could be prohibitive. There is so much that could thwart it. Imagine!

But that is what Eva and Patty and Nora and Kelly and a long succession of devoted students have taught us to do. It starts in a library, where we learn to imagine. And so we dare to continue to do.

By Rebecca Eckard

The Library introduced me to two ideas that inform my professional and my personal life: the concept of process and the concept of capturing stories. Although I believed in "process over product," I fully experienced the practice of this idea while researching and rehearsing for *The Library*. The process of our discourse in creating the play highlighted the process that was the careful formulation of the Nuremberg laws and other discriminatory Third Reich policies.

The Library also instilled in me the importance of capturing and recording personal stories. To blur the binary of good and evil, to move away from a world recorded as black and white, winners and losers, we must listen to individuals. By scribing these stories—of major events or of daily struggles—we receive a glimpse into the formation of our collective consciousness. The collection of oral testimony is vital for our pursuit of understanding. Eva's story and the stories of others who experienced the Shoah helped me to understand that my pursuit of knowledge and the truth is a process in and of itself: we all must be explorers seeking stories.

This idea of process and story must remain a "work in progress," a lifetime pursuit that does not condone complacency, ignorance, or apathy.

By Zachary Einstein

I actually joined *The Library* fairly late in its process. There was a need for a male to play the part of David, so I was asked by Kelly, Abby, and Shannon (who were all in my group of friends) to consider helping out by enrolling in the class. I spoke to Patty about it and decided that it, in fact, was worth getting up early in the morning, not only because my friends needed help, but because I quickly saw how important it was that the project take flight.

Being a part of *The Library* sparked my love for teaching. While I had been a religious school aide in high school, I had never traveled to schools with a show as a teaching tool. My experience working on *The Library* influenced my post-graduation decision to become a Resident Actor/Intern at the Civic Theatre of Allentown, Pennsylvania. In that position, I was a member of the Outreach Company, performing in three shows—one of which is a Holocaust-related piece—concurrently in schools in the Greater Lehigh Valley and occasionally in New Jersey.

By Kelly Howe

I was seventeen years old when I walked into my interview for the college course that would lead to the script and first production of *The Library*. That decision to interview was pivotal on so many counts. I owe so much of the activist, teacher, and artist I continue to become to my involvement with *The Library*.

As Patty and others have recounted, we began our semester by researching the Holocaust via books, documentaries, and museum visits. We were, like so many others, collectively horrified by the vastness of the devastation leveled by the Third Reich. We quickly realized, however, that learning about the Holocaust in a macrohistorical way—one that pans out rather than pans in—might be just as overwhelming for the students seeing the play as it was for those of us who would be performing it. We needed to acknowledge the scale of the brutality and lives lost, but we needed also to focus in a microhistorical way—one that pans in and allows students to see all of the seemingly small choices and circumstances that helped pave the way to enormous atrocities.

We asked ourselves, why are we here? Why are we doing this project? We finally came to the conclusion that we wanted students to know the past, but that we also wanted them to work toward better futures. To do that, we knew we had to "personalize" the past for the audience, so that spectators would not be tempted to distance themselves from that past as something so horrible and so "other" from them that there was no need to worry about it ever happening again.

The most influential stage of our research for me happened when we met Eva and Inge. Hearing from these passionate women renewed my sense of purpose. While I would like to think I would have cared every bit as deeply about anti-prejudice education as I do now merely on principle, I'm not sure I ever would have had the same level of investment had I not, for example, met Eva. Her unflinching honesty about what she had lived through—coupled with the incredible sense of hope and purpose she brought to every interaction with us—changed me irrevocably. If she could take the risk of hoping for a better world, how could I—blessed with, it would seem, so many more reasons to be optimistic—not follow her example? Eva made me believe that people can actually learn from history—and evolve in the ways that they treat one another as a result of that learning.

When the play was finally ready to be performed, we toured to a large handful of schools. It was in the talkback sessions that followed our performances that I first began to learn to be a teacher. Facilitating those sessions was exhilarating and frustrating, as perhaps all teaching should be. (At least that's how I still experience my best teaching almost a decade later). While other members of our group were more drawn to compiling our study guide or collecting our props and costumes, I became engrossed in planning our discussions with the students. Patty is fond of recalling a night when I called her at a rather inappropriately late hour, rapidly chattering on about how we needed more clarity in the talkbacks' structure. I couldn't sleep for thinking about it, so I guess I wasn't going to let her sleep, either.

I wanted to shape the discussion questions to strike a very particular balance: On the one hand, I wanted to guide the students toward certain realizations about their power to make changes in the worlds around them. On the other hand, I didn't want the questions to be too leading or manipulative. I didn't have the language then to know that what I was doing was learning how to guide open-ended inquiry—the most important skill I possess as a teacher today.

Many of the questions we ultimately asked the students had to do with what it means to be a bystander and what it takes to be an ally. Some examples included:

Which characters help Rachel? Why? And at what cost?

Which characters hurt Rachel? Why?

Which characters might have been able to help Rachel but instead do nothing?

Why might those characters—those bystanders—have made such choices?

What might have been the cost of becoming Rachel's ally? Why?

I vividly remember ending several of the talkbacks by saying to the students, "To be a builder or a breaker of fellow humans—that is a choice you all have, in some form or another." In retrospect, I realize that my language was overly simple and ahistorical. My word choices might not have always sufficiently acknowledged the systemic pressures that were sometimes acting on individuals and shaping their behavior in certain ways. Still, I'm glad to have erred on the side of suggesting that each person can be powerful. I'm also glad we focused on how each of the play's characters is connected in some way. The project underscored how we are all, simultaneously, individuals *and* community members.

It was while working on *The Library* that I began to interrogate what it means to use theatre as a venue for working for social justice. I asked a question so many people working for social change have asked: How possible is it to use theatre as activism? Under what circumstances? Would any of the students change how they thought or behaved? Would *we* change how we thought or behaved—as artmakers and global citizens? I am confident that the answer to the latter question is, for the most part, yes. As for the other questions—the ones about our student audience members—it's difficult to say what they took away from the play experience. On some days, our interaction with students felt especially lively and successful; on other days, it was less so. That, of course, is the precarious nature of any potentially rich educational experience, and this project helped me consider the value of effecting change that might be so incremental that it won't always be easily perceptible. The questions I mention above led to others, like: Why do history? For whom? What is the role of empathy in learning? What *should* the role of empathy be in learning? I still ask these questions, and my answers tend to change daily.

The Library shaped not only my short-term future choices but my long-term ones as well. During the rest of my years at Muhlenberg, I continued to perform in the play's cast occasionally, and I worked as a facilitator at the college's Youth & Prejudice Conferences, where I met many survivors and second-generation survivors. In my final two years of undergraduate school, in conversation with Patty Carlis, I wrote a teacher's guide to a curriculum for staging *The Library* in middle-school and high-school classrooms. The guide and the curriculum presume that the most deeply felt learning to be done in relation to *The Library* is the learning that happens for and to the performers themselves. I compiled the guide with the hope that it would help students learn about Holocaust-related content in embodied ways they would be unlikely to soon forget.

Today, I am a PhD student in the Performance as Public Practice Program at the University of Texas at Austin, where my interests extend to a wide variety of types of performance. All of them, however, are related to asking how theatre can be involved in the process of bringing about better, more just worlds. Since *The Library*, my theatre-making and my activism have remained inextricably intertwined. I hope that one day I will be a professor who will help at least some of her students discover that the same is true for them.

The class in which we helped devise *The Library*'s script included five students, all of whom stumbled bleary-eyed into our first early morning session knowing each other but not necessarily all knowing each other well. Today all those students remain cherished friends with bonds borne out of, among other things, shared commitments to social justice. As for Eva, her friendship has shaped my life in ways that move me just to think about. I will never forget the moment she asked me to work with her on this book. She let me into her life so generously, just as she does with all the other students she encounters. I love her not as my friend but as my family.

Working on this book with her—a long process she has pushed through with admirable resolve—has taught me that real change, deep and abiding change, requires nothing short of *relentlessness*, with ourselves and with others. Confronting the complications of the past makes us all the more responsible to the future, and on that score we must never relent. We must *always* presume the world is not fine or okay as it is. And even working for tolerance is not enough; such a word still summons connotations of some groups having the power to do the tolerat*ing* and others being the merely tolerat*ed*. We must work instead for nothing less than peaceful, egalitarian coexistence.

All this said, Eva and I have talked over the years about how we want to teach tolerance, so part of me fears she might be surprised to hear me question that word we have used so often. But I have faith that she will give me her blessing to question *even that*. She, maybe more than anyone else, is the one who taught me to question in the first place.

Before I Close:
A Few More Acknowledgements

In the process of writing this book, I had to leave out many people in my life that I have been fortunate to call friends. I couldn't find a place for them in this short account thus far, but I want to mention three of many such friends before I close.

First, I would have to say that I owe a lot to my friend Ruth, who took me under her wing when I first joined the League of Women Voters and I was really wet behind the ears. She introduced me to her social circle. Because of her, I gained a lot of social confidence.

Second, my friend Frida. Third, my friend Olga, more a sister than a friend. Frida and Olga were always there for me.

But without naming all others, it is in my heart to acknowledge what they have contributed to my life.

Epilogue

*"It is extraordinary how nothing ever dies completely,
even the evil that was Nazi Germany's and which today
is gaining ground in this land."*
–Yehudi Menuhin, violin virtuoso, from an interview in
France's newspaper Le Figaro.

"[T]here ought to be limits to freedom."
–Then-presidential candidate George W. Bush,
May 21, 1999

I continued my association with the Youth and Prejudice conference until 2008. Now I am at a point in my life where I feel that, for
the most part, I have accomplished what I set out to do. That said, the
work is not yet done; finishing this book and having others read it remain important goals. Documenting my life thus far took an immense
amount of determination and an unaccountable amount of fortitude.
It was a daunting task. I tried to avoid being bogged down with minute
details. I have hoped instead to emphasize how life my life has been
a strange mix of having power and having no power at all. However,
while some elements of life we cannot control, we often can control
how we *respond* to them. We can choose to act in our own interests
only—or to act in the interests of something larger than ourselves.

I also wanted to write this book because, since September 11, 2001,
the leadership of this country has frequently left me with a sense of

combined photos of message board I carried to protest the war in Iraq

*On one side of the poster: " People can always be brought to the bidding of the leader.
Tell them they are being attacked and denounce the pacifists for lack of patriotism"*
—Herman Goering

*The other side of same poster: "An evil exists that threatens everymen. Woman and
child in this great nation. We must take steps to ensure our domestic security and
protect our homeland."*
—Adolf Hitler writing about the creation of the Gestapo in Nazi Germany

déjà vu. The Bush Administration's constant use of the politics of fear
began to make me feel like I was back in Hungary in the 1930s. In my
opinion, when leaders rule with fear, it is a sign that they want to have
total control. I have worried about the increasing threat to civil liber-

ties in our nation, and the ways that the lives lost on 9/11 have been used to justify that threat. I came to this country because I felt safe to do so. I believed the Constitution protected the rights of the people, but I believe the Bush Administration has particularly compromised that safety net. All these concerns I have identified—along with my worry that religious beliefs are encroaching too much on our public educational system—relate to *The Library*'s cautionary tale. We need to be alive and responsive to the seemingly small changes that chip away at freedom. Such subtle changes have scared me, not for myself, but for the future of this country and for the world.

As I finish *Sparks from the Fire*, Barack Obama has just been elected the 44th President of the United States. I am proud of his election. Time will tell where he is able to lead us, but I am cautiously optimistic that he will be a President who cares about freedom, peace, and justice. Nevertheless, he cannot fight for those things without us. I hope this book can ignite (or stoke) interest in guarding those values. I hope you will all be its sparks.

Printed in the United States
218959BV00002B/51/P